creaturely POETICS

creaturely POETICS

ANIMALITY AND VULNERABILITY IN LITERATURE AND FILM

ANAT PICK

COLUMBIA UNIVERSITY PRESS  NEW YORK

COLUMBIA UNIVERSITY PRESS

Publishers Since 1893

New York   Chichester, West Sussex

Library of Congress Cataloging-in-Publication Data

Pick, Anat.

Creaturely poetics: animality and vulnerability in literature and film / Anat Pick.

p. cm.

Includes bibliographical references.

ISBN 978-0-231-14786-6 (cloth: alk. paper) —ISBN 978-0-231-14787-3 (pbk.)

1. Animals in literature. 2. Human-animal relationships in literature. 3. Animals in

motion pictures. 4. Human-animal relationships in motion pictures.

5. Philosophical anthropology. I. Title.

PN56.A64.P53   2011

809'.93362—dc22   2010038193

Casebound editions of Columbia University Press books are printed on permanent and

durable acid-free paper.

Printed in the United States of America

c 10 9 8 7 6 5 4 3 2 1

p 10 9 8 7 6 5 4 3 2 1

To my parents

I would like to make it, not less painful, only clearer.

—Simone Weil, *Letter to a Priest*

If the sadness of life makes you tired
And the failures of man make you sigh
You can look to the time soon arriving
When this noble experiment winds down and calls it a day
Time has come now to stop being human
Time to find a new creature to be
Be a fish or a weed or a sparrow
For the earth has grown tired and all of your time has expired
All the gardens are sprouting with flowers
All the treetops are bursting with birds
And the people all know that it's over
They lay down all their airs and they hang up their tiresome words

—Thinking Fellers Union Local 282, "Noble Experiment"

CONTENTS

ACKNOWLEDGMENTS

My biggest thanks to Wendy Lochner at Columbia University Press for taking on the project and seeing it through to its completion. Susan Pensak's meticulous editorial eye helped transform it from a manuscript into a book. It has been a pleasure working with her.

A number of people contributed, knowingly or otherwise, to the writing of this book: Dana Pick, Dorit Barchana-Lorand, Shira Weisz Avivi, Miki Avrahamer, Michal Don, Neta Brenner, Naama Harel, Michele Aaron, Mark Schofield, Katie Joice, Gali Gold, Jane Hatfield, and Rima Dapous. For their particular insights and general support I am grateful to Maud Ellmann, Jeri Johnson, and my colleagues at the University of East London: Paul Dave, who got me thinking again about Bazin and realism, Yosefa Loshitzky, Susannah Radstone, Haim Bresheeth, and Eyal Sivan, whose "common archive" project inspired some of my own reflections on the Holocaust and commemoration. My fellows at the Centre for Cultural Studies Research at

UEL continue to provide a tangible sense of academic community: Mica Nava, Maggie Humm, Tim Lawrence, Debra Benita Shaw, Ashwani Sharma, Jeremy Gilbert, Roshini Kempadoo, Sarah Baker, and Jamie Hakim. Cary Wolfe pointed me in the direction of Cora Diamond, which proved decisive.

Erica Fudge, Tom Tyler, Hilda Kean, and the other participants in the British Animal Studies Network sustained a lively platform for debating animal ethics. I wish also to thank Lisa Saltzman, Kate Thomas, and Bethany Schneider of Bryn Mawr College for inviting me to speak on "scientific surrealism" at Bryn Mawr's Center of Visual Culture. My gratitude to Marcel Schwierin, Alissa Timoshkina, and Silke Panse for helping out with hard-to-come-by copies of films by Vladimir Tyulkin, Kira Muratova, and Frederick Wiseman.

The University of Oxford's Rothermere American Institute under the directorship of Paul Giles hosted the lecture series on posthumanism and American culture where some of these ideas began to take shape. It was during my time at the Rothermere that I was fortunate enough to meet Richard Ford; chapter 2 could not have been written without him, since he left me a copy of William Golding's *The Inheritors* in what can only be described as an act of gratuitous generosity.

Three anonymous reviewers for Columbia University Press read the proposal and manuscript with unfailing rigor and care; their comments and suggestions were an integral part of the writing process. Louise Blanks, Maren Hobein, and Anthony Bale read and commented on chapter drafts. And Ingrid Scherübl read through the entire manuscript and pointed out its problems and pitfalls, most (or some) of which I hope I have managed to redress.

A shorter version of chapter 3 originally appeared as "*Pigscripts*: The Indignities of Species in Marie Darrieussecq's *Pig Tales*" in *Parallax* 12.1 (2006): 43–56.

creaturely POETICS

INTRODUCTION *Creaturely Bodies*

> The vulnerability of precious things is beautiful because vulnerability is a
> mark of existence. —Simone Weil, *Gravity and Grace*

This is a book neither strictly about humans nor about animals. It does
not set out to show what is after all by now an accepted wisdom, that
the distinctions between humans and animals are conceptually and
materially indecisive. I start off from the double premise that 1. the
human-animal distinction is a site of contestation, anxiety, and ritual
(philosophical, scientific, religious, and artistic) and that the concrete
relations between human and nonhuman animals have been—increas-
ingly since the age we call modernity—an area of sharp separation, a
zone in which the upkeep of human integrity, as it were, exacts a dev-
astatingly violent price on animals; and 2. that the human-animal
distinction constitutes an arena in which relations of power operate
in their exemplary purity (that is, operate with the fewest moral or
material obstacles). This disparity of power has not lessened with the
dawning of the so-called posthuman age, when the human itself comes
under unprecedented pressures from advances in cognitive science and

biotechnology (and the concurrent rise of bioethics) that render classical humanity all but obsolete.[1]

A growing body of work in the relatively new field of "animal studies" has in recent years contributed to the interrogation and unsettling of the human/animal divide as a specifically posthumanist and post-anthropocentric task. In *Zoographies*, his lucid analysis of a main trajectory within continental philosophy, from Heidegger to Lévinas, Agamben, and, finally, Derrida, Matthew Calarco suggests that the ultimate dismantling of the human-animal boundary is not only desirable, but an inevitable outcome of this philosophical tradition. "Surely," writes Calarco, "Derrida's thought, inasmuch as it is *philosophical* and follows through on the implications of his ethical and ontological analyses, would bring us to the conclusion that the human-animal distinction should be abolished or, at the very least, be treated with considerable caution and suspicion" (143). As a genuinely original field of inquiry, animal studies entails more than "a historical and genealogical analysis of the constitution of the human-animal distinction and how this distinction has functioned across a number of institutions, practices, and discourses" (Calarco 140). It should aim for an "alternative ontology of animal life, an ontology in which the human-animal distinction is called radically into question" (141), in line with Derrida's deconstructions of the (always already untenable) divisions between human and nonhuman life, while avoiding "reductive accounts of animality" (141).

The sway of the current study is, I hope, both "antireductive and antianthropocentric" (Calarco 141). My theoretical itinerary emerges vis-à-vis two dominant threads within animal studies: extensionism (an essentially liberal ethics of extending moral consideration to animals based on their shared capacities and characteristics with human beings) and the more decidedly posthumanist project to tackle and alleviate what Cary Wolfe called the "fundamental repression" (*Animal Rites* 1) of nonhuman subjectivity. Wolfe's critique of the "discourse of species" works its way *internally* through "the 'inside,' the site of what used to be called the 'self' and the 'subject'" (*Animal Rites* 193). While I am certainly indebted to the sort of posthumanism Wolfe has been painstakingly developing, the present argument proceeds in the opposite direction, *externally*, by considering the corporeal reality of living bodies.

To redirect the conversation to the exteriority of bodies, I turn to the thought of Simone Weil (1909–1943). "The vulnerability of precious things is beautiful because vulnerability is a mark of existence," Weil wrote in her posthumous collection *Gravity and Grace* (1952).[2] This deceptively lyrical statement is in fact the basis of a radical aesthetics and an equally radical ethics. If fragility and finitude possess a special kind of beauty, this conception of beauty is already inherently ethical. It implies a sort of sacred recognition of life's value as material and temporal. What follows in this book is an attempt to think through this single statement by Weil in the context of human and nonhuman lives, since the relationship between vulnerability, existence, and beauty necessarily applies across the species divide and so delivers us beyond the domain of the human.

Weil is impossible to classify. In her introduction to Weil's Penguin anthology, Siân Miles bemoans the tendency "to make of Simone Weil a latter-day saint, an absurd absolutist or to impose upon her stereotypes with which every woman is familiar" (65). Leslie Fiedler speaks of "the terrible purity of her life" ("Introduction" vii), and Susan Sontag (wrongly) identifies in her a "dedication to martyrdom" ("Simone Weil" 60). Mario von der Ruhr places Weil in the canon of Christian thinkers, and T. S. Eliot suggests that "agreement and rejection" of her views "are secondary: what matters is to make contact with a great soul" (Weil, *The Need for Roots* viii). The idea of contact is not only central to the experience of reading Weil but is the very fabric of her thought. Contact with the flesh and blood vulnerability of beings— whether human or not—is the nexus within which the readings in this book take shape. They provide a corrective of sorts to the major trends within animal studies that center on the "content" or structure of otherness and less on the meanings of what Weil sees as the creaturely abandonment to "pitiless necessity."

Weil's writings return in different formulations to the interchangeability between vulnerability, reality, and beauty. That which exists must be loved, and loved because it exists, because it is subjected to necessity: "Compassion for every creature, because it is far from the Good. Infinitely far. Abandoned. God abandons our whole entire being—flesh, blood, sensibility, intelligence, love—to the pitiless necessity of matter" (Weil, "Epilogue" 142). Love, compassion, and beauty are a response to and a mode of confrontation with the concrete conditions of life, which Weil equates with divine absence. The beauty of necessity is glimpsed once one conceives of creation as an act of benevolent retreat: God's *letting be* of the world, which abandons it to the blind laws of matter. Weil's rhetoric presses together powerful contrasts (abandonment, love) into a resounding affirmation: "The absence of God is the most marvellous testimony of perfect love, and that is why pure necessity, necessity which is manifestly different from good, is so beautiful" (GG 106).

Animals have traditionally been perceived as pure necessity, material bodies pitted against human mindfulness and soulfulness. And yet there is nothing specifically "animal" about the susceptibility of mind and body alike to earthly forces—all that Weil summed up as the movement of *gravity*. Weil's writing abounds with the tautologies of necessity, which Maurice Blanchot saw as expressions of "certitude," Weil's proceeding via a series of affirmations in response to a "rigorous exigency" (Blanchot 106). "I should not love my suffering because it is useful. I should love it because it is" (GG 80). Of life's "nameless horrors," Weil says that "we have to accept the fact that they exist simply because they do exist" (GG 80). In human psychology too, necessity reigns. She calls it "human mechanics" (GG 5). Nor is the social sphere free of the same gravitational mechanism. "To be dependent on an alien will," she writes, "is to be a slave. This, however, is the fate of all men" (GG 155). "Man is a slave in so far as between action and its effect, between effort and the finished work, there is the interference of alien wills" (GG 155). Human (and other) bodies are indiscriminately subject to natural necessity and powers from without. As Weil puts it in the section "Necessity and Obedience": "The sun shines on the just and on the unjust. . . . God makes himself *necessity*. There are two aspects of necessity: it is exercised, it is endured: the sun and the cross" (GG 43).

Natural law (the sun) and affliction (the cross) determine the creaturely estate of all human (and nonhuman) beings. What aesthetic forms and narrative devices give expression to this view of living creatures? To frame the question somewhat differently: How might literature and film "appear"—and how do "man" and "animal" appear (and disappear) within them—as subjects of necessity? And how might a creaturely poetics come to mean in light of the connections Weil sees between beauty, fragility, and reality? These are the principal questions of this study.

The creature, then, is first and foremost a living body—material, temporal, and vulnerable. The modality Weil names *attention* (and Walter Benjamin attentiveness) to the bodily and the embodied determines my readings, whose sum as critical practices is the poetics I am calling creaturely. In her nuanced study of Weil, Sharon Cameron understands attention as "regard without motive" (115): "Attention brings into being without determining the nature of this being. . . . The difficulty is not one of perceiving, but rather one of arriving at an orientation that, once you arrive at it, eliminates difficulty, but not through understanding. Seeing like this—without identification—is seeing that resists 'reading'" (116–117). Attention is antiphilosophical; it does not produce arguments or truth claims about its object. Vulnerability as an object of attention does not yield a moral "reading." I am interested instead in the ramifications (for thought and also for action) of being oriented toward vulnerability as a universal mode of exposure. I will come later on to the possible problems of approaching animals in this powerless way. Before I do so, however, I want to provide a context and an outline for the poetics I am proposing. What does a creaturely poetics amount to conceptually and practically?

Reading through a creaturely prism consigns culture to contexts that are not exclusively human, contexts beyond an anthropocentric perspective. It recognizes in culture more than the clichéd expression of the "human condition" but an expression of something *in*human as well: the permutations of necessity and materiality that condition and shape human life. A work's formal qualities as well as its conceptual and historical contexts are fundamentally stamped by this altered perspective. Being human is grappling with what is inhuman in us. Stanley Cavell would have perhaps put it differently as the need to stop escaping our humanness: stop philosophizing in a manner that both steers and covers up the tracks of the escape.

Tracing the logic of flesh in examples across image and text reveals how culture makes sense (and use) of the body as a wager of species identity in the service of what Wolfe called the "*institution* of species*ism*" (*Animal Rites* 2). Embodiment undermines institutionalized speciesism in two ways: first, it provides a critical space for thinking of the human outside Cartesian abstractionism, as rigorously material. Second, embodiment makes for a different sort of aesthetics and ethics along the rudimentary lines Weil suggests. It is important to add that it is not a matter of taking the body out of discourse as some pure precultural entity, but of looking at how notions of embodiment—the material, the anonymous, and the elemental—provide a powerful antidote to anthropocentrism.

Instead of interrogating and expanding the possibilities of (non-human) subjectivity, I propose to explore the regions deemed animal (even vegetative) that lurk within the human itself. The gesture is one of *contraction*: making ourselves "less human," as it were, whilst seeking to grant animals a share in our world of subjectivity. Animal studies at its most ambitious could be thought as a way of reshaping (contracting) the humanities and social sciences under the sign of *dehumanization*.[3]

Dehumanization as a strategy of oppression has a long and iniquitous history.[4] Few if any events in recent European history illustrate the negative workings of dehumanization more profoundly or decisively than the Holocaust. I am interested in whether and how dehumanization can be reclaimed as, at least partly, positive. My opening argument is that while the Holocaust performed a violent unraveling of human identity, disclosing human contingency and the genocidal impulses inherent in striving for human perfection, much of the scholarly and popular legacy of the atrocity has been, oddly, the restitution and rehabilitation of humanism. A creaturely reading retrieves the Holocaust's disavowed animality as central to the ethics of memory.

The thinkers and witnesses at the center of this study—Simone Weil and Walter Benjamin among them—cluster around the (post) war imagination haunted by genocide. But I am not a historian or a Holocaust scholar. My thinking of the Holocaust is as a test case for the deployment of the human. The event also signifies what in her beautiful essay "The Difficulty of Reality and the Difficulty of Philosophy," on which more shortly, Cora Diamond calls a "disturbance of soul" (56) and the mind's "frightful no-man-fathomed cliffs" (54)— the sense that the question of our treatment of nonhuman lives is both painful and urgent.

Part 1 of this study, "The Inhumanity of Literature" (chapters 1–3) reads several works of fiction especially attentive to the body. These texts are, by nature, antipsychological and antipersonalist. They are examples of the flight from interiority toward an exteriority that renders the human as commonly understood unintelligible. Part 2, "The Inhumanity of Film" (chapters 4–6) turns to cinema and to modes of observation and seeing that push against the endeared viewing positions in the visual arts: identification and exchanged looks. I show how our concepts of the cinematic object, the spectator, and the practice of criticism can be revised by a creaturely cinema.

Animal Studies: Rights to Lives

J. M. Coetzee's groundbreaking novella *The Lives of Animals* (1999) helped reorient philosophical discussions in animal ethics away from utilitarian, reason, and rights-based approaches (that still occupy the center ground of the debate) toward what I am calling creaturely thinking. The five essays that make up *Philosophy and Animal Life* (2008) elegantly track the shift, punctuated five years earlier by the publication of Wolfe's *Animal Rites*.[5] Wolfe's critique of the rights and capabilities approach is by now fairly well established. Moral philosophers like Peter Singer and Tom Regan promote a model that extends only to those "who are (symptomatically) 'most like us'" and so "ends up reinforcing the very humanism that seems to be the problem in the first place" (*Animal Rites* 192). To get beyond the "residual" humanism of rights-based philosophies, Wolfe invoked, amongst others, Wittgenstein, Cavell, and Derrida (though not yet Coetzee).

Philosophy and Animal Life revisits a similar philosophical terrain, this time with Coetzee as its pivotal reference. The collection does not only depart from the (all but) exhausted model of rights, it highlights the exposed, incapable, and vulnerable body as the chief concern of a nonhuman ethics. "Exposures," Wolfe's introduction to *Philosophy and Animal Life*, declares the volume's principal theme: the being open to the physical realities that challenge or confound thought. In Cora Diamond's words, it is a matter of "the difficulty of philosophy, the difficulty of staying turned toward before and after, toward flesh and blood, towards the life of the animals we are" ("Difficulty" 77).

In Coetzee's *Diary of a Bad Year* (2008) an aging male writer is working on piece for a collection called *Strong Opinions*, assisted by a young and desirable secretary. In a section entitled "On the slaughter of animals," the fictional author writes, "Animal flesh looks much the same as human flesh (why should it not?). So, to the eye unused to carnivore cuisine, the inference does not come automatically ('naturally') that the flesh on display is cut from a carcass (animal) rather than from a corpse (human)" (63). The writer of *Diary of a Bad Year* recalls Coetzee's other, better-known writer, Elizabeth Costello. Here as in *The Lives of Animals* and *Elizabeth Costello* (2003), the "strong opinions" Coetzee's aging novelists hold in relation to the treatment of animals are firstly about bodies—about animal carcasses and human corpses and the fact that it takes the force of habit not to see both as the vestiges of living beings. The two protagonists regard themselves as potential "chunks of flesh," which makes it impossible for them to maintain the distinction between a human corpse and an animal carcass. A third, most important similarity between *The Lives of Animals* and *Diary of a Bad Year* is that their "strong opinions" are embedded in states of bodily agitation that mitigate the arguments the writers make. *Diary of a Bad Year* does this by dividing the page into several textual tiers: at the top is the text of *Strong Opinions*. Beneath it in the second tier are the writer's private thoughts and sexual yearnings for the carefree and enticing Anya. Anya's first person commentary at the bottom of the page adds the narrative's third layer. As work on the manuscript progresses, Coetzee's writer muses on how his opinions lose their authority in Anya's presence: "what has begun to change since I moved into the orbit of Anya is not my opinions themselves so much as my opinion of my opinions" (*Diary* 136). Anya's young flesh does not merely contrast with his own but shows off the drabness and sterility of his ideas (like Saul Bellow's Herzog, *Diary*'s aged intellectual rails against life, but he lacks Herzog's exuberant pathos).

More emphatically still than *Diary of a Bad Year*, *The Lives of Animals* presents the writer as an exposed animal whose strong opinions are like scars borne of an encounter with an unbearable reality.[6] Diamond's "The Difficulty of Reality" views the exposure of thought to the painfully baffling as Costello's existential predicament. Costello is "haunted by the horror of what we do to animals." She is deeply "wounded by this knowledge, this horror, and by the knowledge of how unhaunted others are. The wound marks her and isolates her" ("Difficulty" 46).

The question of animals here is no longer properly philosophical at all. It has become a wound, a "rawness of nerves," a physical rather than an intellectual problem. *The Lives of Animals*—as the mixed (and mix-up) commentaries on it suggest—is not just a confounding text, but a text about the state of being confounded.[7] Moreover, the "lives of animals" are not only those of which philosophers debate whether and which rights they deserve, but the life of Costello and in turn also ours. The manner in which the fate of animals figures in and inhabits Costello's life and our own is part of the kind of life forms she and we are: "in the life of the animal she is, argument does not have the weight we may take it to have in the life of the kind of animal we think of ourselves as being" ("Difficulty" 53). Reasoned argument is something we might believe intimately expresses "the kind of animal we think of ourselves as being"—but only *think*. For Diamond, the philosophical argument "may have built into it a distancing of ourselves from our sense of our own bodily life" ("Difficulty" 53). What Coetzee's novella is about, then, are not arguments for or against animal rights, but the possibility that philosophical arguments as such are a form of evasion—what Diamond (borrowing Cavell's term from "Knowing and Acknowledging") calls deflection.

Deflection "happens when we are moved from the appreciation, or attempt at appreciation, of a difficulty of reality to a philosophical or moral problem apparently in the vicinity" ("Difficulty" 57). Exposure and deflection are intimately linked via the bodily vulnerability—the creatureliness—we share with other animals:

> The awareness we each have of being a living body . . . carries with it exposure to the bodily sense of vulnerability to death, sheer animal vulnerability, the vulnerability we share with them. This vulnerability is capable of panicking us. To be able to acknowledge it at all, let alone as shared, is wounding; but acknowledging it as shared with other animals, in the presence of what we do to them, is capable not only of panicking one but also of isolating one, as Elizabeth Costello is isolated. Is there any difficulty in seeing why we should not prefer to return to moral debate, in which the livingness and death of other animals enter as facts . . . not as presences that may unseat our reason?   ("Difficulty" 74)

Two issues arise from the passage: creaturely fellowship and the lures of deflection. First, Diamond understands the connectedness between human and nonhuman animals as the cross-species vulnerability of bodies. In the 1991 essay "Eating Meat and Eating People" Diamond developed the idea of animals as "fellow creatures," a notion that guides me throughout this book, and which Diamond hastens to add "is *not* a biological concept" ("Eating Meat" 328). In "Injustice and Animals" (2001), Diamond turns to Weil's theory of justice. Despite apparent "obstacles to connecting Weil's thought with animals" ("Injustice" 129), her idea of injustice not as the withdrawal of rights but as the relentless crushing of the weak by the strong does not exclude animals. "Weil's thought about injustice should be understood as a response to *communicative pressure*" ("Injustice" 135; my emphasis).

Here Diamond is in accordance with Derrida, who replies to Jeremy Bentham's famous question "can they [animals] suffer?" with an "*undeniable*" yes ("The Animal That Therefore I Am" 397).[8] The reply is emphatically not morally calculating, but responds to what Calarco describes as the "disruptive force in animal suffering" (Calarco 120). To deny the agency of creaturely suffering does not only deflect a difficult reality, but compromises thought. In a powerful passage in "The Animal That Therefore I Am" (which refutes Lévinas's denial of the animal face), Derrida says that "a war is being waged . . . between those who violate not only animal life but even and also this sentiment of compassion and, on the other hand, those who appeal to an irrefutable testimony of pity" (397). To "think the war" is not just an ethical obligation but a philosophical task par excellence, since it involves the primordial source of thought in the appeal of the other (animal): "I say 'to think' this war, because I believe it concerns what we call 'thinking.' The animal looks at us, and we are naked before it. Thinking perhaps begins there" (AIA 397).

Weil's thought begins there. Her refusal to deflect from the communicative pressures of vulnerability renders her an exemplary thinker of exposure. Diamond reads Weil and Cavell, each in their way, as philosophers "concerned with deflection from the difficulty of reality" ("Difficulty" 75) who refuse the "consolations of philosophy."[9] Consolatory thinking (intellectual, psychological, or religious), Weil warns, comes at the expense of appreciating reality and must therefore be overcome. Reality is the passionate meeting point between blind necessity (gravity) and a loving (and absent) God (grace). Politics, ethics, and art materialize at this difficult crossroad (the cross is for Weil the literal intersection between gravity and grace). Attitudes and actions may be judged according to their orientation toward reality: the extent to which they seek to avoid (deflect) or else perceive and receive the real.

While there are obvious points of contact between Diamond and Derrida—I am characterizing this as the move *from rights to lives*—there are also significant differences, which for Wolfe reside in Diamond's attachment to a certain "internal theoretical and methodological level that recontains and even undermines an otherwise admirable philosophical project" ("Flesh and Finitude" 8). The difference between Diamond and Derrida emerges "in the articulation of this peculiar thing called 'the human'" ("Exposures" 20). Several examples from Diamond's earlier essays "Experimenting on Animals" and "Eating Meat and Eating People" illustrate the importance that a sense of being human still exerts for her. She writes, for example, that the "response to animals as our fellows in mortality . . . depends on a conception of *human* life" ("Eating Meat" 329).

Derrida undoes this sort of self-transparency of the human in the face of the very finitude that is so crucial to Diamond. Quoting Richard Beardsworth, Wolfe explains: "For Derrida . . . 'no relation to death can appear as such,' and 'if there is no "as" to death,' then the 'relation to death is always mediated through an other. The "as" of death always appears *through* an other's death, *for* another' (Beardsworth, *Derrida*, 118)" ("Exposures" 22). The Lévinasian primacy of the other over the self in the impossibility of my being-toward-death, as the radical limit to any sense I might have of my own finitude, joins a second limit: that of language. In its "radically ahuman technicity or mechanicity" ("Exposures" 26), language sets a further limit to notions of a self-knowing, transparent humanity—including the sense of physical finitude that Diamond's earlier work invokes as a condition for the ethical appreciation of nonhuman life. In Derrida,

> "we" are always radically other, already in- or ahuman in our very being—not just in the evolutionary, biological, and zoological fact of our physical vulnerability and mortality, our mammalian existence, of course, *but also in our subjection to and constitution in the materiality and technicity of a language that is always on the scene before we are, as a precondition of our subjectivity.* ("Exposures" 27; my emphasis)

Derrida's familiar notions of the trace, iterability, and *différance* that constitute language are also what mark its inhumanity. (It is in this sense, by the way, that Wolfe and Calarco maintain that Derrida's work from its very inception was concerned with the animal). The internal foreignness of language—language as an open system of differences—fissures the identity and self-presence of the human, cutting through the appreciation of embodiedness fundamental for Diamond.

The final and most crucial tension between Derrida's philosophizing, on the one hand, and Diamond (and Cavell's), on the other, pertains to Derrida's "derivation of a general economy or 'law' of 'heteronomy'" ("Exposures" 34) in the appreciation of the two forms of finitude—language and death. "For Cavell," writes Wolfe, "the problem with the Derridean general economy . . . is that it continues the project of metaphysics while announcing metaphysics' demise, and it does so in flight from the 'ordinary,' the 'everyday'" ("Exposures" 35). Derrida's gesture, rehearsed with considerable ingenuity throughout all of his writing, has the effect of shoring up philosophy and rather snugly affirming its authority, albeit in a different tone. Put plainly, Derrida retreats from the encounter with wounding finitudes into the relative haven of a general system. Wolfe explains:

> In Derrida's derivation of a general economy or "law" of "heteronomy" . . . Diamond and Cavell would no doubt find him seeking his own kind of solace, engaging in his own kind of "deflection" by the force of reason that they see their philosophy as dedicated to resisting. For what is lost in such a foreclosure, in their view, is the rawness testified to by an Elizabeth Costello and the ethical stakes of attending to that rawness. ("Exposures" 34–35)

Ethics discloses the presence of a crisis (Costello's "rawness of nerves," Weil's response to a "rigorous exigency") whose source is the ordinary—yet extraordinary—living encounter. The meaningful difference between Derrida and Diamond emerges around the breakdown of thought in the face of the first of the two limits: the flesh and blood nature of reality. We might therefore observe that while Diamond and Derrida both touch on the question of animals, their philosophies signify different ways of being touched by it. Diamond resists retrieving a system or a law (such as Derrida's subjective economy of "carnophallogocentrism") from what she describes as the "coming apart of thought."[10] What she holds fast to instead is—like Weil—the *force of the blow*: the "*how much* that coming apart of thought and reality belongs to flesh and blood" ("Difficulty" 78; my emphasis).

Vulnerability

I want to briefly address a likely objection to the kind of poetics I am proposing, whose main trope of vulnerability might appear overly negative. To begin with, why treat embodiment solely in the locus of vulnerability? And why approach animals in this way, as radically vulnerable? This would appear to foreclose the possibility of animal agency (and resistance), limit the variety of relations we have with them, and reduce animals to the status of superlative victims. I will address each objection in turn.

In *Corporal Compassion*, Ralph R. Acampora develops an ethics he calls "embodied conviviality" (96), whose foundation is the "specifically somatic core of cross-species moral experience" (xiv). While vulnerability does figure in this scheme (79–84), it is conviviality as "intercorporal cohabitation" (78) on which relations and potential relations between humans and animals are founded. In responding to "a certain affective/somatic deficit in animal ethics" (74), Acampora aligns himself in part with feminist care ethicists such as Josephine Donovan and Carol J. Adams. Where Donovan stresses the "dialogical nature of care theory" (Donovan 360), based on attention (not quite in Weil's sense) to animals, Acampora adds that "this experience is originally mediated by physical sensibility" (Acampora 74). The physically dialogic "space of convivial worldhood" enables, even favors, what Acampora calls "somaesthetic caring" and "symphysis" (78)—not as part of a normative ethics but designating the "(pre-) moral texture of conviviality" (73).

Acampora refers to vulnerability in the work of philosopher Edith Wyschogrod, for whom vulnerability "constitutes a proscriptive 'corporal plea' against violence, as if the other's body were saying 'do not injure me'" (Acampora 80). There are obvious Lévinasian and Weilian inflections to this "plea," which locates the ethical response to bodies in their nakedness and exposure. But vulnerability is not a privileged condition of possibility, and Acampora's aim is, in a more Nietzschean vein, to reclaim the body as a positive plenitude.

What invites a "protectionist" rather than an "instrumentalist/ exploitative" stance toward other animals is not a moral injunction

(Singer, Regan) or a metaphysical structure (Lévinas), but what Acampora describes as "fitting-relations" whose "apprehension can be given more or less phenomenologically rigorous descriptions . . . in or through a mental process of imaginatively empathetic identification" (75). Nonetheless, Acampora admits that it is possible, indeed easy, to disrupt intersomaticity. Laboratory animals are a good example. They are isolated in cages that effectively replace their bodies; in this case, says Acampora, "the carceral overtakes the carnal" (100) and undermines the potential for corporal compassion. In one sense, then, vulnerability dispassionately denotes the condition of being embodied as necessarily limited, and limited by necessity, but always already encompassing the dialogic relation between bodies that underlies caring. Within this vulnerable range are possible all kinds of experiences, many of which fit Acampora's "convivial" ones.

It is clear, however, that my use of vulnerability is closer to Agamben's bare life and the powerful violations it invites and to the workings of pitiless necessity at the center of Weil's thought. There are several reasons for placing animals in a context of such extraordinary powerlessness. First, as Wolfe reminds us in *Animal Rites*, the logic of speciesism, while applicable to humans, is disproportionate in relation to nonhuman animals. *Creaturely Poetics* opened with the assertion that, when it comes to animals, power operates with the fewest of obstacles. Thus animals constitute an exemplary "state of exception" of species sovereignty. To speak of animals' vulnerability in this context is to draw attention to their outstanding position in the judicial, political, and moral orders.

That said, I do not regard animal life as absolutely bare. In the course of my argument, ideas of bare life act more as a permanent but permeable threshold than as a foundation upon which life's other functions are built and to which life returns when these are taken away. *All* life is bare in the sense of being susceptible to the interventions of power. As Weil put it: "to be a created thing is not necessarily to be afflicted, but it is necessarily to be exposed to affliction" (*Simone Weil* 66).[11] My use of vulnerability belongs to the ethicoreligious exploration of creaturely exposure.

Theorists like Slavoj Žižek and Alain Badiou recently warned against a "culture of victimization" that elevates suffering to bolster conservative and interventionist policies.[12] Vulnerability does not entail such an appeal to humanitarian sympathies. It comes into being in a very different climate from the one Žižek has in mind. Attentiveness to vulnerability is produced in the state Weil calls "perfect detachment." As the discussions that follow shall invariably show, there is a degree of affinity between Žižek and Badiou's criticisms and my own antihumanitarianism. Despite its "soft" connotations, vulnerability offers a fundamental challenge to liberal humanism, both in terms of the rejection of the notion of rights and in a radical critique of subjectivity.

In his essay on Paul, Badiou quotes from the First Epistle to the Corinthians:

> For the foolishness of God is wiser than men, and the weakness of God is stronger than men. . . . God chose the foolish things of the world to confound the wise, and God chose the weak things of the world to confound the strong; God chose what is base and despised in the world, and even things that are not, to bring to nought things that are, so that no one might glorify himself in his presence.[13]
>
> (1 Cor. 1:25–29)

These may look like inversions—the weak is the powerful, the mad is the sane—but they are not. They enunciate not as philosophical argument but as what Badiou calls a "subjective disposition" (45), a novel discourse that altogether transcends the (Jewish) economy of signs and the (Greek) economy of wisdom. A similar "ontological subversion" (47) lies at the heart of Weil's thought. Absolute powerlessness and foolishness (impersonality, inhumanity even) are for Weil the path out of the clutches of power: subjection to the illusions of selfhood and, I would add also, the illusions of species. Not only does Weil attempt a renunciation of her own powers, she insists that the "act of creation is not an act of power. It is an abdication" ("Are We Struggling for Justice?" 123). Following Weil, then, vulnerability proceeds by doggedly pursuing the most vulnerable argument. As I hope each chapter will nonetheless show, the most vulnerable argument can yield compelling critical insights.

In "Companionable Thinking" Cavell writes that Elizabeth Costello's "revelation of the woundedness that marks being human . . . has roughly the logic of a voice in the wilderness, crying out news that may be known (inordinately) to virtually none, but to all virtually. It is a voice invoking a religious, not alone a philosophical, register: it is uninvited, it goes beyond an appeal to experiences we can assume all humans share, or recognize, and it is meant to instill belief and a commentary and community based on belief, yielding a very particular form of passionate utterance, call it prophecy" (111). Much can be said about this passage, which leads Cavell to diagnose in Costello a deepseated human antipathy, perhaps even misanthropy. But what the passage affirms is the place of religious discourse in the sort of realities Costello—and Weil—is communicating.

What is Weil's contribution, not just to the arguments concerning our ethical obligation to animals, but to what Cavell called the "register" in which we approach the subject? Diamond and Derrida (as well as Coetzee) suggest that the philosophical register deflects (or to use Badiou's term, forgoes fidelity to) the event of nonhuman suffering. Thus a new register is required, which complements, but also keeps philosophy in check.

The materialist perspective I have been proposing does not recognize species as a definitive (or especially significant) mark of identity. It invariably transforms the ways we think about relations between humans themselves and between humans and other animals. And yet the creaturely is not simply a synonym for the material and corporeal. It carries within it (as inflection, as horizon) an opening unto a religious vocabulary of creation and created, and so attempts a rapprochement between the material and the sacred. Weil's contribution, then, resides in breaking what Françoise Meltzer called the "taboo against religion" (Meltzer 620), and, as chapter 1 will make clear, in linking the political with the mystical: "Weil is the only writer I can think of, in what Derrida calls the Tradition (that is, Western metaphysics), for whom the mystery of the sacred is inextricable, not only from the idea of responsibility (as in Lévinas), but from political activism" (Meltzer 621).

It is no accident that Žižek and Badiou, in books like *The Puppet and the Dwarf* and *Saint Paul*, are recasting revolutionary politics in the light of Christian mystical discourse (something Weil both practiced and preached).[14] Calarco is surely right to point to the "implicit anthropocentrism" (Calarco 12) of these theorists' reconfigurations of subjectivity. But there is, I believe, great potential to the "rehabilitation" of religious discourse in the articulation of a fundamentally new politics and ethics, a new language and art—all that Calarco rightly sees as the most radical promise of confronting the question of the animal. The task at hand, I would therefore argue, is not only posthumanist and postanthropocentric, but also, and no less significantly, postsecular.

Chapter Outlines

Chapter I examines the unraveling of the human in the Holocaust and argues that a resuscitation of humanism in the post-Holocaust task of remembrance is neither possible nor desirable. The chapter reads closely several key texts by Weil alongside texts by Primo Levi, Agamben, and Alain Finkielkraut, claiming Weil as an important theoretician of atrocity.

The problem of genocide's "inheritance" returns in chapter 2 on William Golding's 1955 novel *The Inheritors*, in which Golding experiments with a form of embodied language to render palpable the final days in the lives of Neanderthals. I compare Golding's pictorial method to Temple Grandin's "thinking in pictures" and ask whether and how their respective visualities attend animals' lives. The latter part of the chapter turns to Walter Benjamin's materialist-messianic analysis of history. Drawing on the work of Beatrice Hanssen and Eric Santner on Benjamin's creaturely attentiveness, I rethink Golding's novel as a natural history narrative that retrieves the prehuman history of the vanquished.

"The Indignities of Species in Marie Darrieussecq's *Pig Tales*" introduces metamorphosis and the indeterminacy of species as writing, through the novel's notion of *écriture de cochon* (pig writing). Forfeiting interiority in favor of materiality, Darrieussecq sculpts the bodies of her fictional universe out of an array of forms, from the *nouveau roman*, through naturalism, pastoral, science fiction, and pornography. Her writing is concerned with material transformation as a source of literary innovation.

Chapter 4, "Cine-Zoos," revisits the work of theorists of the visual animal, John Berger, Steve Baker, Akira Mizuta Lippit, and Jonathan Burt. The tension inherent in the animal image between the simulated and the real leads me back to the film theory of André Bazin in the context of the recent "realist turn" in film studies. Bazinian realism, I argue, must be thought as profoundly *zoomorphic*. A close look at examples of zoomorphic cinema indicates some of the ways in which cinema defies dominant humanist watching habits.

Chapter 5 looks at Georges Franju's *Le Sang des bêtes* (1949) and Frederick Wiseman's *Primate* (1974) as documentary studies of biopolitics. Both films center on institutions—the abattoir and the primate research center—whose chief product is the clear hierarchy of species. In their visual strategies both films display a convergence between scientific and surrealist imagery, which Raymond Durgnat described as "scientific surrealism" and Paul Virilio condemned as a "pitiless art."

The final chapter turns to the cinema of Werner Herzog, who works with and against the sort of creaturely poetics I have been developing. While Herzog's films involve what Gertrude Koch called "extreme situations" that expend and engulf the human, many also invoke the tradition of male exploration and heroism that posits man squarely against nature. I argue that Nietzsche (rather than Weil) is more suitable for thinking about creatureliness and the tragic in Herzog's work.

1 THE INHUMANITY OF LITERATURE

1 Humanity Unraveled, Humanity Regained

The Holocaust and the Discourse of Species

And the wolf shall dwell with the lamb, and the leopard shall lie down
with the kid; and the calf and the young lion and the fatling together; and
a little child shall lead them.   —Isaiah 11:6

We are in the midst of a humanistic revival or at least a neohumanist burst
of energy. . . . Issues of how humans live and what they live for become
central because they are what concern us as readers and teachers—some-
times in spite of ourselves.   —Daniel R. Schwarz, *Mapping the Ethical Turn*

Liberation

Primo Levi's *The Truce* recalls the first days of the liberation of Aus-
chwitz with an anecdote. A cow delivered by the Russian army to feed
the camp's survivors is swiftly set upon, torn apart, and eaten:

> About midday a frightened child appeared, dragging a cow by the
> halter; he made us understand that it was for us, that the Russians
> had sent it, then he abandoned the beast and fled like a bolt. I
> don't know how, but within minutes the poor animal was slaugh-
> tered, gutted and quartered and its remains distributed to all the
> corners of the camp where survivors nestled.   (*Truce* 191)

The scene is a sort of freakish reworking of the prophecy of Isaiah, a book
whose theme is salvation at a time (the late eighth century BC) of Jewish
dejection and exile. In Isaiah, too, a child—symbol of a heavenly truce—
leads the animal. Was Levi thinking of Isaiah when he noted the "poor

animal" whose violent death is oddly concurrent, perhaps even synonymous with, the liberation of Auschwitz? The passage from *The Truce* and the prophecy of Isaiah are mirror images of emancipation: the liberation of Auschwitz marked the *Häftlinge*'s return into history and humanity, while the biblical vision glimpses a final escape from history and from the dictates of species. If presenting this passage from *The Truce* and the prophecy of Isaiah as twin tales seems gratuitous, the irony with respect to liberation is, I would argue, implicit in Levi's text.

Cultural anxiety over species identity determines the ways the Holocaust is and is not represented. Holocaust discourse is uncannily doubled: on the one hand, animals permeate the Holocaust. We find them in the perpetrators' denial of the humanity of the Jews and in the reverse commonplace that the Nazis "behaved like animals," in the image of Jews as "lambs for the slaughter," clichés about Nazi animal lovers (and Hitler's supposed vegetarianism), and most potently, perhaps, in the resounding question of Holocaust literature of how to retain one's humanity in the face of Auschwitz. But if the Jews died like cattle, cattle do not die like Jews. Comparing the fate of animals to that of Jews is considered ethically repugnant (Cavell calls it "indecorous"). Sifting legitimate from illegitimate Holocaust imagery is part and parcel of the work of memory, and it discloses a profound insecurity specifically around the notion of species.

Daniel Schwarz, for example, "want[s] to show how [Holocaust] narratives are about humans, by humans, and for humans" (*Imagining the Holocaust* 4). The human in discussions of the Holocaust acts as a persistent but ultimately floating signifier: "if ever a past needed a human shape," says Schwarz, "it is the Holocaust; yet as we shall see, putting a human shape on inhuman behavior challenges our ability to imagine evil and to represent it linguistically" (6). Does it? If we must "keep the Holocaust human," this is precisely because the event radically erodes human legibility. To simply reject as iniquitous the analogy between Jews and animals is also to refuse to engage fully with the Holocaust itself.

Much Holocaust writing is devoted to the moral salvaging of humanity from the wreckage of the Second World War. Restoring humanity (defined through the familiar tropes of free will, rationality, morality, and language) from what in *Remnants of Auschwitz* Agamben called the "shipwreck of dignity" (62) is the reparative principle behind a large portion of Holocaust commentaries. In *The Holocaust in American Life*, Peter Novick says that in the United States suffering has become "the path to wisdom—the cult of the survivor as secular saint" (11).[1] To be sure, this humanist project is by now so habitual as to have become intuitive and unquestionable. It is also seductive, since its goal is to assert human dignity in the face of atrocity. But such a project is, I would argue, a vacant one. Even for Levi, "by temperament, education, and class, the quasi embodiment of the Enlightenment humanist subject" (Druker 11), human identity after Auschwitz is not simply recoverable.

The significance of the Holocaust's uncanny animality is, as Agamben has already shown, profound. The mania for racial purity, the ghettos, deportations, and camps claimed the human itself as an embattled zone, an identity whose instability fueled the urge for demolition and reinvention. The battle over the human being did not, however, end with the defeat of the Third Reich. It survives as dutifully and as passionately in the post-Holocaust task of remembrance. The result is that in post-Holocaust rhetoric, too, human and animal, humanity and inhumanity continue to circle one another in contagious proximity. Schwarz's affirmation of a "neohumanist burst of energy" somewhat wishfully indicates that Holocaust memory today shoulders the great weight of species identity as its ethicopolitical epicenter.

This chapter begins with Primo Levi, who bore witness to the Holocaust's unraveling of human identity, and continues with Simone Weil's important notion of "affliction" (*malheur*), a striking elaboration of which I find in Levi's memoirs *If This Is a Man* and *The Truce*. Affliction both illuminates and presents a challenge to the standard understanding of the Holocaust's radical transgressiveness. My discussion then turns to a comparison between Weil and Alain Finkielkraut's formulations of radical injustice. Finkielkraut's call for a clearly defined category of "crimes against humanity" to address the "boundless crime" of genocide bears some resemblance to Weil's understanding of ultimate injustice as a violation of the sacred. In Weil's formulation, however, the particularity of the human gives way to a less anthropocentric ethics of creaturely life. The chapter closes with a look at fiction by I. B. Singer, who reinstates the animality of the Holocaust by linking the abject figure of the survivor to the downtrodden animal. My aim in this chapter is to follow a less predictable train of thought, beyond the binaries of humanity/inhumanity, historiography/testimony, representable/inexpressible. In so doing, I also consider Weil's original contribution to the thinking of atrocity.

The Bathers

On three occasions in "The Main Camp" chapter of *The Truce*, Primo Levi and his fellow prisoners are made to bathe by the military authorities under whose control they come. The first of these "christenings" takes place on arrival to Auschwitz. The second is on liberation by the Red Army and the third in American custody. "I am not questioning that a bath was opportune for us in our condition," Levi remarks, but "at each of those three memorable christenings, it was easy to perceive behind the concrete and literal aspect a great symbolic shadow, the unconscious desire of the new authorities, who absorbed us in turn within their own sphere, to strip us of the vestiges of our former life, to make of us new men consistent with their new models, to impose their brand upon us" (194).

The three christenings—unseemly inversions of the painted bathers of Renoir, Courbet, or Cézanne—produce "new men" whose identity each time reflects the peculiarities of an ideology. In the tenebrous world of the Lager, the baths conflate mythic ritual with the practices of modern hygiene. While the Germans imposed a "bath of humiliation," a "grotesque-devilish-sacral bath," and a "black mass bath," the Russian bath was "extemporaneous and crude" (194). The Americans, dressed in chemical suits, sprayed the naked survivors with DDT, "a functional, antiseptic, highly automatized bath" (194). Each baptism is a rebirth: scrubbing away the residues of an improper humanity and producing it anew.

Much of *If This Is a Man* and *The Truce* illustrates the conscious efforts required to produce, retain, or retrieve one's humanity in the face of its unraveling. In its doing and undoing, the human is shown to be a tenuous, fragile construct. In chapters like "Chemical Examination" (*If This Is a Man* 107–114), humanity is pragmatically conferred on Levi by the German authorities as a function of his scientific expertise—a classically rationalist, ability-based definition of humanity, though certainly not a universal one (Levi knows that failing the chemistry exam means certain death). Earlier, in "On the Bottom" (28–43), Levi charts the "demolition of a man" (32) on entering the foreign universe of the Lager. In the Dantesque "The Canto of Ulysses" (115–121), Levi clings to recitations of Dante's "Inferno" as precious shreds of his civilized existence. Yet Levi also believes what Agamben will later develop into a systematic study of the legacies of Auschwitz, that "the Lager was pre-eminently a gigantic biological and social experiment" (93).

At the second bathing, the hefty Russian women encounter a "serious obstacle":

> a shadow, a bald little figure, twisted like a root, skeleton-like . . . like an inanimate block . . . Charles and I, naked and streaming, watched the scene with compassion and horror. When one of his arms was stretched out, we saw the tattooed number for a moment: he was a 200,000, one of the Vosges: "*Bon dieu, c'est un français!*" exclaimed Charles, and turned in silence towards the wall.
>
> (*Truce* 195)

This is one of Levi's "submerged" or "drowned" figures, a *Muselmann*: Auschwitz slang for the ruined human of whom little remains but the final flickering of biological life.[2] The episode is followed by the often-quoted passage on Hurbinek:

> Hurbinek was a nobody, a child of death, a child of Auschwitz. He looked about three years old, no one knew anything of him, he could not speak and he had no name; that curious name, Hurbinek, had been given to him by us, perhaps by one of the women who had interpreted with those syllables one of the inarticulate sounds that the baby let out now and again. He was paralyzed

from the waist down, with atrophied legs, as thin as sticks; but his eyes, lost in his triangular and wasted face, flashed terribly alive, full of demand, assertion, of the will to break loose, to shatter the tomb of his dumbness. The speech he lacked, which no one had bothered to teach him, the need of speech charged his stare with explosive urgency: it was a stare both savage and human, even mature, a judgment, which none of us could support, so heavy it was with force and anguish. (*Truce* 197)

When Hurbinek dies, Levi writes that "nothing remains of him: he bears witness through these words of mine" (198). This testimony signals "the disjunction between two impossibilities of bearing witness" (*Remnants* 39): Levi's impossible rendering of Hurbinek's impossible speech. The *Muselmann*, claims Agamben, embodies Auschwitz's "radical refutation of every principle of obligatory communication" (*Remnants* 65).

Though Agamben may be the most arresting of them, several commentators take up Levi's wrestling with liberal humanism as key to a post-Holocaust ethics. Jonathan Druker recently argued that "while Levi scholars have usually noted the memoir's humanist agenda, in which reason and culture are only redemptive, they have seldom taken into account the counternarrative embedded in the text, which corroborates that after Auschwitz, the Enlightenment conception of man, and the ethical guarantees the word implies, have been irreparably damaged" (Druker 72).[3] The erosion of man is underway even before the book begins, in the title's maimed grammaticality: *If This Is a Man*.[4]

What is exemplary about Levi is not just the quality of his writing (we know that he saw himself as chemist first and writer second). His work embodies the lacuna by which "the witness must in some way submit his every word to the test of an impossibility of speaking" (*Remnants* 157). This idea of witnessing is, I would argue, central to inter- and postwar literature whose modernity resides in the attempt to draw nearer to the slaughtered millions. "Perhaps every word, every writing is born, in this sense, as testimony" (*Remnants* 38).

In the use of an episodic structure, naturalism and modernism, and the theme of the epic, picaresque sojourner through worlds, Levi is surprisingly close to another work of witnessing, Louis Ferdinand Céline's *Journey to the End of the Night* (1932). Céline's semiautobiographical narrator is witness to a world that would soon descend to the horrors of Auschwitz:

We had reached the end of the world, that was becoming obvious. We couldn't go any further, because further on there were only dead people.

The dead began on the Place du Terre, two steps away. From where we were it was easy to see them . . . you've got to know how to find them—namely, from inside you with your eyes almost closed, because the electric signs with their great copses of light make it very hard to see the dead, even through the clouds. . . . There were old patients of mine here and there, male and female, that I'd long stopped thinking about, and still others, the black man in a white cloud, all alone, the one they had given one lash too many down there in Topo. (322–323)

Levi the chemist, Céline the physician; their professions enter their books. Chemistry does not just save Levi from the gas chambers, but lends an elemental dimension to his prose (full-blown in *The Periodic Table*). Céline's accounts of the degradations of existence, of bodies marred by poverty, war, and disease are filtered through the physician's gaze of Bardamu, *Journey*'s first-person narrator and medicine man of the *banlieues*.

If we can speak of realism in Levi and Céline, it is not as a literary convention but as an attitude. Both keep their eyes fastened on the condition of creaturely exposure amplified by the two world wars that frame their work. It is no accident that *Journey to the End of the Night* includes several extraordinary passages on cruelty to animals (250–251, 259).[5] Céline's later collaborationism and the seething antisemitism of his pamphlets (*Bagatelles pour un massacre* [1937], *L'école des cadavers* [1938], and *Les Beaux Draps* [1941]) should not deter us from comparisons with Levi. On the contrary, to a postwar readership in the shadow of totalitarianism and declining the apologist path, Levi and Céline share a common historical tragedy.[6]

Affliction

The connection Levi makes between the Holocaust and inarticulacy does not spring from the insufficiencies of language. Experience in all its varieties, appalling, joyous, or prosaic, is difficult to put into words. Not finding the words is an expression of the kind of creatures we are. It is also an expression (and an experience) of our loneliness. In what sense, then, is the Holocaust uniquely positioned outside language? "Why confer on extermination the prestige of the mystical?" (*Remnants* 32). Unsayability for Agamben is the paradox of witnessing, the site where language meets nonlanguage. Speaking about the Holocaust is not therefore a matter of making language express a special content that categorically defies language—for there is no such content—but of making language open to the excessive reality of the event.

The Hurbinek episode epitomizes what for Weil is a general problem of communicating injustice, that "those who most often have occasion to feel that evil is being done to them are those who are least trained in the art of speech" ("Human Personality" 73). Both the *Muselmann* and the lacuna of testimony are uncannily prefigured in the condition Weil called "affliction."[7] "Affliction is by its nature inarticulate. The afflicted silently beseech to be given the words to express themselves. There are times when they are given none; but there are also times when they are given words, but ill-chosen ones, because those who choose them know nothing of the affliction they would interpret" ("Human Personality" 85). Affliction is by far Weil's most suggestive contribution to the field of Holocaust studies, and it has yet to be worked through and reckoned with systematically.[8]

Weil's most important thoughts on affliction are found in the essay "The Love of God and Affliction," written in 1942, the year of Levi's deportation to Auschwitz. It begins by distinguishing between suffering and affliction: "*affliction is something apart, specific,* and irreducible. It is quite a different thing from simple suffering. It takes possession of the soul and marks it through and through with its own particular mark, the mark of slavery" (67). This recalls Levi's description of arriving to Auschwitz: "Imagine now a man who is deprived of everyone he loves, and at the same time of his house, his habits, his clothes, in short, of everything he possesses: he will be a hollow man, reduced to suffering and needs, forgetful of dignity and restraint, for he who loses all often easily loses himself" (*If This Is a Man* 33). Affliction is sorrow stripped of all its "possessions" (the people we lost, our house, our habits, our clothes) and reduced to its nakedness. Sharon Cameron explains that "'affliction' cannot be mitigated in that its source—distance from God—is irremediable" (121). The afflicted, "a being struggling on the ground like a half-crushed worm" ("Love of God" 69), like Levi's *Muselmann* and Agamben's *homo sacer*, is bare life abandoned and forsaken. In Weil and Agamben, it is important to stress, these figures do not function as "limit cases" but serve to illuminate a general situation (*Remnants* 48–50). Unlike Agamben, however, affliction in Weil is not part of the anatomy of sovereignty but a "divine technique" ("Love of God" 81), a sort of theological gateway. For once the particular features of suffering have been cleared and suffering stripped bare, affliction "converts the person's *separation* from God to his *inseparability* from God" (*Impersonality* 122).

"Those who are persecuted for their faith and are aware of the fact are not afflicted, although they have to suffer" ("Love of God" 73). To become affliction, suffering must cease to make sense ("affliction is ridiculous" ["Love of God" 73]). An illogical and random persecution commutes the sufferer's identity, since their suffering is comprehensible neither as martyrdom nor as heroism. The afflicted is no longer strictly a person (he "will keep only half his soul" ["Love of God" 69]), but an anonymous focal point of pain.

This has bearing for that common question of post-Holocaust theodicy (How could God let Auschwitz happen?). "It is not surprising," writes Weil, "that the innocent are killed, tortured, driven from their country, made destitute, or reduced to slavery, imprisoned in camps or cells, since there are criminals to perform such actions. . . . But it *is* surprising that God should have given affliction the power to seize the very souls of the innocent and to take possession of them as their sovereign lord" ("Love of God" 69). The atheist is right: God is absent from the world. But this absence for Weil does not signify a failed or malevolent Creator. The existence of the world is synonymous with the possibility of affliction: a "blind mechanism, heedless of degrees of spiritual perfection, continually tosses men about and throws some of them at the very foot of the Cross. *It rests with them to keep or not to keep their eyes turned toward God through all the jolting*" ("Love of God" 73; my emphasis). This is not, Cameron insists, the masochistic reinscription of pain as love. Love, understood as "a direction and not a state of the soul" ("Love of God" 81) is rather "generated in spite of the pain and by what the pain can't touch—'the greatest suffering' being insufficient to disturb 'the acquiescent part of the soul, consenting to a right direction'" (*Impersonality* 122). I take this to be at stake in the "October 1944" chapter of *If This Is a Man*, in which a religious man called Kuhn thanks God for sparing him during selection. This is a rare occasion on which Levi foregoes his usual decorum:

> I see and hear old Kuhn praying aloud, with his beret on his head, swaying backwards and forwards violently. Kuhn is thanking God because he has not been chosen.
>
> Kuhn is out of his senses. Does he not see Beppo the Greek in the bunk next to him, Beppo who is twenty years old and is going to the gas chamber the day after tomorrow and knows it and lies there looking fixedly at the light without saying anything and without even thinking anymore? Can Kuhn fail to realize that next time it will be his turn? Does Kuhn not understand that what has happened today is an abomination, which no propitiatory prayer, no pardon, no expiation by the guilty, which nothing at all in the power of man can ever clean again?
>
> If I was God, I would spit at Kuhn's prayer.   (135–136)

Kuhn's prayer expiates suffering by denying the reality of affliction. His gratitude is thus a perversion of prayer, which far from "consenting to a right direction" and keeping his "eyes turned toward God through all the jolting" attributes to God personal preference and caprice in the meting out of suffering. What sort of a God is Kuhn thanking in this way? Levi the atheist recognizes in Kuhn's prayer a scourge on both God and man.

There is a second way in which affliction alters how we might wish to think about the Holocaust. It concerns the problem of evil. Affliction, we have seen, is the "mark of slavery." The afflicted are deprived of personality and made into things ("Love of God" 73). A loss of autonomy, indeed of humanity, also befalls the perpetrators of affliction. But there is a structural difference between the evildoer and the victim in the possibility, however small, of the afflicted turning their gaze toward and not away from God. The criminal for Weil is not a "monster"; he has simply looked away. "Human crime, which is the cause of most affliction, is part of blind necessity, because criminals do not know what they are doing" ("Love of God" 73–74). It is vital to add that Weil's notion of evil does not remove responsibility from the evildoer. Like Hannah Arendt after her, Weil is concerned with understanding evil beyond the mystifications of monstrosity.

Levi's encounter with the cold-eyed German Dr Pannwitz, for whom Levi no more and no less "belongs to a species which it is obviously opportune to suppress" (*If This Is a Man* 112), illustrates Weil's contention that "evil dwells in the heart of the criminal without being felt there. It is felt in the heart of the man who is afflicted and innocent" ("Love of God" 70). No one is further from God than the afflicted, since in Weil's economy the greater the distance, the more intense is God's absence, the only form his presence can take in the world. As presence, God could only be imaginary or false (idolatrous); his absence is his only reality. It follows that the criminal is not distant from God: "sin is not a distance, it is a turning of our gaze in the wrong direction" ("Love of God" 73).

Freedom for Weil operates in the tiny radius of a gesture: the look turned toward God while still consenting to necessity. Though the question of agency is admittedly difficult to tease out of the workings of affliction, Weil maintains that "where everything else is equal, a man does not perform the same actions if he gives his consent to obedience as if he does not; just as a plant, where everything else is equal, does not grow in the same way in the light as in the dark" ("Love of God" 77). In typical fashion, Weil affirms human agency (granting consent) by paradoxically appealing to the vegetative state of the plant; we are speaking about a most liminal kind of agency, snatched from the depths of inertia. Refusal to consent does not release one from the clutches of necessity but, on the contrary, chains one to it all the more blindly: "A creature cannot but obey. The only choice given to men, as intelligent and free creatures, is to desire obedience or not to desire it. If a man does not desire it, he obeys nevertheless, perpetually, inasmuch as he is a thing subject to mechanical necessity" (76). The criminal is a creature who obeys without knowing.

Commandant of Auschwitz was written in 1946 as Rudolf Höss awaited trial in British custody. What makes this autobiographical narrative especially chilling are not its factual inaccuracies, but the sincerity of its unknowingness—the dull-witted account of abominations, which seems strangely automated. Höss is self-righteous. He decries the unnecessary cruelty and low morals of his colleagues and subordinates and proclaims himself a tough but just man. In the context of Dachau, Sachsenhausen, and then Auschwitz, such proclamations are preposterous. We see Höss for what he is, a delinquent nurtured by a criminal regime. But despite its paramilitary peculiarities, Höss's story entails a more general lesson. Levi, who wrote an introduction for Commandant of Auschwitz, agrees. Was Höss no more than a monster, Levi asks? "This question is thoroughly answered by Hoess's book, which shows how readily evil can replace good, besieging it and finally submerging it—yet allowing it to persist in tiny, grotesque islets: an orderly family life, love of nature, Victorian morality" (Commandant 19). Höss's guilt, Levi continues, "which was not inscribed in his genes or in his German birth, lay entirely in the fact that he was unable to resist the pressure exerted on him by a violent environment even before Hitler's takeover" (20). Commandant of Auschwitz is superbly ironic not because of Höss's willful enslavement to Nazi ideology but for his unknowing enslavement to the blind laws of matter. According to Weil, when "a man turns away from God, he simply gives himself up to the law of gravity. Then he thinks that he can decide and choose, but he is only a thing, a stone that falls" ("Love of God" 75). At the very moment he believes he is choosing an ideology and a way of life, Höss is reduced into a thing. "Those whom we call criminals," Weil says, "are only tiles blown off a roof by the wind and falling at random. Their only fault is the initial choice by which they became such tiles" ("Love of God" 75).

Weil's analysis both invites and resists comparisons with Arendt's famous notion of the "banality of evil." But for Weil the "monotony of evil" (GG 69) is not fully explained by the presence of a technocratic apparatus. Evil is not banal only in its peculiar *modernity*. A state's criminal bureaucracy is already a reflection of the submission to the mechanistic that a misunderstanding of necessity effects. When the necessary and the good are confused, evil triumphs as mechanical monotony.

A genuine and effective system of justice would have to avoid a mere "transference of evil from the penal apparatus itself to the condemned man" and redress evil through what Weil calls "compensatory purification" (GG 73). The idea that evil can be transferred (and conserved) rather than alleviated by the legal system already anticipates some of the controversies that surround trials of Nazi criminals not only in the immediate aftermath of the war but in decades to follow.

Remembering in Vain

> Above those institutions which are concerned with protecting rights and persons and democratic freedoms, others must be invented for the purpose of exposing and abolishing everything in contemporary life which buries the soul under injustice, lies, and ugliness.
>
> They must be invented, for they are unknown, and it is impossible to doubt that they are indispensable.
>
> —Simone Weil, "Human Personality"

In 1987 the first trial for crimes against humanity took place on French soil against Klaus Barbie, the "Butcher of Lyon." Two years later Alain Finkielkraut published an attack on the trial and Barbie's defense team led by attorney Jacques Vergès. A densely argued polemic, *Remembering in Vain* raised many of the key issues of post-Holocaust European attitudes: the significance of the Holocaust in a postcolonial, postmodern France and the fate of humanity left battered by the Nazi genocide.[9]

Finkielkraut saw a tendency of postcolonial, multicultural discourse to refuse confrontation with the Holocaust not through silence or denial but, on the contrary, through the Holocaust's vociferous invocation. By a sort of Orwellian newspeak, the Holocaust as a distinct event disappears amongst a "competition of memories" (19) between different groups, each vying for a place in the pantheon of human suffering. Vergès's team did not defend Barbie so much as challenge France's legitimacy to try him. France's colonial violations in Algeria and Indochina, and its continued support of Zionist oppression in Palestine, Vergès argued, exposed French hypocrisy and double standards. The Jewish Holocaust as the be-all and end-all of calamities is enshrined by those who refuse to see it for what it is: a crime committed by Europeans against Europeans. Atrocities Europeans (and their descendents) commit against nonwhites and non-Europeans go unpunished and unremembered. How anomalous, Finkielkraut proclaimed, that Barbie's defenders—nonwhite, leftist lawyers—are the very people Nazi doctrine deemed "subhuman." What cultural malaise and collective forgetting make possible such an anomaly?[10]

For Finkielkraut the error lies in a senseless extension of "crimes against humanity" that conflates all acts of oppression in a single compassionate sweep. Postwar universal humanism (promising "never again"), which totalizes all inhumanities "under the guise of a great reconciliation with democratic ideals" (59) and seeks justice "for all the victims of inhumanity" (56), whiffs of totalitarianism, born of a naive understanding of humanity:

> Try as we may to be henceforth—and so ardently!—democratic anti-Nazis, antitotalitarians, antifascists, antiracists and antiapartheid—we have not yet learned to be wary of the beatific smile of fraternity. In spite of Patocka, Kundera, Hannah Arendt, or Thomas Mann, the lesson of this century has not been heard: we continue to consider life in unison as the very apotheosis of being. . . . When confronted with the racist . . . we are all brothers, next-of-kin, buddies; we are all uplifted by the same feelings, our bodies move to the same rhythm of a great "Euro-world dance," our "ten billion ears"

are enchanted by the same harmonies, our pulses accelerate simultaneously, a like energy electrifies us, and . . . we sing, by the glimmer of cigarette lighters, the same hymn of hope and love across the entire face of the earth. (58–59)

Finkielkraut does not mince his words: a similar romanticism informed National Socialism's own messianic humanism, whose conclusion was the murder not only of countless human beings but of the very idea of humanity.

Of special importance in the Barbie trial was a distinction between the categories of war crimes and crimes against humanity. Alice Vansteenberghe, a resistance fighter and one of Barbie's victims, explained:

"We in the Resistance knew the risks we were taking, and I accept everything that I suffered. But in the cell where I was thrown there were other people. I saw a Jewish woman and her child, well-groomed, very blond, with a barrette in her hair. Well, one day Barbie walked in and came to take this mother from her child. *This is not warfare—it's something unspeakable, beyond all bounds.*"
(Vansteenberghe qtd. in Finkielkraut 22; my emphasis)

This "something unspeakable, beyond all bounds" is what the legal category of crimes against humanity attempts to contain.[11] Whereas in reference to war crimes we may still speak of agents, crimes against humanity imply the eradication of agency. This, according to Vansteenberghe, is one crucial difference between the Resistance fighter (whose fate corresponds to a choice or an act) and the Jew (for whom no such correspondence exists), even when both identically suffer deportation and death.

"Finkielkraut's most essential formulation," Alice Y. Kaplan explains, "is that we once thought that individuals died but humanity itself continued unimpaired. The Holocaust taught us that humanity itself is mortal. The notion of crimes against humanity is the juridical trace of the coming to consciousness of humanity's *mortality*" (Kaplan 84). "Crimes against humanity" reflects the law's noble attempt to seize that "something unspeakable, beyond all bounds." It addresses the considered (rather than frenzied) assault on humanity by Germany's "exterminating bureaucracy" and "criminal public service" (Finkielkraut 4). Since by targeting people not for what they did but for who they were Nazism overwrote the "laws of humanity" (Finkielkraut 2), crimes against humanity legally restores "Thou shalt not kill" as a fundamental universal commandment. Crimes against humanity call for a truly "Kantian program of international justice" (Finkielkraut 10). They are not the affair of any particular state (or people). Though it remains unclear what form Finkielkraut intends this "program" to take, his call echoes Weil's insistence on the need for institutions—as yet uninvented and perhaps unimagined—to expose and abolish "everything in contemporary life which buries the soul under injustice, lies, and ugliness."[12] For Weil, they will be placed *above* those existing institutions "concerned with protecting rights and persons and democratic freedoms." "Above" does not designate recourse to a higher legal authority but to a different ontological order. Both Weil and Finkielkraut acknowledge in the judicial an appeal to a fundamental and incorruptible ethical realm. But they envisage this realm in significantly different terms.

Finkielkraut's fundamental ethical law is at the same time decidedly and historically French: "By referring, beyond the diversity of concrete laws, to eternal principles—to laws of humanity applicable to all nations—the judges at Nuremberg were following the classical tradition of the Rights of Man that Montesquieu defined as the 'civil code of the Universe,' in the sense that every people is a citizen thereof" (Finkielkraut 5). In "The Crisis of French Universalism" Naomi Schor points out that the characteristic "Frenchness of universalism" (43) does not, in fact, originate with the French Revolution (as Finkielkraut seems to imply). Its roots lie deeper, within France's Catholic Church. We ought to see the Revolution of 1789 more accurately as the continuation of an older French universalism by other means (44).[13] The inventiveness of the French Revolution lay not in universalism per se but in its superimposition of rights: "What the French Revolution crucially instituted was the association of universalism and human rights; what was missing from pre-Revolutionary accounts of universalism was the modern humanistic doctrine of universal human rights" (Schor 46). Since the 1990s, French universalism has been embroiled in the "French culture wars" between the "upholders of the Republic [Finkielkraut] and the advocates of French multiculturalism and democracy [Vergès]" (Schor 48). The proceedings of the Barbie trial, in which a legal team made up of France's former colonial subjects (the French-Vietnamese Vergès, Congolese Jean-Martin M'Bemba, and Algerian Nabil Bouaita) indicted France for colonial crimes equal to those of Nazism, epitomized the debates on France's national identity and colonial heritage vis-à-vis its universalist humanist credentials. But do the universal Rights of Man and their progeny, the curiously phrased "crimes against humanity," truly exhaust the boundless violations of Auschwitz?

Inhumanity and the Sacred

> When the infliction of evil provokes a cry of sorrowful surprise from the depth of the soul, it is not a personal thing. Injury to the personality and its desires is not sufficient to evoke it, but only and always the sense of contact with injustice through pain. It is always, in the last of men as in Christ himself, an impersonal protest.
>
> There are also many cries of personal protest, but they are unimportant; you may provoke as many of them as you wish without violating anything sacred.   —Weil, "Human Personality"

In a telling passage toward the end of *Remembering in Vain,* Finkielkraut dismisses calls to televise the Barbie trial for the supposed edification of the French citizenry. The "pedagogical and therapeutic virtues of the television screen" (70) are misconceived because

> the same principle, in fact, holds true for justice as for religion, for theatre or for the act of teaching—it can be done anywhere (a table suffices), but only by isolating the time and the space of

these interactions from their secular settings. Therefore it is doubly absurd to want to televise judicial proceedings in order to educate people. For far from reproducing this fundamental *separation*, television presents the sacred as food for the secular, and puts the outside world at the mercy of the private world. (70)

The consecrated courtroom is at the heart of the contractual humanity that Finkielkraut espouses. It is a reminder of the sacred origins of the law, prefigured for Finkielkraut (as for Lévinas) in the face-to-face encounter between the self and the wholly other person.

Weil's essay "Human Personality" ("La personne et le sacré": the person and the sacred) also appeals to the sacred origins of justice. With "Are We Struggling for Justice?" and *The Need for Roots*, "Human Personality" is Weil's most explicit critique of rights as the foundation of justice. Written in 1942–43, concurrent with the Nazi horrors but before their ultimate unfolding, "Human Personality" touches on several of Finkielkraut's contentions about the Holocaust's judicial and ethical legacies. Weil's opinions on themes ranging from Marxism to the USSR, colonialism, and Judaism intersect provocatively with Finkielkraut's. As children of assimilated middle-class Jews (both attended Lycée Henri IV and the École Normale Supérieure), their thinking is shaped, albeit differently, by France's educational and political culture.

"Human Personality" begins with the assertion that "something is amiss with the vocabulary of the modern trend of thought known as Personalism" (70). "I see a passer-by in the street. He has long arms, blue eyes, and a mind whose thoughts I do not know, but perhaps they are commonplace. It is neither his person, nor the human personality in him, which is sacred to me. It is he. The whole of him. The arms, the eyes, the thoughts, everything" (70–71). Profound injustice offends neither the man's body nor his personality (his intelligence or character). Nor even is his singularity defined by his human capacities and attributes. The "whole of him" is larger than the sum of his parts and makes it "impossible to define what is meant by respect for human personality. It is not just that it cannot be defined in words.

That can be said of many perfectly clear ideas. But this one cannot be conceived either; it cannot be defined nor isolated by the silent operation of the mind. To set up as a standard of public morality a notion which can neither be defined nor conceived is to open the door to every kind of tyranny" (71). Next, Weil considers the combination of "human personality" with a second erroneous notion: rights. The universal principle of human rights amounts to a double inadequacy, whose source is the French Revolution and its Rights of Man, the very legacy Finkielkraut champions as enshrining humanity's "eternal principles": "The notion of rights, which was launched into the world in 1789, has proved unable, because of its intrinsic inadequacy, to fulfil the role assigned to it. To combine two inadequate notions, by talking about the rights of human personality, will not get us any further" ("Human Personality" 71). Weil's rejection of rights-based humanism weakens the disparity between Finkielkraut and Vergès, both heirs to the French Revolution. From this perspective, French Republicanism and postcolonialism seem locked in a struggle over the interpretation and application of universal rights, exposing the congenital link between rights and power: "Rights are always asserted in a tone of contention; and when this tone is adopted, it must rely upon force in the background, or else it will be laughed at" ("Human Personality" 81).

In bracketing off rights and human personality as sources of the sacred, Weil is already signaling toward what I would call creaturely reflections on the Holocaust. Weil's question "What is it, exactly, that prevents me from putting that man's eyes out *if I am allowed to do so?*" ("Human Personality" 71; my emphasis) recognizes the Third Reich's self-suspension of law (which Carl Schmitt called the "state of exception").[14] Weil replies that "at the bottom of the heart of every human being, from earliest infancy until the tomb, there is something that goes on indomitably expecting, in the teeth of all experience of crimes committed, suffered, and witnessed, that good and not evil will be done to him. It is this above all that is sacred in every human being" (71). Although the language is emphatically humanist here, Weil's understanding of justice is not. As Cora Diamond argues in "Injustice and Animals," Weil offers a powerful model for animal ethics because "what underlies the animal rights movement is a responsiveness to the vulnerability of animals in the face of the relentless exercise of human power, and . . . the articulating of that responsiveness calls for a grammar akin to the grammar of justice as Weil describes it" (120). Weil's grammar of justice *is*, it seems to me, profoundly inhuman. Creaturely life is material and vulnerable and so oriented toward life and not toward destruction. This orientation constitutes the "expectation" (or plea) Weil distinguishes from the eligibility for rights: "this profound and childlike and unchanging expectation of good in the heart is not what is involved when we agitate for our rights" ("Human Personality" 72).

In *The Need for Roots* Weil maintains that "it makes nonsense to say that men have, on the one hand, rights and on the other hand, obligations. . . . A man left alone in the universe would have no rights whatever, but he would have obligations" (3–4). Rights and obligations are not symmetrical. It is not a matter of simply shifting perspectives in which what looks like my right is another's obligation. Obligations are primary and removed from the order of facticity. Rights come into being only "when obligations descend to the realm of fact" (4) and are therefore "related to certain conditions. Obligations alone remain independent of conditions. They belong to a realm situated above all conditions, because it is *situated above the world*" (4; my emphasis).

As if directly addressing Finkielkraut, Weil continues that the "men of 1789 did not recognize the existence of such a realm. All they recognized was the one on the human plane. That is why they started off with the idea of rights" (4). This mistake "is largely responsible for the present political and social confusion" (4). As we shall see later on, the accusation of a confusion of the realms resurfaces in Weil's critiques of Marxism.

Rights are not merely worldly but economic. Their "commercial flavour" (Human Personality" 81) is due to their origin in Roman property law. Weil's antipathy to Rome (second only to her objections to Judaism) leads to comparisons with Nazi Germany: "The Romans, like Hitler, understood that power is not fully efficacious unless clothed in a few ideas, and to this end they made use of the idea of rights, which is admirably suited to it. Modern Germany has been accused of flouting the idea; but she invoked it *ad nauseam* in her role of deprived, proletarian nation. . . . The Greeks had no conception of rights. They had no words to express it. They were content with the name of justice" (81–82). Weil's syncretic swoops across cultures and periods seem impetuous (she routinely connects Christian mystery with Buddhism and the Greeks), but they are an essential part of her method of attentive contact with ahistorical truths.[15] Since rights, modeled on property law, are a euphemism for power, they can only yield victor's justice— *Vae victis* or *Siegerjustiz*.

Weil begins "Are We Struggling for Justice?" with a quote from the "Melian Dialogue" in book 5 of Thucydides' *History of the Peloponnesian War*. The exchange between the Athenian generals and the besieged representatives of Melos famously sums up Greek *Realpolitik*: "The examination of what is just is carried out only when there is equal necessity on each side. Where there is one who is strong and one who is weak, the possible is done by the first and accepted by the second" (120).

The truth that "when someone does not have the capacity to refuse, one is not going to look for a way of obtaining his consent" (121) is not just Machiavellian but describes precisely the workings of interspecies justice, the truth of which mainstream animal rights discourse has in fact inverted: the drama of unequal power (arguably, necessity/natural law operates equally, if differently, on humans and nonhumans, only humans refuse to acknowledge it) and animals' incapacity to refuse is recast as the drama of animal otherness (nonhuman subjectivity) misrecognized or misconceived by the human mind. *A drama of force becomes a story about poorly understood concepts.*

When in *The Lives of Animals* Elizabeth Costello says that "we point to the Germans and Poles and Ukrainians who did and did not know of the atrocities around them. . . . We like to think that in their nightmares the ones whose suffering they had refused to enter came back to haunt them. . . . But probably it was not so. The evidence points in the opposite direction: that we can do anything and get away with it; that there is no punishment" (35), she suggests that a similar *Realpolitik* operates also at the level of conscience. Before rejoining Weil, I want to briefly look at one example of post-Holocaust cinema that examines Costello's dark vision.

Passenger (*Pasazerka,* 1961–63), by the Polish director Andrzej Munk, remembers the Holocaust through Liza, a former German SS supervisor in Auschwitz. While on a holiday cruise with her husband some ten years after the war, Liza catches sight of a woman she believes to be Marta, a Polish political prisoner in the camp. Fearing exposure, Liza confesses to her husband in the form of two flashbacks. She first presents herself as a victim of circumstance and describes her efforts to save Marta. The second flashback is a more accurate version of Liza's revenge after failing to "recruit" Marta. Liza's two narratives, the film's voiceover suggests, are reminders that "justifying oneself is only human": "what is this recollection of a game . . . between overseer and chosen prisoner; an apology, an escape from cruelty and evil, only too human? In the vague, unreal background, people die, silently, casually, anonymously, as others perform their duty. . . . Victims trampled into the mud, over whom she walked, unseeing."[16] *Passenger* focuses on daily life in Auschwitz, shunning the more ideological narratives of resistance typical of earlier Polish Holocaust films. The film is indebted to the writings of Tadeusz Borowski, for whom the camp world swallows up both perpetrator and victim, leaving them in what Primo Levi dubbed the "gray zone," a morally ambiguous space that corrupts all who inhabit it.

When Marta disembarks at the next port, the disturbance is over. Life goes on, crime goes unpunished. Liza's confessions, sparked partly by fear, vaguely by guilt, reframe notions of memory, witnessing, and testimony in a transient, fleeting light. Neither imprisoned nor tormented by her past, Liza has successfully reintegrated in life. When pressed, she remembers with a mixture of admission and self-justification. *Passenger* affirms the "mechanicity" Weil sees as shaping human behavior. It allows one to carry on, beyond trauma and guilt. If the human drama is most frequently defined as the internal conflict between conscience and circumstance, Weil sees it no less as the external drama and mystery of *force*.[17]

Weil wrote one of her finest essays, "The *Iliad* or the Poem of Force," between 1940–41, early in the war, some two decades since Rudolf

Höss first associated with the notorious *Freikorps* and seven years after he joined the SS and began an illustrious career of running concentration camps.[18] One way of reading Weil's text is as an essay on the anthropomorphizing of force, whose effect is always, in turn, a deforming of the human. "To define force—it is that x that turns anybody who is subjected to it into a *thing*" ("Iliad" 183). Homer's war epic is an ingenious illustration of the desire to humanize force and the result of being dehumanized by it. Homer achieves this by making the inhuman—rather than the human—the poem's protagonist: "the true hero, the true subject, the centre of the *Iliad* is force. Force employed by man, force that enslaves man, force before which man's flesh shrinks away. In this work, at all times, the human spirit is shown as modified by its relations with force, as swept away, blinded, by the very force it imagined it could handle, as deformed by the weight of the force it submits to" (183). Weil's idea that "force is as pitiless to the man who possesses it, or thinks he does, as it is to its victims" (191) is close to Levi's (and Borowski's) view of the camp as a morally corrupting force field.

As early as 1934, in the essays comprising *Oppression and Liberty*, Weil presented an analysis of the "play of blind forces" (74) and their relation to structures of social oppression. Throughout her writing, Weil retained the notion that human action is mechanistically determined:

> there are no other restraints upon our will than material necessity and the existence of other human beings around us. Any imaginary extension of these limits is seductive, so there is a seduction in whatever helps us to forget the reality of the obstacles. That is why upheavals like war and civil war are so intoxicating; they empty human lives of their reality and seem to turn people into puppets. That is also why slavery is so pleasant to the masters.
>
> ("Human Personality" 72)

This vision (indebted to, yet already exceeding, Marxist historical materialism) sees human action as regulated first by obstacles—the play of forces—not by ideas (not even the idea of class struggle). War and revolution create the illusion of human mastery of force and a canceling out of obstacles. When, in the sway of force, one meets with weak or no resistance, it is easy to forget one's own essential vulnerability.

This radically materialist vision of human action is integral to Weil's thoughts on justice. The "Iliad" essay makes the connection plainly: "The man who is the possessor of force seems to walk through a non-resistant element; in the human substance that surrounds him nothing has the power to interpose, between the impulse and the act, the tiny interval that is reflection. Where there is no room for reflection, there is none either for justice or prudence" ("Iliad" 193). Justice is possible only in the form of a disturbance to the crushing impulses of power. This disturbance consists in the recognition of the reality of vulnerability and its relation to the sacred—a religious recognition. It alone can deliver justice or liberty that are not a mere reshuffling of power. Thus, in Marxism's disavowal of religiosity Weil recognizes an invitation to tyranny:

> When force changes hands, it still remains a relation of stronger to weaker, a relation of dominance. It can go on changing hands indefinitely, without a single term of the relation being eliminated. At the moment when a political transformation occurs, those who make ready to take over power *are already in possession of a force*, that is to say a dominance over weaker men. *If they possess none at all, power will not pass into their hands, unless an effective factor other than force should intervene*; which Marx did not admit as possible.
>
> (*Oppression and Liberty* 149; my emphasis)

Political power never materializes ex nihilo. The problem with revolutionary politics (perhaps with politics as such) is that it *always comes too late*. If Marx's laboring masses have assumed power, this is not because they obtained it at will, but because they were already in possession of force. Weil distinguishes here between *force* (the natural laws governing motion and rest) and *power* anthropomorphized, incarnated in particular human structures and institutions (the distinction will also be made by Arendt). Once in possession of power, the proletariat is already no longer itself: it has become embroiled in the very dynamic of domination against which it rose up in just indignation. To transform social injustice, a principle wholly other than force is required. Yet "Marx's revolutionary materialism consists in positing, on the one hand, that force alone governs social relations to the exclusion of anything else, and, on the other hand, that one day the weak, while remaining the weak, will nevertheless be the stronger. *He believed in miracles without believing in the supernatural. From a purely rationalist point of view, if one believes in miracles, it is better to believe in God as well*" (*Oppression and Liberty* 149–50; my emphasis).

It is customary these days to denounce Marxism as a religion and link its totalitarianism to this religiosity, as if religion and totalitarianism were interchangeable. Weil's point is different: the horrors of Stalinism are proof that Marxism was not religious enough. Not seeing through to its logical conclusion to its own materialist principles, Marx ended up with some very bad theology. Not owning up to the implications of his own analysis, by which the play of material forces miraculously yields the good, Marx attributed to matter (gravity) the qualities of divine intervention (grace): he attributed to matter itself the capacity for moral transformation while denying the reality of God; he may have thought that no one would notice his leap of faith. "Man cannot bear to be alone in willing the good. He needs an all-powerful ally. If this ally is not spirit, it will be matter. It is simply a case of two different expressions of the same fundamental thought. But the second expression is defective. It is a badly constructed religion" (*Oppression and Liberty* 154). Weil considered Marxism a "religion devoid of *mystique*" (154). As with Montesquieu's "civil code of the Universe," which I discussed earlier, the confusion of levels between here and elsewhere produces an empty religion of the Rights of Man. For Weil, therefore, the natural and spiritual orders are not in opposition. Rather, the logicality and integrity of each requires their total separation. Separation does not denote incompatibility; on the contrary: "The idea of working out a mechanics of social relationships had been adumbrated by many lucid minds. It was doubtless this that inspired Machiavelli. As in ordinary mechanics, the fundamental notion would be that of force. The great difficulty is to grasp this notion. *Such an idea contains nothing incompatible with the purest spirituality; it is complementary to it*" (*Oppression and Liberty* 155; my emphasis).

Strict adherence to the mechanics of social relationships, Weil insists, makes the sacred possible as separation. On both sides of the infinite partition, something inhuman is at work. Both power and justice are conceived nonanthropocentrically. Humanity's susceptibility to the inhumanities of force (gravity) and to the good (grace) has little to do with the faculties of reason or language. The material and the supernatural meet for Weil in the reality of vulnerable bodies whose oppression is not a crime against humanity but a violation of the sacred.

Animality and the Holocaust

Herman Gombiner, I. B. Singer's main character in the short story "The Letter Writer," lost his family in Europe and lives alone in a crammed New York apartment. When he discovers a mouse in the flat, Herman leaves her food and names her Huldah (Hebrew for "rat," and the name of the biblical prophetess). Herman is haunted by the Holocaust, which returns in his memories, dreams, and philosophical musings. Interiorizing the Holocaust in this way reinforces Herman's sense of life's interconnectedness, which makes the mouse "just as much a part of God's creation as the planets, the stars, the distant galaxies" (225).

Fearing that Huldah has died, Herman eulogizes her in the story's famous "eternal Treblinka" passage: "What do they know—all those scholars, all those philosophers, all the leaders of the world—about such as you? They have convinced themselves that man, the worst transgressor of all the species, is the crown of creation. All other creatures were created merely to provide him with food, pelts, to be tormented, exterminated. In relation to them, all people are Nazis; for the animals it is an eternal Treblinka" ("Letter Writer" 234). The pairing of the Jewish Holocaust with the puny life of a mouse is not immediately contentious (as it is in *The Lives of Animals*). Singer's refugees themselves often make the analogy. It is a sign of their altered perspective on the laws of the universe, their loss of faith, or divergence from ordinary Judaism.

When the lonely Herman finally accepts the love of Rose Beech-man, the woman who well-nigh miraculously saves his life, he is "filled with love both for the mouse and for the woman" ("Letter Writer" 237). This bemuses Lawrence S. Friedman, who writes that "at some risk of trivializing Herman's epiphany, Singer insists upon juxtaposing the sudden surge of love for Rose with the love for a mouse" (*Understanding* 211). Friedman believes that the "eternal Treblinka" passage is no more than an expression of Herman's mental crisis. Yet nothing in the story suggests that Herman's love for the mouse is more "trivial" or silly than, say, his belief in the occult or Rose's insistence that her dead grandmother speaks to her. To argue as much is to misrecognize the peculiarities of Singer's universe, in which shtetl humor and fairy-tale elements fuse with modernist mores, and where the Holocaust acts as an irrevocable cosmic intervention.

"Like so many of Singer's Jewish refugees who have lost their families in the Holocaust," writes Friedman, "Herman is prematurely aged, physically decrepit" (209). Singer describes Herman as a "short man, in oversize pajamas, emaciated to skin and bone, with a scrawny neck and a large head. . . . His forehead was wide and deep, his nose crooked, his cheekbones high. . . . The remaining strength in Herman Gom-biner's body—a body worn out by illnesses and undernourishment—seemed to be concentrated in his gaze" ("Letter Writer" 208). Herman suffers from memory loss (207) and "tremors of the hands and feet" (210) and feels himself a "corpse returning from its own funeral" (222). His pneumonia is accompanied by resignation in the face of pain and death. In his anorectic-apathetic state Herman resembles not the archetypal survivor but that other central figure of the Holocaust, the *Muselmann*.

When Rose cares for the dying Herman, she is helping the one who, like the *Muselmann*, does not ask for help, who is very nearly beyond help. Reading Herman as a *Muselmann* throws light on what some critics dismiss as the story's curious lowly ethics. For the *Muselmann* is the ruin of Enlightenment morality: "The *Muselmann* has . . . moved into a zone of the human where not only help but also dignity and self-respect have become useless. But if there is a zone of the human in which these concepts make no sense, then they are not genuine ethical concepts, for no ethics can claim to exclude a part of humanity, no matter how unpleasant or difficult that humanity is to see" (*Remnants* 63–64). For Singer (and his characters), however, the challenge of the *Muselmann* is not confined to a "zone of the human," but projected unto creation as a whole. The Holocaust in Singer never functions simply as the cause of the characters' psychology. It enters as a cosmic upheaval, shaking the characters' faith and turning them into skeptics or else into occultists.[19] But both positions—materialism and spiritualism—lead to the practice of vegetarianism, not as the attainment of what Calarco calls an "ethical ideal" (*Zoographies* 135) but as an ethical *foundation*: a creaturely fellowship grounded in the vulnerability of living bodies that the Holocaust laid bare.[20]

Herman "couldn't take a bit of meat if his life depended on it" ("Letter Writer" 210). When Herman Broder, of *Enemies, a Love Story* (1972), to which "The Letter Writer" is a kind of prelude, discovers that his lover Masha prepared a meal of meat, he protests: "'You promised me not to cook meat any more.' 'I promised myself, too, but without meat, there's nothing to cook. God himself eats meat—human flesh. There are no vegetarians—none. If you had seen what I have seen, you would know that God approves of slaughter'" (166). And a visit to the zoo reminds Herman Broder of the camps: "Herman often compared the zoo to a concentration camp. The air here was full of longing—for deserts, hills, valleys, dens, families. Like the Jews, the animals had been dragged here from all parts of the world, condemned to isolation and boredom. Some of them cried out their woes; others remained mute" (177).

As is widely acknowledged, National Socialism was not simply opposed to ideas of Enlightenment humanism. Rejecting some, it nonetheless shared the happy vision of humanity's improvability. "Human progress is like ascending an endless ladder," wrote Hitler in *Mein Kampf* (122). In the name of progress, the Holocaust drained not only the idea of humanity but of inhumanity as well of their intelligible powers. It took to its limit the violence inherent in the distinction between human and inhuman. For if the Holocaust proves anything at all, it is that Jewish (and other) bodies are animal bodies. The monotony of assembly-line production of corpses and the withered physique of *Muselmänner* do not, in effect, reveal anything new.

We go to great lengths to forget the Holocaust's systematic demystification of human identity. In much academic and popular Holocaust discourse, this forgetting takes the paradoxical form of grandiose remembrance. As I have tried to show, remembering the Holocaust in this way amounts to a "remembering in vain." To bear the weight of an "eternal Treblinka" is to approach the Holocaust with something other than the stillness of human commemoration. I have been arguing—not as mere semantic quibbling—that in trying to address its specific and excessive transgression, the notion of "crimes against humanity" in fact obscures the Holocaust's fundamental unraveling of the human. Weil's understanding of affliction and the sacred is an invitation to think through the insufficiencies of a humanist project of remembrance whose implications for the practical pursuit of justice for living beings are as far-reaching as they are debilitating.

2 Neanderthal Poetics in William Golding's *The Inheritors*

To Richard Ford, with thanks

A poem is stored energy, a formal turbulence, a living thing, a swirl in the flow.   —William Rueckert, "Literature and Ecology"

William Rueckert's recycled lines from Gary Snyder's *Turtle Island* on the biopoetic nature of verse get one thinking about Golding's second novel *The Inheritors* (1955). Recounting the final days of a group of Neanderthals on the eve of their extinction at the hands of Cro-Magnon man, *The Inheritors* is quite literally a story about ecology and evolution. The novel's central character is Lok, who with the rest of his tribe comes across a strange group of "new people." The encounter proves deadly. One by one the People are killed, until only Lok, the last of his kind, remains. *The Inheritors* does not imagine but rather *becomes* (in Deleuze and Guattari's sense) Neanderthal. Written almost entirely from the Neanderthals' perspective in a language crafted especially for them, the story switches view in the final chapter, to look out of the eyes of modern man.

The Inheritors is poised against H. G. Wells's *The Outline of History* (1920) and "The Grisly Folk" (1921), gothic texts that depict the

Neanderthal as beastly and ruthless. As his epigraph, Golding quotes from *The Outline of History*:

> " . . . We know very little of the appearance of the Neanderthal man, but this . . . seems to suggest an extreme hairiness, an ugliness, or a repulsive strangeness in his appearance over and above his low forehead, his beetle brows, his ape neck, and his inferior stature. . . . Says Sir Harry Johnston, in a survey of the rise of modern man in his *Views and Reviews*: 'The dim racial remembrance of such gorilla-like monsters, with cunning brains, shambling gait, hairy bodies, strong teeth, and possibly cannibalistic tendencies, may be the germ of the ogre in folklore . . . '"

Golding dismissed Wells's text as "the rationalist gospel *in excelsis*" and went on to tell Virginia Tiger that "it seemed to me to be too neat and too slick. And when I re-read it as an adult I came across his picture of Neanderthal man, our immediate predecessors, as being these gross brutal creatures who were possibly the basis of the mythological bad man . . . the ogre. I thought to myself that this is just absurd. What we're doing is externalizing our own inside" (Golding qtd. in Tiger 71). But Golding's rejection of teleological anthropology that depicts the destruction of the Neanderthals as a beneficial stage in civilized progress does more than reflect shifting attitudes in the Neanderthal debate.[1] *The Inheritors* is a bold ecopoetic experiment that gives rise to a new kind of literary sentience.

Although Golding's method involves literary subversion, intertextuality does not diminish the remarkable autonomy of his prose. Craig Raine has argued that Golding's sources stretch far and wider than Wells or Ballantyne. Raine finds Golding in the company of Aldous Huxley, Anthony Beavis, Dostoevsky, Henry James, Robert Southwell, and Kipling.[2] But sources finally "account for very little of any great work of art, however interesting they might be" (Raine 107), and Golding's novels are their own solid sources—lonely creatures. Their unbrotherly, island prose is at times plainly weird. No wonder that so much in him concerns castaways and the shipwrecked. Golding's mixed reception (the singling out of *Lord of the Flies* at the expense of his other work) is testimony to this singularity of his. In critical terms, too, *The Inheritors* is generous. It closely links postcolonialism and ecocriticism, critiques whose mutual affinities are only now beginning to be considered.[3] Despite the tender evocations of the natural world, however, nature in Golding criticism often means the nature of man. Perhaps this is why *The Inheritors* produced few if any ecocritical readings but found avid readers in the neighboring area of science fiction.[4]

The fictional retrieval of an extinct sensibility (an ecopoetic feat par excellence) is the novel's most astute and touching achievement. It is what I propose as the novel's Neanderthal poetics. Golding's is the first postcolonial fable, the "original sin" of colonization and genocide that inaugurated the vexed relations between man and nonman, relations whose deadly machinations can be traced in the rest of Golding's postwar fiction written under the sign of Belsen and Hiroshima.[5]

The Inheritors is far ahead not only of its time but also of ours in that it exists—as a text and as a work of art—in the possibility of transcending the distinctions of species. Rather than combine human and nonhuman, Golding explores different modes of perception, Neanderthal and human being in the world. In Wells's *Outline of History* and "The Grisly Folks" as well as *The Time Machine* (1895) and *The Island of Dr Moreau* (1896)—science fictions that ostensibly deal with hybrid species—Wells nonetheless remains rooted in human perception. Dr Moreau is the archetypal mad professor whose godlike ambition finally destroys him. *Moreau* contains some powerful passages on the horrors of vivisection, but the novel's humanized animals ultimately serve to critique the giddiness that scientific rationality can arouse in excellent but uninhibited minds. They offer little by way of an alternate sensibility.

Not species, but perception, then. What is this new way of being alive to the world that *The Inheritors* renders so palpable? I begin by discussing Golding's commitment to material description and to the visual. Visuality has been especially pertinent in recent debates on nonhuman subjectivities, and I compare and contrast Golding's ocular logic to Temple Grandin's "thinking in pictures." In the final section of the chapter I consider the relevance of Walter Benjamin's concepts of natural history and the creaturely to *The Inheritors*' own counterhistorical narrative.

Style of Stone

Neanderthal perception is concrete and pictorial rather than abstract. It is a non-Cartesian sensibility rooted in embodied experience. Because of this, the People practice a commonality impossible for beings with a solitary consciousness. *The Inheritors* is a literary example of what Ralph Acampora calls "intersomatic" and "intercorporeal" relations.[6] There is nothing paranormal about the People's communication. Their intersubjectivity is continuous with their intercorporeal existence. Despite the Neanderthal's fate, the novel's tragedy is finally Cro-Magnon's—our tragedy—the result of their constitution as mentally disparate entities, doomed to solipsism and that distinctly modern malaise, alienation.

Throughout most of the novel, the reader is immersed in Lok's world as he sees and feels it, without narrational assistance. It takes some acclimatizing to appreciate emotional as physical states. We read, for example, that Lok "watched the water run out of her [Nil's] eyes" (*The Inheritors* 69).[7] There is no need to disclose an internal world with its furnishings of sadness, grief, or loss. These can be conveyed as colors and shapes, transposed from the inner to the outer world. So the "lights"

faint as the starlight reflected in the crystals of a granite cliff. The lights increased, acquired definition, brightened, lay each sparkling at the lower edge of a cavern. Suddenly, noiselessly, the lights became thin crescents, went out, and streaks glistened on each cheek. The lights appeared again, caught among the silvered curls of the beard. They hung, elongated, dropped from curl to curl and gathered at the lowest tip. The streaks on the cheeks pulsed as the drops swam down them, a great drop swelled at the end of a hair of the beard, shivering and bright. It detached itself and fell in a silver flash, striking a withered leaf with a sharp pat.   (*TI* 220)

In the essay "Golding's Pity" Barbara Everett explains that the "'pity' of *The Inheritors* is not in Lok's tears alone; it is in our witness and understanding of what causes them. The book requires the participation of the observer, the visitor to the Zoo—the reading self which, at first wholly absorbed in the People, at last comes to recognize itself in the New Men, our direct and destructive ancestors" (Everett 116). I find the reference to the zoo in this passage suddenly intrusive in the jarring of the urban depressiveness of zoos with *The Inheritors'* feral setting. But the zoo is intended to negotiate the interspecies drama in *The Inheritors* and our position as readers within it. The image invokes the colonial subtext, which the novel shares, however loosely, with zoos. Everett speaks visually of the "observer," not the reader, but vision is preceded by *witnessing*, an ethically and historically charged concept, discussed in some detail in the previous chapter. Everett suggests that we "see" these Neanderthals as we see zoo animals, that in both cases we face them with a measure of colonial guilt. More can be made of the analogy between readers and zoo-goers (as between novels and zoos), but I want to keep with Everett's thread. "When Lok weeps," she goes on, "something as much ape as man suffers—and we suffer with him that pain of the animals so hard to endure because inarticulate, out of reach or inconsolable" (Everett 117). The sentence falters a little between a creaturely approach that takes Lok and us (and inevitably also the Cro-Magnons) as fellow sufferers, commonly embodied beings—"suffering with him that pain of animals"—and that more conventional view of animal suffering as somehow other and remote.

Golding, however, does not treat nonhuman suffering as incommunicable. After losing his female partner Fa, Lok's anguish is described in terms of physical momentum—but when an inarticulate, wordless howl is finally released from inside Lok, Golding calls it "man-sound": "Lok began to bend. His knees touched the ground, his hands reached down and took his weight slowly, and with all his strength he clutched himself into the earth. He writhed himself against the dead leaves and twigs, his head came up, turned, and his eyes swept round, astonished eyes over a mouth that was strained open. The sound of mourning burst out of his mouth, prolonged, harsh, pain-sound, man-sound" (*TI* 190). Golding starts here conservatively enough (the animal as movement without language). Then comes the miniature coda: "man-sound." This correction, this adjusting of the passage also reforms our assumptions about human articulacy and unintelligible animal "noise," and it applies not only to this passage but to the novel as a whole. *The Inheritors* proceeds through such man-sounds, or animalized speech, as Neanderthal expression.

At the root of *The Inheritors'* affective power, Everett finds W. H. Auden's "the sadness of the creatures" (Auden qtd. in Everett 115): "our capacity to register in detachment the suffering of the creaturely estate, which men and animals have in common" (116).[8] Pity for creatures—animal, human, Neanderthal—is "by virtue of their intense, their in fact humiliating existence in their own bodies" (117–18). In Everett's essay "creatures" heal the rift between human and nonhuman, placing *The Inheritors* exquisitely in the interval—the open—the reconciliatory nonplace that Agamben described as "Shabbat of both animal and man" (*The Open* 92). The creature, then, is a figure that belongs at once to the distant past and the unforeseen future, which makes *The Inheritors* prehistoric science fiction.

If *The Inheritors* experiments with creaturely embodiment, the gesture is reversed in Golding's subsequent novel *Pincher Martin* (1956), about a man struggling to stay alive on a tiny rock in the Atlantic. The narrative is nothing more than the unfolding of a mind, willing itself to survival in the icy water. Here Golding refutes Wellsian rationalism by the opposite means: stripping thought (and the castaway narrative) of all body. As Virginia Tiger points out, while Lok perceives without understanding, Pincher Martin is conscious without perceiving. Lok, who "attends scrupulously to the concrete" (Tiger 77), *lives* strictly through sense perception with only the slightest abstract consciousness of this life, while Pincher Martin purely and powerfully *thinks*, without living (76). As formal inversions, then, *The Inheritors* and *Pincher Martin* produce impossible knowledge of radical states. As a creature whose life is rendered solid and palpable, Lok signals a place where, thought free, only the body remains as pure vitality. Martin's thought, conversely, achieves total bodilessness when, in the novel's coda, we discover that he is actually dead.

The Inheritors' language is elemental and aquiline; Golding's strength is description: "I'd say I'm passionately interested in *description*, the exact description of a phenomenon. When I know what a wave looks like or a flame or a tree, I hug that to me or carry the thought agreeably as a man might carry a flower round with him" (Golding qtd. in Tiger 75). The novel is full of examples of language tracing the contours of a thing, state, or place. Trailing their way through the forest, the People reach the clearing of a dead tree: "Ivy had taken over, its embedded stems making a varicose entanglement on the old trunk and ending where the trunk had branched in a huge nest of dark green leaves. Fungi had battened too, plates that stuck out and were full of rain-water, smaller jelly-like blobs of red and yellow so that the old tree was dissolving into dust and white pulp" (*TI* 21–22). When Lok hears the new people speak, description renders the "shapes" of his incomprehension: "He could hear their speech and it made him laugh. The sounds made a picture in his head of interlacing shapes, thin, and complex, voluble and silly, not like the long curve of a hawk's cry, but tangled like line weed on the beach after a storm, muddled as water" (104).

The Inheritors belongs alongside the best of nature writing, from Thoreau to J. A. Baker, but description can also verge on the fantastic. Describing (rather than explaining) things gives them integrity and a life of their own. So, "there were many birds on the island and they resented the people so that Fa and Lok began to move with great care" (127). When Lok dreams, Golding writes:

> Lok's ears spoke to Lok.
> "?"
> But Lok was asleep. (43)

The book opens mid-motion (like a film), with Lok "running as fast as he could": "Lok's feet were clever. They saw. They threw him round the displayed roots of the beeches, leapt when a puddle of water lay across the trail" (11). These are animistic rather than anthropomorphic descriptions. They do not attribute human qualities to animals or body parts. They simply describe Neanderthal reality as it is experienced, determined by a sense that the various natural elements are interconnected, responsive, each alive in its turn, from birds to ears and feet. The world of *The Inheritors* is, then, a richly diverse but single plain. The multiplicity of elements implies an equivalence of value—a kind of moral flatland. Animals, plants, and things exist singularly, neither lower nor higher than the rest.

The most powerful way of achieving this evenness of life—the dignity of exteriority—so central to *The Inheritors* is through what Mark Kinkead-Weekes and Ian Gregor called the novel's "visualizations" (73). Pictures are Golding's most important means of natural description and the heart of the novel's Neanderthal poetics. Pictures replace ideas. When Fa grows impatient with Lok, the novel's gentle buffoon, she tells him he is less clever than a baby: "you have fewer pictures than the new one" (*TI* 134). Tiger points out that "the 'picture' renders, as no other device could, the life of the senses and instinct since the impression the reader receives of the outside world is of *a series of still images*" (83; my emphasis). John Bayley has argued that Golding's uniqueness paradoxically lies in his impersonality. The weakness of a personal style results in what Dostoevsky called a "deeper realism," which "could be described in terms of the properties physicists now associate with matter itself" (129). Deeper realism is unlike realism or naturalism, both of which—in the classic examples of Zola or Balzac—retain the author as meticulous chronicler or social scientist. Golding's absence from his narrative breaks the contractual intimacy between author and reader and pushes the writing from realism toward what Bayley calls "actuality": "the refusal of a writer like Golding to satisfy the reader's expectation of a novel's choreography of action into spectacle. It is the difference between 'reality,' which is a created matter, and 'actuality,' which is not" (132).

What interests me about Tiger and Bayley's otherwise very different remarks is their shared *technicality*. Tiger's "series of still images" and Bayley's "actuality" do not belong to the world of literary criticism but to the mechanical world of film. Golding's style, then, is peculiarly cinematic. The perceptual, visual focus of the narrative is not simply realistic, but photographic. The earliest films, made between 1895–1902, are known as "actualities," a term that predates the division between the documentary and fiction film and captures at its purest the Bazinian essence of cinema as a photographically realist medium.

Consider the following passage describing Lok's "thinking" process as the cinematic viewing of moving images. Smelling the presence of "another," Lok follows the scent to the water's edge, whereupon "one of the farther rocks began to change shape": "Lok stood and let the pictures come and go in his head. One was a picture of a cave bear that he had once seen rear itself out of the rock and heard roar like the sea. Lok did not know much more about the bear than that because after the bear had roared the people had run for most of a day. This thing, this black changing shape, had something of the bear's slow movement in it. He screwed up his eyes and peered at the rock to see if it would change again" (*TI* 79). Lok is not connecting the idea of the bear with the idea of the unknown intruder. He is rather following an arrangement or sequence of images—editing—a strictly visual recording in his head. An even stronger example of Lok's fidelity to the series of stills and his (and initially our) inability to construct a general concept out of them (the problem of Antonioni's photographer in *Blow-Up*) is his encounter with one of the new people:

> Lok steadied by the tree and gazed. A head and a chest faced him, half hidden. There were white bone things behind the leaves and hair. The man had white bone things above his eyes and under the mouth so that his face was longer than a face should be. The man turned sideways in the bushes and looked at Lok along his shoulder. A stick rose upright and there was a lump of bone in the middle. Lok peered at the stick and the lump of bone and the small eyes in the bone things over the face. Suddenly Lok understood that the man was holding the stick out to him but neither he nor Lok could reach across the river. . . . The stick began to grow shorter at both ends. Then it shot out to full length again.

> The dead tree by Lok's ear acquired a voice.
>
> "Clop!"
>
> His ears twitched and he turned to the tree. By his face there had grown a twig: a twig that smelt of other, and of goose, and of the bitter berries that Lok's stomach told him he must not eat. This twig had a white bone at the end. (*TI* 106)

I do not want to push too far this analogy to the cinema but for one final point: the collective function or "picture sharing" among the People, which is an essential part of their particular form of life. Early in the novel, Nil, Fa, and Ha are trying to resolve the problem of crossing a river. "The three of them stood and looked at each other. Then, as so often happened with the people, there were feelings between them. Fa and Nil shared a picture of Ha thinking" (14). Watching the group's elder Mal, the People realize his impending death in a kind of telepathic mise en abyme of pictures within pictures:

> Quite without warning, all the people shared a picture inside their heads. This was a picture of Mal, seeming a little removed from them, illuminated, sharply defined in all his gaunt misery. They saw not only Mal's body but the slow pictures that were waxing and waning in his head. One above all was displacing the others, dawning through the cloudy arguments and doubts and conjectures until they knew what it was he was thinking with such dull conviction.
>
> "To-morrow or the day after, I shall die." (38–39)

And after Ha disappears by the river, having spotted one of the new people, Lok in his confusion "had no pictures" (78). The people are shaken by the incident, and this disrupts their instinctive togetherness, causing them to lose one another to an unfamiliar solipsism. The dread of separateness is brought home to Lok when he sees the group's wise matriarch pass him by without noticing. Lok senses something is wrong: "all at once Lok was frightened because she has not seen him. The old woman knew so much; yet she had not seen him" (78). The looming presence of the new man marks the onset of the skeptical challenge of the separateness of minds. It makes Lok feel that he

> was cut off and no longer one of the people; as though his communion with the other had changed him he was different from them and they could not see him. He had no words to formulate these thoughts but he felt his difference and invisibility as a cold wind that blew on his skin. The other had tugged at the strings that bound him to Fa and Mal and Liku and the rest of the people. The strings were not the ornament of life but its substance. If they broke, a man would die. All at once he was hungry for someone's eyes to meet his and recognize him. (78)

The passage is heartbreakingly prophetic. Gestures and images (the frosty bite of wind, the tugging at strings) show not only what is inside Lok's mind but the vital importance of the "how-ness" of his thinking: the binding ties between the People are not a metaphor (a political metaphor, for instance, of some social ideal). Intercorporeality is the form of their existence; if severed, the People's existence is no longer possible.

This scene is also one of the first intimations of the change in Lok that encountering his modern successor brings about, the "upheaval in the brain" that makes him feel "proud and sad like Mal" (191). The only way Lok can understand this strange mutation is by situating it in a particular body: "Mal thinking" (193). Lok's thinking is stretched from the montagelike linking of images toward an abstract connecting of elements whose meaning arises from the idea of likeness:

> Lok discovered "Like." He had used likeness all his life without being aware of it. Fungi on a tree were ears, the word was the same but acquired a distinction by circumstances that could never apply to the sensitive things on the side of the head. Now, in a convulsion of the understanding Lok found himself using likeness as a tool as surely as ever he had used a stone to hack at sticks or meat. Likeness could grasp the white-faced hunters with a hand, could

put them into the world where they were thinkable and not a random and unrelated irruption. (194)

This shift in thinking is from metaphor (fungi are ears) to simile (fungi are *like* ears). Lok revels in his new capacity for invisibly linking things by inserting a ghostly likeness between them. But this new and fabulous tool brings to an end the multiplicitous singleness of Lok's world. No longer do things occur in the world as singular and independent. They now belong to a system of elements linked by "likeness," subject to an ordering hierarchy. The world coheres into a thinkable whole at the same time that it divides into higher and lower categories of being. To be systematic rather than irruptive, then, things must lose their singularity, their integral life as objects, and become parts of a general metaphysical order of Being.

On observing the new people's frantic rituals, their wild romps and the drinking of a putrid, intoxicating liquid, Lok rehearses his new similes, which finally yield the meaning of the new people:

"The people are like honey trickling from a crevice in the rock" . . .

"The people are like honey in the round stones, the new honey that smells of dead things and fire" . . .

"They are like the river and the fall, they are a people of the fall; nothing stands against them." . . .

"They are like Oa." (*TI* 195)

Golding's language follows the gradual shift away from the pictorial to the "half-knowledge, terrible in its very formlessness" that "filtered into Lok as though he were sharing a picture . . . but had no eyes inside his head and could not see it" (173). Abstraction itself is visualized as lacking eyes. Next, Golding describes Lok's noting the new people's canines, proof of their carnivorousness: "they were teeth that remembered wolf" (174). How easy it would have been for a less attentive writer (Wells?) to put down "recalled" instead of "remembered." And how compromised the sentence would have been by this choice. For

Lok, as yet unaccustomed to practicing likenesses, it is the man's teeth themselves who do the remembering.

Thinking in Pictures: Golding, Grandin, and Animal Studies

Pictorial thinking has become something of a hobbyhorse in animal studies as a path to "other" subjectivities, ungrounded in abstract reasoning or linguistic ability. "Thinking in pictures," popularized in the work of Temple Grandin, also suggests (as yet undeveloped) connections between disability and animal studies. Grandin is an animal scientist and best-selling author who has written widely about her experiences as an autistic person in a nonautistic world. *Thinking in Pictures* (1995) and *Animals in Translations* (2005) both reached a wide readership.

I first came across Grandin in Errol Morris's *Stairway to Heaven* (1998), one of his First Person documentary films featuring a typically zany American coterie.[9] The film's title refers to an improved cattle ramp and conveyor restrainer system Grandin designed for a large meatpacking plant at the beginning of her long career in the meat industry. With its penchant for the bizarre and the garish, Morris's film is morally ambiguous, an ambiguity that all but dissipated as Grandin entered the mainstream.

In his foreword to *Thinking in Pictures*, Oliver Sacks describes Grandin as a "designer of livestock equipment, struggling for the humane treatment of animals" (xiv). Her story offers "a glimpse, and indeed a revelation, that there might be people, *no less human than ourselves*, who constructed their worlds, lived their lives, in almost unimaginably different ways" (xviii; my emphasis). But the human community need not be viewed in this way (the "normal" implied readers and the disabled whom Grandin's experience in a sense speaks for). Community can be divided along very different, multiple, or multiply overlapping lines. How might an ethical vegetarian, for example—whether autistic or not—relate to Grandin's story?

In contrast to Sacks, Cary Wolfe's "Learning from Temple Grandin, or Animal Studies, Disability Studies, and Who Comes After the Subject," takes pictorial thinking as demonstrating the possibility of other subjectivities, ones not "drawn from the liberal justice tradition and its central concept of 'rights,' in which ethical standing and civic inclusion are predicated upon rationality, autonomy, and agency" (110). For Wolfe, what is at stake in Grandin's work is precisely the transcending of a human community whose commonality overrides the appearance of difference. Wolfe is operating instead within a "fundamentally posthumanist set of coordinates" (110) that enable a provocative but fruitful encounter between animal studies and disability studies in line with earlier movements for social critique and reform, from civil rights to feminism and gay liberation, which transformed our understanding of society, culture, and the subject (110).

While agreeing that animal studies and disability studies intersect in potentially interesting ways, I have serious misgivings about the value of Grandin's contribution to discussions of human-animal relations.[10] Wolfe's appropriation of Grandin rather problematically defers what I would argue are the essential ethical questions. It is worth stopping to look more closely at Grandin's work in light of Golding's *The Inheritors*, since both Golding and Grandin reach toward what Wolfe calls a "shared trans-species being-in-the-world" (122) that emerges out of modes of life explicitly or implicitly deemed "disabled."

The Inheritors' thinking in pictures underlies the reader's experience of the novel's protagonists, who could easily enough be considered "subnormal." But the similarity between Golding and Grandin renders their differences all the more striking. It also implies that championing ulterior subjectivities does not in itself generate a new ethics if the question of power is left unaddressed. As Everett showed, Golding's text places creaturely pity at its center. Pity is a very different thing to "humane treatment" and far closer to Weil's notion of the "vulnerability of precious things." In chapter 1 I discussed Weil's distinction between justice and rights. Welfare is equally foreign to the notion of justice.

Grandin attributes her lifelong connection with animals to her autism, manifested in part by her hypervisual thinking and tactile sensitivity. Her identification with cattle perception—and the emphasis in this case significantly falls on animals' perceptual models, not on animals' lives—allows Grandin to design "better" (more humane and more efficient) devices for industrial packing plants. Grandin never doubts that animals have an internal world, since she sees her own mental life as mirroring that of animals:

> When a well-respected animal scientist told me that animals do not think, I replied that if this were true, then I would have to conclude that I was unable to think. He could not imagine thinking in pictures, nor assign it the validity of real thought. Mine is a world of thinking that many language-based thinkers do not comprehend. . . .
>
> It is very likely that animals think in pictures and memories of smell, light, and sound patterns. In fact, my visual thinking patterns probably resemble animal thinking more closely than those of verbal thinkers. It seems silly to me to debate whether or not animals can think. (*Thinking* 186–187)

But does thinking in pictures really get one closer to the being of a cow? Cows have elaborate social structures and complex familial attachments. Their *lives* rather than their *minds* are significant in ways that Grandin barely addresses. *Thinking in Pictures* is the story of a mind's becoming transparent to itself, an avowedly Cartesian story, which quickly turns into a tale of betrayal. Grandin's ability to see from a cow's point of view allows her to enter into their midst like a spy. Her insider's perspective makes killing them easier. Grandin's story raises many questions, some of which are the ones that interest Wolfe, but others seem to me more fundamental: questions about the relationship between subjectivity and ethics, about the industry Grandin is involved in, and about our own relationship to the masses of animals killed by that industry. Ultimately the question is this: *What would these animals have to become, and become in our eyes, to be creatures that it is forbidden to kill?*[11]

If Grandin's story is about the *en*abling power of *dis*ability, there is a kind of "virtual autism" that her work actively (if unintentionally) fosters when the most pressing ethical questions are skipped. Wolfe speaks of "inattentional blindness," the fact that "what we think of as 'normal' human visuality does not see—and it (necessarily) does not see that it does not see" ("Learning" 113). An inattentional blindness is evident in the responses Grandin's work often provokes in the mode of "not asking" rather than of "not seeing."

The theme of unasked questions is explored in Coetzee's *The Lives of Animals*. When the psychologist Wolfgang Köhler conducted his behavioral studies of apes in Tenerife, Costello tells her audience, he wanted to see whether apes could think instrumentally.[12] Bananas suspended from the top of the cage, just out of reach, prompted the chimpanzees, the most talented of whom was called Sultan, to pile up crates to reach the food. Costello points out that the experiment could have triggered any number of questions for the apes, of which "How does one use the crates to reach the bananas?" is the least interesting. Sultan could have thought: "Why is he starving me?" or "What have I done?" or "Why has he stopped liking me?" (*TLOA* 28). "At every turn," Costello concludes, "Sultan is driven to think the less interesting thought. From the purity of speculation (Why do men behave like this?) he is relentlessly propelled toward lower, practical, instrumental reason (How does one use this to get that?) and thus toward acceptance of himself as primarily an organism with an appetite that needs to be satisfied" (*TLOA* 29). By inquiring into the learning capacities of apes, Köhler wards off—in himself as much as in his experimental subjects—a set of questions that belong to a different category of thought, which Costello unashamedly ascribes to the higher order of pure speculation. For Costello such purity of speculation is more likely to arise in Sultan than in Köhler. This sort of speculation is not Cartesian, but reminds one of Weil's creaturely cry of the heart against injustice: "Why am I being hurt?" ("Human Personality" 93). This question never surfaces in Grandin's work, and there is no reason to assume that she hears it. Instead, Grandin is concerned with the practicalities of injustice: the administration, management, and minimization of suffering. "But the cry 'Why am I being hurt?' raises quite different problems, for which the spirit of truth, justice, and love is indispensable" ("Human Personality" 93).

Like Sultan, readers of Grandin are propelled toward the less interesting thought when otherness becomes a functional rather than an ethical issue. Like Sultan, we locate ourselves at the instrumental level and reject speculating about the consequences that a creaturely fellowship with animals (which Grandin readily acknowledges) might entail. I am not suggesting Grandin is disingenuous in claiming a connection with animals. But this affinity is rooted in an instrumental, precisely *inattentive* relationship, in which fellowship and love are displaced, allowing Grandin to make her home in an industry that turns animals into food.

In pivotal moments in her narrative, and despite being an atheist, Grandin describes her work in spiritual terms. For Grandin, moreover, the industry maintains its dignity partly through an appeal to religious animal sacrifice. At the end of the book, Grandin describes a dream of placing her hands on the white walls of the Swift meat packing plant as "touching the sacred alter" (*Thinking* 227). In another passage (which Wolfe too finds richly troubling), Grandin is at a kosher plant equipped with the restraining chute she designed:

> I had to force myself to relax and just allow the restrainer to become part of my body, while completely forgetting about the levers. . . .
>
> Through the machine, I reached out and held the animal. When I held his head in the yoke, I imagined placing my hands on his forehead and under his chin and gently easing him into position. Body boundaries seemed to disappear, and I had no awareness of pushing the levers. The rear pusher gate and head yoke became an extension of my hands. (*Thinking* 25)

Grandin continues a little further down:

> the parts of the apparatus that held the animal felt as if they were an extension of my own body. . . . During this intense period of concentration I no longer heard noise from the plant machinery. I didn't feel the sweltering Alabama summer heat, and everything seemed quiet and serene. It was almost a religious experience. It was my job to hold the animal gently, and it was the rabbi's job to perform the final deed. I was able to look at each animal, to hold

him gently and make him as comfortable as possible during the last moments of his life. I had participated in the ancient slaughter ritual the way it was supposed to be. A new door has been opened. It felt like walking on water.[13]   (25–26)

A rare comment on the killing of animals from Weil's *Letter to a Priest* is worth citing in this context: "people must have thought in very ancient times that God is actually present in animals killed to be eaten; that God in fact descends into them for the purpose of offering himself as food to man. This notion turned animal food into a communion, whereas otherwise it is a crime, unless we adopt a more or less Cartesian philosophy" (*Letter* 11). Weil concedes that animals killed for food outside a communion are killed immorally, unless one accepts Descartes's feeble notion of animals as mere automata. Golding's Neanderthals share a similar distaste for unreflective, automated consumption of flesh. They eat discarded meat, but ask forgiveness from the animal whom they devour. Meat consumption in *The Inheritors* is both graphic and subject to a prohibition:

The doe was wrecked and scattered. Fa split open her belly, slit the complicated stomach and spilt the sour cropped grass and broken shoots on the earth. Lok beat in the skull to get at the brain and levered open the mouth to wrench away the tongue. They filled the stomach with tit-bits and twisted up the guts so that the stomach became a floppy bag.

All the while, Lok talked between his grunts.

"This is bad. This is very bad." ... "This is bad. But a cat killed you so there is no blame."   (54)

The Neanderthal goddess Oa does not require sacrifice to bridge the chasm between heaven and earth. Communion needs no ritual, because it is a living fact. This is why the prehistoric world of *The Inheritors* is also premystical. The prohibition on meat is thus the affirmation of unimmediated contact between creatures and creator. In this sense alone the Neanderthals' world is prelapsarian. With the arrival of the new people, we are immediately transported to the symbolic order of ritual sacrifice (and cannibalism), a mystical world empty of God.

Despite their common emphasis on the picture as a gateway to nonhuman alterity, then, Grandin and Golding offer starkly different versions of the idea of communion. Quite unlike Golding, whose object of pity and love is the vanquished and downtrodden creature, Grandin's breakthrough moments, during which she reaches something approaching religious ecstasy ("like walking on water") are not moments of communion with other lives. They are moments that celebrate the body-made-docile by a feat of technology. Wolfe is quick to relate this moment of seamless assemblage of the human, animal, and mechanical to Donna Haraway's idea of the *cyborg* ("Learning" 117). The kosher slaughter scene can be read as a hybrid site of encounter, not simply in terms of merging organic and inorganic matter through the killing apparatus but in terms of the histories, traditions, and myths that enmesh the lives of all of Haraway's critters. But Grandin's veneration of smooth contaminations remains morally numb. Her accounts disclose what Diamond describes as "a kind of pitilessness at the heart of welfarism, a willingness to go ahead with what we do to the vulnerable, a willingness to go on subjecting them to our power because we can, because it suits us to do so, and it has suited people like us for millennia" ("Injustice and Animals" 141).

A final aspect of Golding's "thinking in pictures" has to do with the issue of historical consciousness. *The Inheritors* takes the form of a memory, an image sparked by the sudden and visceral presence of the past. Golding is reminiscent of Benjamin, who wrote that "the true picture of the past flits by. The past can be seized only as an image which flashes up at the instant when it can be recognized and is never seen again" ("Theses" 247). *The Inheritors* does not lay claims to factual accuracy about Neanderthal existence. At stake for Golding is not history itself but the nature of historical knowledge. And in this book and others Golding regards history, conservatively, as essentially tragic.

Golding's Counterhistories

> What moments of terror and triumph! What acts of devotion and desperate wonders of courage! And the strain of the victors was our strain; we are lineally identical with those sun-brown painted beings who ran and fought and helped one another, the blood in our veins glowed in those fights and chilled in those fears of the forgotten past.
>
> —H. G. Wells, "The Grisly Folk"

The slightly maniacal passage toward the end of the "The Grisly Folk" illustrates Wells's comportment toward the historical. In their sense of what constitutes historical consciousness, Golding and Wells stand at opposite ends of Benjamin's historiographical models in "Theses on the Philosophy of History": on the one hand *historicism,* with its primarily social democratic and progressive agenda, and on the other *historical materialism*, which for Benjamin looks to the fragmented and catastrophic past in order to salvage it in the name of revolutionary-messianic hope.[14]

Golding calls historicism into question in three ways. First, he rejects the idea of rational progress, which propels Wells's vision of human evolution. Second, *The Inheritors* allegorically transcends its prehistoric setting by, as it were, foreshadowing modern European genocide. If, as Golding believes, Wells's monstrous Neanderthals are none other than our own projection, then historiography must proceed reflexively to expose the truth that "there is no document of civilization which is not at the same time a document of barbarism" (thesis 7, "Theses" 248). Last, Golding rejects anthropocentric history and opens up the historical to a nonhuman dimension, which, in his own historical reflections, Benjamin called the creaturely.

First subversion. *The Inheritors* responds to what Coetzee described as Benjamin's "call (in the 'Theses') for a history centered on the sufferings of the vanquished, rather than on the achievements of the victors" (*Inner Workings* 64). History told from the perspective of the winners is not really history at all. Ronald Beiner's observation that Benjamin's "historiography is an unremitting struggle on behalf of the dead" (427) is remarkably suited to *The Inheritors* as an attempt to mend a broken past. "Where the historicist sees an inert 'chain of events,' the historical materialist sees a broken vessel in need of repair, a ruined past in need of salvation, *a forsaken ancestor in need of awakening* (thesis IX)" (Beiner 427; my emphasis). *The Inheritors* is not merely a tale about forsaken ancestors but a bridge in time, linking the ruined prehuman past with Europe's postwar present. It is no accident, then, that Golding treats the "subhumans" of a bygone era with such profound pity, since he is writing from a future in which celebrating what Wells called "true men" proved deadly false. From past to present, then, human progress is delusional.

In thesis 13, Benjamin rejects progress because it implies movement "through a homogeneous, empty time" ("Theses" 252). Progress subdues time under the banner of the Future. As deeply ideological, the idea of progress denies whatever introduces difference into humanity's steady onward march. Belief in progress paradoxically excludes the possibility of what Benjamin called a "messianic" intervention, which is, after all, history's saving grace: the idea that history does not merely rehearse as eternal the transitory dogmas of the present but throws up each moment (miraculously) anew as a temporality rent from the continuum of history and so pregnant with the possibility revolution: "Historicism gives the 'eternal' image of the past; historical materialism supplies a unique experience with the past. The historical materialist leaves it to others to be drained by the whore called 'Once upon a time' in historicism's bordello. He remains in control of his powers, man enough to blast open the continuum of history" (thesis 16, "Theses" 254). In an altogether more whimsical tone (befitting Benjamin's *Arcades* project rather than the "Theses"), Golding describes history as a hodgepodge of objects washed up by time. "We stand among the flotsam," he says at the end of "In My Ark," "the odd shoes and tins, hot-water bottles and skulls of sheep or deer. We know nothing. We look daily at the appalling mystery of plain stuff. We stand where any upright food-gatherer has stood, on the edge of our own unconscious, and hope, perhaps, for the terror and excitement of the print of a single foot" (105).

Golding avoids the pitfalls of narrative history (the "once upon a time") by rendering the past pictorially as a fleeting, fatal moment of farewell. Like Benjamin, Golding also writes from a sense of history's alterity. It is fitting, therefore, that *The Inheritors* draws to a close with man's failure to see. As the new man, Tuami ("tu-ami": you/r friend), journeys forth into the unknown, Golding switches from solid land to water. Man's ascent is replaced by the horizontal pushing through darkness: "Tuami looked at the line of darkness. It was far away and there was plenty of water in between. He peered forward past the sail to see what lay at the other end of the lake, but it was so long, and there was such a flashing from the water that he could not see if the line of darkness had an ending" (*TI* 233).

To discuss Golding's second and third subversions of historicism, I turn to Benjamin's concepts of natural history (*Naturgeschichte*) and the creature (*Kreatur*) as considered by two influential commentaries on Benjamin. In *Walter Benjamin's Other History* Beatrice Hanssen proposes to reinterpret much of Benjamin's work "in light of an aspect of his philosophy of history . . . the ethico-theological call for another kind of history, one no longer purely anthropocentric in nature or anchored only in the concerns of human subjects" (1). Natural history, as Benjamin used it, "referred to a process of transience and to a logic of decay that radically undermined Enlightenment and post-Enlightenment conceptions of human history, anchored in categories of human freedom and historical teleology. . . . Benjamin's positive validation of natural history was meant to overcome the limitations of historical hermeneutics, whose category of 'meaning' (*Sinn*) remained grounded in the understanding of a human subject" (Hanssen 3). Benjamin recognizes in history a foreign element, a kind of natural growth, which sweeps human legibility into history's catastrophic pileup. Benjamin's 1928 (failed) Habilitation thesis *The Origin of German Tragic Drama* (*Trauerspiel*) "spelled out this original conception of a natural, nonhuman history, coupling it with a critique of the philosophy of the subject, which would culminate in his redefinition of the theological concept *Kreatur*" (Hanssen 1–2).[15] Benjamin replaces the agent—the one who, as we say, "makes history"—with the creature overtaken by or lost in history. Natural history does not simply admit nature as a backdrop or mise-en-scène. It reveals nature as what is fundamentally temporal about history—mutability, transience, and decay—the passing of the historical order into ahuman nature, the passing of man into nonman, of soul into matter.

We can begin to appreciate *The Inheritors* as an exercise in Benjaminian historiography that refutes human teleology by attending not to historical subjects but to creatures of history—Neanderthal and Cro-Magnon alike—whose lives are a snapshot of the past and the demand for a new kind of history. This is how, in "A Left-Handed Blow: Writing the History of Animals," Erica Fudge formulates Benjamin's importance for a nonanthropocentric view of history: "History and humanity are, as the humanists proclaim, coterminous, but a history can be written that does not celebrate the stability of what was, what is, and what shall be. Instead history should reinterpret the documents of the past in order to offer a new idea of the human. No longer separate, in splendid isolation, humans must be shown to be embedded within and reliant upon the natural order" (Fudge 15). Creaturely history, then, reabsorbs the human in nature and paves the way for radically other histories inclusive of nonhuman life.

Eric Santner's *On Creaturely Life* takes a different view of the significance and ramifications of natural history and the creaturely. By *Naturgeschichte* Santner understands Benjamin to be exposing the ahuman opacity at the heart of human history, signaling—as Agamben does—a creaturely dimension *within* the human. "In Benjamin's parlance," Santner explains, *Naturgeschichte* does not simply allude to the idea that "nature also has a history but to the fact that the artifacts of human history tend to acquire an aspect of mute, natural being at the point where they begin to lose their place in a viable form of life (think of the process whereby architectural ruins are reclaimed by nature)" (Santner 16). One can think of natural history as a sort of double take: a thing that survives beyond its historical context is reified as a natural object (it "lives" beyond the death of its symbolic order). But, seen from the other direction, an expired historical context leaves relics seeming "denaturalized" (since history is to us a kind of "second nature"). The lifeless object is merely "historical," while the historical relic is purely elemental: "natural history is born out of the dual possibilities that life can persist beyond the death of the symbolic forms that gave it meaning and that symbolic forms can survive beyond the death of the form of life that gave them human vitality. Natural history transpires against the background of this space between real and symbolic death, this space of the 'undead'" (Santner 16–17). This undead historical space gives rise to a new historical subject. No longer an agent at home in history, this new subject is *Unheimliche*, or creaturely.

The difference between Hanssen and Santner emerges at this point. Santner reads creatureliness in the tradition of German Jewish writing (Benjamin, Kafka, Scholem, Freud, and leading up to W. G. Sebald) profoundly marked by the experience of fascism: "For Benjamin, natural history ultimately names the ceaseless repetition of such cycles of emergence and decay of human orders of meaning, cycles that are, for him—and this is where the Schmittian background can be felt—always connected to violence" (17). As the reference to Carl Schmitt makes clear, the creaturely assumes a distinctly political or biopolitical flavor. Creatureliness is "less a dimension that traverses the boundaries of human and nonhuman forms of life," as it does for Hanssen, "than a specifically human way of finding oneself caught in the midst of antagonisms in and of the political field" (xix).

Located at the point of an evolutionary/colonial handover, *The Inheritors* brings together biology, politics, and history in one seamless gesture. Critics tend to overlook the political import of Golding's work, focusing instead on its universal and existential dimensions. Yet Golding's use of natural images, materials, and locales (islands, water, rocks) is not as symbolic "Anywheres" but is also historical. "Although set in the distant past," Paul Crawford writes in *Politics and History in William Golding*, "and lacking the surface details specific to World War II . . . *The Inheritors* powerfully suggests the sociopolitical context of contemporary genocide" (Crawford 69).[16] *The Inheritors*, then, is not an escape from history into fable but an example of "the mutual imbrication of nature and history" (Hanssen 16) whose meaning can only be transcribed allegorically.

Benjaminian allegory is inherently linked to natural history: "Benjamin's theory of allegory," writes Hanssen, "unearthed the debris of human history. . . . Under Benjamin's critical gaze, allegory was transformed into the figure of natural history" (15). For Adorno as well, "allegory was to be understood as a constellation that comprised the ideas of nature, history, signification, and transience—a constellation that, without fusing these terms, preserved their facticity and uniqueness" (15). How precisely is this constellation worked out in *The Inheritors?*

Much has been written on Benjamin's notion of allegory, most often in the context of his critique of modernity. Bainard Cowan explains that allegory is an experience rather than a concept, arising from "an apprehension of the world as no longer permanent, as passing out of being" (Cowan 110). Richard Stamelman writes that "allegory could be called the trope of death: the language of fragmentation, decay, and erosion which death speaks or writes. . . . In allegory, an absent and unrecoverable meaning is joined to an excessive and overdetermined language" (*Lost Beyond Telling* 53). Hanssen points to Benjamin's characteristically convoluted and idiosyncratic use of allegory at the end of *The Origin of German Tragic Drama* (97–102). She exposes the redemptive dimension of allegory as a leap from the contemplation of the ruination of meaning in the world to the realm of divine resurrection (100–101). Redemption is implicit for Benjamin precisely in the allegorical apprehension of the unbridgeable gap between the sign and transcendent reality. This is a negative theology (again reminiscent of Weil) that is at once pessimistic and yet structurally open to mystery.

In Richard Ford's novel *The Sportswriter* (1986), about a man's life following the death of his young son, Ford's main character, disillusioned novelist-turned-sportswriter Frank Bascombe, says to his ex-wife (known only as X): "there are no transcendent themes in life. In all cases things are here and they're over, and that has to be enough. The other view is a lie of literature and the liberal arts" (Ford 22).[17]

As a novel about transience, *The Inheritors* avoids the consolations of literature that Frank Bascombe dislikes. Golding opens mid-motion with the drumbeat of Lok's feet (thorn bush in hand) and ends with Lok's body pressed sideways against the hollowed earth (*TI* 221). If there is transcendence here, it is lowly, not vertiginous. Like Ford's novel, *The Inheritors* is an exploration of a terrain. In Golding we are most probably in northern Europe, while Ford's novel is filled with the minutiae of suburban New Jersey. In *The Sportswriter*, familiar American tropes (highways, late-night bars, driveways, and motels) are never conventionally iconic, and the novel's scrupulous descriptions are mainly domestic (mail-order catalogues, backyards and street curbs, the faintly lit windows of the family home spied from inside a parked car).

There is also the theme of the dead child. In *The Inheritors*, Lok cannot see what Fa already knows—that Liku, the little Neanderthal girl captured by the new people, has been cannibalized:

> "Now there are only Fa and Lok and the new one and Liku."
> For a while she looked at him in silence. She put out a hand and he took it. She opened her mouth to speak but no sound came. She gave a shake of her whole body and then started to shudder. He could see her master this shudder as if she were leaving the comfort of the cave in a morning of snow. She took her hand away.
> "Come!"   (*TI* 198–199)

Although parenting for the People is a communal, not a couple's, affair, Golding makes the loss of the child strike at the core of life, as shattering a blow as could be imagined in the confines of the nuclear family. Some thirty thousand years separate Golding's wild savannah from Ford's New Jersey suburb, but the distance is dwarfed by the sense in both novels of the inevitable and indifferent passing of time, the true sense of life's "inheritance": "Some things can't be explained. They just are. And after a while they disappear, usually forever, or become interesting in another way. Literature's consolations are always temporary, while life is quick to begin again. It is better not even to look so hard, to leave off explaining. Nothing makes me more queasy than to spend time with people who don't know that and who can't forget, and for whom such knowledge isn't a cornerstone of life" (Ford 229–230).

After Fa's death, Lok curls up on the ground clutching the ancient Oa and prepares to be swallowed up by time. In the closing passages the new people strive blindly on, urged by restlessness and fear. Golding and Ford are writing of persons struggling to understand the losses they incur in a world whose precise workings are temporal and opaque. Contingency is where allegory and natural history coincide and where the so-called realism of Ford meets Golding's so-called fantasy: "The great achievement of the allegorical mode of representation was, as Benjamin put it . . . that it rendered a sense of life bereft of any secure reference to transcendence, life utterly exposed to the implacable rhythms of natural history" (Santner 18). Santner's explanation rings as true for Golding as it does for Ford and sums up all the sorrow and the pity cooped up in these two understated works.

3 The Indignities of Species in Marie Darrieussecq's *Pig Tales*

> The humanist discovery of man is the discovery that he lacks himself, the discovery of his irremediable lack of *dignitas.*
>
> —Giorgio Agamben, *The Open*

> It is facile, virtually meaningless, to demand that literature stick with the "human." For the matter at stake is not "human" versus "inhuman" (in which choosing the "human" guarantees instant moral self-congratulation for both author and reader) but an infinitely varied register of forms and tonalities for transporting *the human voice* into prose narrative.
>
> —Susan Sontag, "The Pornographic Imagination"

Fictionalizing with a Scalpel

From Ovid to Kafka, narratives of the transformations of species have served as a vehicle for discussing human identity, its failings and flaws. Marie Darrieussecq's debut novel *Pig Tales* (*Truismes*), published in France in 1996, may at first appear as a clever addition to the corpus of metamorphosis literature. Told from the point of view of a grown sow, *Pig Tales* also seems to rehearse the classical mode of the animal fable, which, through thick anthropomorphic haze, confronts us with uncomfortable truths (truisms) about our human selves.[1] The novel is narrated in the first person by a woman who has turned into a pig, and who, on the first page of the book tells us she is literally struggling to hold pen to paper to transcribe her strange ordeal:

> Simply holding a pen gives me terrible cramps. I haven't enough light, either, so I have to stop at nightfall, and I write very, very

slowly. I won't tell you about the problems I had getting this notebook or about the mud, which dirties everything and dilutes ink that's barely dry. *I hope that any publisher patient enough to decipher these piggle-squiggles* [*cette écriture de cochon*] *will graciously take into consideration the enormous effort I'm making to write as legibly as possible.* Even the act of remembering is quite difficult for me. But if I concentrate hard and try to think back as far as I can . . . I manage to recover some images.[2]   (*Pig Tales* 1; my emphasis)

From the outset, then, *Pig Tales* sets up the literary act of writing as a corporeal rather than psychological event. Only an act of supreme patience and goodwill on the part of the well-bred editor can confer on such pig writing (these "piggle-squiggles") the status of a literary autobiography. The unlikely author of the text is pigheaded enough to press on against the odds, and, as Michel Lantelme pointed out, the novel partly works as a thinly veiled allegory on the "birth of the writer."[3] But *Pig Tales* is far more than that. In the novel "pigscripts"—*écriture de cochon*—stands for a particular approach to literature whose orientation is exterior rather than interior: writing that does not express the humanistic self-awareness of the autobiographical subject, lacks self-transparency, and partakes of the creaturely opacity of language.[4]

On its publication, *Pig Tales* struck a chord with the reading public and literary critics alike.[5] Shirley Jordan notes how the novel "gave the French publishing world its phenomenon for the beginning of the 1996 literary year" (Jordan 142). Though indisputably unique (its economy and confidence give the impression of having been written in a single stroke of the pen), *Pig Tales* need also be read in the context of the bold new fictions of the generation of French writers who came to the fore in the 1990s (the best known of whom in France and the English-speaking world alike is Michel Houellebecq), fictions which for Frédéric Badré warranted the title "Une nouvelle tendance en littérature."[6]

"Why a sow?" Darrieussecq opens her 2006 collection of short stories *Zoo* with this brief prologue:

Of all possible questions, except maybe "how are you?" this is the one posed to me most often since the publication of *Pig Tales* in 1996. I haven't really a reply, except statistically. We treat women as sow more often than mare, cow, monkey, viper, or tigress; more often still than as giraffe, leech, slug, octopus, or tarantula; and far more often than as a centipede, female rhino, or koala. It's simple. But does that answer the question? So often posed, it's that it points elsewhere, questions someone or something else. We tap at the window. But is anyone in, while writing?[7]

(*Zoo* 7–8; my translation)

Darrieussecq moves away from the statistical facts of women's cultural animalization to the issue of writing in general (not even that of the woman writer). Fiction is portrayed by Darrieussecq as written in an empty house, absent-minded and ghostly, occasioned by something other than the writer herself as the one who can definitely say "why a sow." The passage helps approach *Pig Tales* as a novel about animality and about writing—and about a certain animality *of* writing that exceeds the state and stakes of the female writer.

Commentaries on *Pig Tales*, by and large, treat the theme of metamorphosis as the opening of *Zoo* first implies: metaphorically. Animalization is the figure of female oppression and degradation. The metamorphic "fall" from humanity expresses women's cultural othering within the dynamics of modern biopower. As Jeanette Gaudet explains: "The literary trope of metamorphosis explicitly illustrates the radical re-organisation of the female body by the sociosymbolic structures in which it is enmeshed" (Gaudet 183). The body as the locus of both oppression and transgression has become a major point of reference in recent French writing (and filmmaking) by women, which makes metamorphosis a useful device for exploring female corporeality and identity (Rye and Worton 14). In *Pig Tales*: "the heroine's porcine transformations keep the struggle over the meanings of the female body firmly at the centre of this complex text. Cleverly standing in metaphoric relation to a wide range of experiences from puberty to menopause, they allow Darrieussecq to explore a collective sense of feminine identity through highlighting one woman's relationship—sometimes painful, sometimes joyous—with her physical self" (Jordan 143–144).

Gender is immediately central to Darrieussecq's thematics of transformation. Hired as part masseuse, part prostitute by a dubious establishment (Perfumes Plus) in a futuristic and barely recognizable Paris, the protagonist's metamorphosis seems like mere accompaniment to her everyday experiences in which she is subjected to physical violations by the male management and clientele, violations that specifically "animalize" her. Yet it seems to me that a reluctance to radically literalize the workings of metamorphosis in the novel, reluctance to acknowledge the specificity of species alongside the registers of gender and sex, commits interpretation to an unduly narrow feminist conundrum.[8] "On the one hand," claims Jordan, "the novel seems deeply pessimistic . . . of the worst in women's experiences, riddled with soft-porn images and sexual violence, and with a narrator who is unpardonably light-hearted and too insouciant to denounce the social order. From this perspective the ultimate outrage is that . . . Darrieussecq . . . appears to indicate that bodies of feminist knowledge have not percolated down to ordinary women: it is as if they were an irrelevance of history" (Jordan 146). Read positively, however, "*Truismes* could be said to exemplify Lidia Curti's equally persuasive argument that the freakish body can be 'a derisive counterpoint to stereotypes of the feminine'" (Jordan 146).[9]

The "ultimate outrage" suggested by Jordan's negative reading calls for a separate discussion, as it is crucial not merely to this novel and its feminists concerns but to the bulk of contemporary fictions I have just mentioned, including Houellebecq. That feminism, along with other liberal and "liberationist" discourses (especially those pertaining to sexual liberation), have in some grave sense failed is, I would argue, a possibility Darrieussecq's text goes some way to articulate. An even more explicit and sneering indictment of liberal ideas and the emancipatory campaigns of the 1960s (in particular 1968) powers many, if not all, of Houellebecq's novels, most famously in *Les particules élémentaires* (*The Elementary Particles*).[10] There are some interesting similarities between Darrieussecq and Houellebecq, not least in their questioning of the meaning and destiny of the human in narratives of the near future.[11]

Jordan and Gaudet share a strongly metaphorical understanding of the transition from human to animal. While these readings admit that such a transition in *Pig Tales* remains incomplete (the heroine is neither strictly pig nor strictly woman), they do not entertain hybridity at the literal level of species, nor, therefore, do they consider hybridity as complicating the very notion of a clear human/animal divide. As metaphor, the transformations of species denote crises in human affairs (social, sexual, political, or personal) while brushing aside the overwhelmingly physical trauma of metamorphosis: the crisis of the human form.

In its audacity (and pitilessness) *Pig Tales* refutes the bad faith of anthropomorphism. For does not anthropomorphism first and foremost carry through the becoming-human of human beings? Do not literature, the arts, and the "humanities" at large reflect the incomplete becoming—the struggle of the human to assume and to inhabit a definite form? To come to terms with and give shape to an entirely incidental embodiment? It is only after this initial humanizing that other animals can be brought into the field of human semblance. This secondary anthropomorphism (a bone of contention within animal studies as well as in the discourse of animal rights) serves to erase the primary act of anthropomorphic appropriation. To make other animals "like us" entails forgetting that humans begin by making themselves "like us." This primary anthropomorphism is neurotically betrayed (repressed and revealed) in the book of Genesis, which, in its subconscious and subtextual anxiety about the human form, resorts to molding man alone in the image of God.

In *Twilight of the Idols* Nietzsche wryly mocks Judeo-Christian monotheism for precisely such blatant reversals of cause and effect: "There is no error more dangerous than that of confusing the *consequence with the cause*: I call it the real ruination of reason" ("Four Great Errors" 26). The creation story, rooting human form in the divine rather than in the animal, reveals the space of hesitation in which mankind seeks to redeem the contingency of its own form and tear itself away from its own animal being. Yet, with this primary act of self-invention safely forgotten, making other animals like us becomes for humanists a denial of human extraordinariness and, for some animal advocates, a dismissal of animal otherness. A variety of studies have more recently challenged the notion that anthropomorphism is scientifically unfounded or inappropriate.[12] As literary tropes, nevertheless, anthropomorphism and metamorphosis remain locked in the untenable binary of a species divide. I want to see what happens when the metaphorics of body politics give way to a literal reappraisal of the human form—what happens, that is, when gender and species come together under the rigorous literalism of metamorphosis.

As I have suggested, *Pig Tales* begins by making the relationship between species and writing one of its chief concerns. Parodying the generic courtesies of literary confessionals, the pig narrator opens with an apology: "I know how much this story might upset people, how much distress and confusion it could cause. I suspect that any publisher who agrees to take on this manuscript will be heading for trouble—heading for prison, probably—and I'd like to apologize right now for the inconvenience. But I must write this book without further delay, because if they find me in my present state, no one will listen to me or believe what I say" (*Pig Tales* 1).

Gaudet cites Antonin Artaud as a reference point for Darrieussecq's central idea of *écriture de cochon*. Artaud asserted that "Toute l'écriture est de la cochonnerie" (Artaud qtd. in Gaudet 181).[13] At the end of her essay, Gaudet lists the possible interpretations of *écriture de cochon*: beyond the fantastical facts of a pig who can write, the phrase could mean "writing that is good only for pigs" (190). The pigs for whom the narrative is intended are none other than the readers. And so, from the outset, *Pig Tales* is written simultaneously by and for pigs.

Darrieussecq's unassuming narrator (her voice is intentionally "unliterary," deadpan and colloquial; she repeatedly stresses her lack of education and political awareness) highlights the effort to bestow human form on an animal existence, a project of which, in a sense, all writing partakes. *Pig Tales* is, then, not merely a fictional narrative about species exchange but a metafiction on the forging of the human through language, through writing.

Darrieussecq is interested in how identities (human, pig, woman, whore) linger, travel, and seep into one another, flickering, as it were, in their own difference, their own becoming. *Pig Tales* and the truisms it espouses, I want to argue, veer away from the binary rationale of metamorphic transformation, by which one thing becomes another, in an act of conversion or, in a Christian-humanist sense, of transubstantiation. The novel also refuses the didactic offloading of human frailties onto nonhuman creatures. Thematically and formally, it invites a different reading of species indeterminacy, not as a metaphor for the degeneration of the human—even if this degeneration ultimately signals the always already degenerate state of the so-called human—but as a probing of the permanent interval of species, the trembling space between the human and the animal—*as* the space of the human.

I begin with *Pig Tales*'s creative working through the anthropomorphic logic of metamorphosis in order to explode it. I then turn to the process of "becoming-human," which for Darrieussecq is inseparable from the question of writing. In closing, and to reach across to the other chapters in this study, I consider *Pig Tales* both as a post-Holocaust and as a fin de siècle text, at this moment of history, and of French literary history, that has been generating relentlessly inventive attacks on liberal humanist ideology.

Humanity as Masquerade

> Becoming produces nothing other than itself.
> —Gilles Deleuze and Félix Guattari, *A Thousand Plateaus*

Freud's essay "The Uncanny" (1919) famously recounts an anecdote of misrecognition. Sitting on the train, Freud catches a glimpse of an unappealing old man in his carriage window. A moment later, Freud tells us, he realized he was looking at his own reflection. The anecdote discloses the amount of untold labor that goes into the sustaining and upkeep of identity. Caught off guard, it would seem, we become strangers to ourselves. Freud's stranger (himself) is suspended somewhere between the metaphysics of self-identity and Deleuze's "becoming-imperceptible," the process of potentially endless differentiation that finally produces a kind of molecular dissolution of all substance, all identity.[14] While Freud is interested in the play between durability and fragmentation of personal identity, a similar uncanniness can be attributed to the collective identity of species.

In *The Open*, Agamben writes of the paradoxical play of recognition and difference that produces the human. The human form is not a given or a unity. Instead, the human can be thought as simultaneously the product and its own producing optical device. This "optical machine" reflects man back to himself as literally "un-manly":

> *Homo sapiens* . . . is neither a clearly defined species nor a substance; it is, rather, a machine or device for producing the recognition of the human. In line with the taste of the epoch, the anthropogenic (or—taking up Furio Jesi's expression—we might say anthropological) machine is an optical one (as is, according to the most recent studies, the apparatus described in *Leviathan*, the introduction to which perhaps provided Linnaeus with his maxim *nosce te ipsum*, or "read thyself" . . .). It is an optical machine constructed of a series of mirrors in which man . . . sees his own image always already deformed in the features of an ape. *Homo* is a constitutively "anthropomorphous" animal (that is, "resembling man" . . .), who must recognize himself in a non-man in order to be human.
>
> In medieval iconography, the ape holds a mirror in which the man who sins must recognize himself as *simia dei* {ape of God}. In Linnaeus's optical machine, whoever refuses to recognize himself in the ape, becomes one: to paraphrase Pascal, *qui fait l'homme, fait le singe* {he who acts the man, acts the ape}. This is why at the end of the introduction to the *Systema*, Linnaeus, who defined *Homo* as the animal that *is* only if it recognizes that it *is not*, must put up with apes disguised as critics climbing on his shoulders to mock him.

(26–27)

Agamben's densely scholastic account of the human as an optical procedure that hinges on differentiation suggests some fascinating parallels with *Pig Tales*. Visual ambivalence is a recurring theme in this novel, in which mirrors and reflections abound. The estranging effect of mirrors registers the human form as a momentary pause in the ongoing fluctuations of species. In the mirror the revelation of animality can be either "chilling" and frightening (32, 69), or positive: "I thought I looked beautiful in the mirrors: somewhat flushed, true, a little chunky, but savage—I don't know quite how to put it. You could see something like pride in my eyes and in my body" (28).[15]

These images yield recognitions that are also misrecognitions, which, it is important to stress, have little to do with Lacan's mirror stage and the impossible cementing of subjectivity. Mirror images in *Pig Tales* pertain to the exteriority of form and to the corporeal definition of and power over bodies. Thus reflections, mirror images, or photo-graphs do not point inwardly to the interiority of mental substance. This is not a novel about consciousness but about contours.

One genuine glimpse of interiority in *Pig Tales* is savagely literal: the view of a young girl's entrails, disemboweled as she hangs from a chandelier during a ferocious bacchanal at Edgar's Palace on the eve of the third millennium (92–96). Another truism for the gentle humanist: inside meat there is only more meat. The narrator-pig dispassionately describes the arrival of her former client the African marabout, a charlatan turned high priest in Edgar's regime, who addresses the exhausted revelers at the culmination of the frenzied possession ritual: "Fortunately for me there was a girl strung up to a chandelier by her hair who was making even more of a racket. Her insides were hanging out, bowels and all—they'd had a fine time with her. In his great goodness, the marabout cut down the girl and blessed the others who were lying around. Gesturing to have all that cleaned up, he said, 'Now go home, my brothers, prepare yourselves spiritually for the coming Third Millennium, and pray that the spirit of the Spiral will wisely inspire our blessed leader'" (96). The scene is Darrieussecq's most exuberant evocation of Sade. The novel as a whole remains true to the pornographic principle of the extinction of personality and psychology in favor of an exploration of the mechanistic intersection of power and sex.

Unwittingly used and abused by Edgar, the leader of Social Free Progressionism (quietly sadistic, surrounded by oversexed socialites and an actress "pal," Edgar is prophetically Sarkozy-like), the narrator discovers herself as the figurehead of Edgar's election campaign. Looking at a large billboard, the narrator confesses:

> I did have some trouble recognizing myself, but there could be no mistake about the look in her eyes. . . . What I thought I saw at first was a pig wearing that beautiful red dress, a kind of female pig—a sow, if you like—and in her eyes was that hangdog look I get when I'm tired. You can understand, though, that it was hard for me to see myself in her. Then I decided that it was only an optical illusion, that the intense red colour of the dress was giving me that deep pink complexion in the photo . . . and I thought I could see how the impression of a snout, slightly protuberant ears, teeny eyes, and so on was simply caused by the rustic atmosphere of the poster, and especially by those extra pounds I'd put on. *Take a perfectly healthy girl, put her in a red dress, have her gain a smidgen of weight, tire her out, and you'll see what I mean.*   (61–62; my emphasis)

The narrator's rationalization of her piggish appearance is one of *Pig Tales*'s many doubled-up ironies. We initially dismiss the explanation as ludicrous, the narrator as a simpleton; we revel in our own knowingness, our own humanity, only to find the explanation, on second thought, entirely perceptive. This is Agamben's optical machine in action, reflecting the contingency and grotesqueness of the human form. If we fail to recognize the pig in the girl, then the joke is on us. Neither silly nor simple, the narrator sees through a different regime of visibility, free from the pretentious burdens of philosophy's desperate pursuit of humanity's essence and art's elevation of the human form, which bracket off the animal trace in the human. The narrator's naïveté, then, is nothing more than the absence of prejudice, the visual prejudice that keeps us from seeing the animal in our own image and that of our fellow humans. Zoomorphic vision replaces presumptions not only about the supposed perfection of the female body but about the inherent dignity of the human form.[16]

Visibility in this scene (simultaneously recognition and misrecognition) arises from the protagonist's heightened perception of differences. She is living out, with absolute precision, the structuralist principle of identity as a system of differences with no positive terms. Darrieussecq takes this notion of identity to its logical/comical extreme: the narrator identifies the pig as female because it/she is wearing a dress (creature + dress = woman). As a concept, then, metamorphosis is really the visualization—the concretion and freezing—of a "structuralist moment": the image of identity *as* difference.

The naive narrator of *Pig Tales* may not engage in philosophical deliberations of the dictum *nosce te ipsum* (in the rigorous manner Agamben suggests), but she does look in the mirror to see herself made and remade across a visual field of differences that form and deform her. She oscillates between regarding her bodily transformations as hideous and as alluring, in full recognition of her incomplete humanity. In her very mindlessness, then, the heroine of *Pig Tales* arrives (perhaps more authentically than the theoretician or the philosopher) at the grotesque becoming of the human.

The narrator's becoming-human and becoming-woman consists in what, in her discussion of the affinities between pornography, science fiction, and the pastoral—the three dominant modes in *Pig Tales*—Susan Sontag called the "rescaling of the human figure" ("The Pornographic Imagination" 89). *Pig Tales* molds humanity, via snout and corkscrew tail, as the imperfect, terrestrial, and fleshy reflection of an animal. Created not in the image of God but in the image of pig, humanity takes its place somewhere amongst the other beasts, in denial of all transcendence. What *Pig Tales* finally asserts is not the descent to the otherness of animality but, to borrow Joan Riviere's famous phrase, "humanity as masquerade."

Darrieussecq also relates this becoming-human to the themes of reading and writing, through which the heroine negotiates her fluctuations (as we do) between human/woman/writer/pig. As a metamorphosis text, *Pig Tales* enacts Agamben's anthropological machine that produces the optical illusion of the human. In this way, the novel whose themes revolve around the visibility and tactility of the body, deformation and deformity, appearance and concealment, and whose tone eschews the pompous (and peculiarly masculine) exceptionalism of the Western Subject, rehearses the process by which the human may be positively constituted as the recognition—abject, farcical, painful—of human animality.

Whereas, however, the figure of the ape in Agamben retained the notion of the conscious subject (it is in all likelihood the ape's face that first strikes us with its uncanny resemblance and makes us pause with equal measures of discomfort and delight), the sow of *Pig Tales* is often seen (and "taken") from her *derrière*.[17] There are, therefore, important differences between Agamben's critique of humanism and Darrieussecq's gender specific parody of the human form: while Agamben's ape clearly signals the threshold of universal and cerebral "man," Darrieussecq's sow does not enjoy the liminal proximity of primates. Apes remind us of ourselves, and if we are reflexive enough we will promptly acknowledge our own "apishness." To recognize ourselves as pigs, however, is a somewhat different optical maneuver that crosses not only the threshold of species but that of gender too.

In *The Pornography of Meat*, Carol J. Adams notes the etymological and cultural connections between women and pigs: in the Greek "*choîros* meant both *pig* and 'female genitalia'" (112), while, "according to the *Dictionary of American Slang*, a pig is *a promiscuous woman, especially one who is blousy and unattractive*" (118). The ethics of *Pig Tales*, in the sense of issuing an encounter with animal alterity, is thus anti-Lévinasian: it is quite literally a *posterior* ethics, not—as in Lévinas—an ethics of the always exclusively human face.[18]

A slightly different exchange between Agamben and Darrieussecq is explored in Andrew Asibong's "*Mulier Sacra*: Marie Chauvet, Marie Darrieussecq and the Sexual Metamorphosis of 'Bare Life.'" Asibong contends that *Pig Tales*'s insistence on the importance of gender and sex revises Agamben's central concepts of bare life and *homo sacer*: "Chauvet and Darrieussecq's disturbing, sexually violent narratives both illustrate and anticipate Agamben's theory of the modern 'camp-like' State, but in doing so problematize Agamben's apparent presentation of its deathly processes as essentially indifferent to the question of sex" (Asibong 169). *Homo sacer* is "sacred in the sense of being outside both social and worldly categorizations and, instead, untouchably 'post-human'" (Asibong 169). The sacred man is utterly forsaken, his exposure to power complete: bare life. The survival of Darrieussecq's sexualized sacred protagonist at the end of the novel leads Asibong to wonder about the subversive potential of bare life as the bearer of a "new politics" (Asibong 176).

Agamben's analyses of the relationship between sovereignty and the living being contain dark (Benjaminian) intimations of a messianic politics. Darrieussecq's story of transformation from woman to sow recovers from bare life a defiant agency. More significantly, however, the process of animalization in *Pig Tales* anticipates Darrieussecq's commitment in her subsequent novels to new forms of physicality (and physics) as privileged narrative realms. Darrieussecq's explorations of material life processes in the novels following *Pig Tales* ultimately distance her from Agamben's biopolitical concerns. Not a politics but rather a *poetics* of material (bare) life becomes Darrieussecq's main project.

Darrieussecq and the "Pornographic Imagination"

Mon roman est tout sauf psychologique.[19]   —Marie Darrieussecq

Though explicit in its graphics of bodily mutations, *Pig Tales* is blasé about the fantastic fact of species crossing. The heroine experiences her lapsed humanity as neither trauma nor loss. *Pig Tales* does not mourn the human. The narrator's animality, in fact, triggers a multitude of other, miniature metamorphoses in those around her. Bestiality features in the novel, but only to the extent that its meaning is gradually obscured. In their sexual encounters, the difference between the woman-pig and her human partners—a difference on which the coherence of bestiality depends—dissolves.[20]

Describing the debauched clients at Perfumes Plus, Darrieussecq piles high the ironies: "They were growing increasingly interested in my derrière, that was the only problem. What I mean is—and I urge all sensitive souls not to read this page, for their own self-respect—that my customers had some peculiar predilections, some completely unnatural ideas, if you follow me. . . . I didn't know, exactly, where I had to draw the line to safeguard public morals" (*Pig Tales* 25–26). As the narrator was becoming a civic-minded sow, so "the customers began carrying on like dogs" (27). After a day's work at the salon "you'd have thought you were in the jungle" (28). Of her client, the African marabout, the narrator says that "we always had to get down on all fours in front of the mirror and make animal noises" (*Pig Tales* 32). Several of the narrator's regulars "always wanted me down on all fours. They sniffed me, licked me, and went about their business while braying or bellowing like rutting stags" (38). Furthermore, the novel's emphasis on anal sex eschews humanity's "proper" reproductive practices. Sodomy marks an economy of power relations across the double threshold of gender/species, by which "man" (masculine/human) subjugates both women and animals.[21]

The world of *Pig Tales* is thus less the world of Gregor Samsa than that of William Burroughs's *Naked Lunch* (1959). Burroughs insists upon an originary cacophony of species and his frequently violent "cut-ups" devote themselves to the excruciating physicalities of *becoming-other*: becoming-insect, reptile, monstrous, excremental. Like some primordial junky, humanity is a poisonous contraction, a spasm, a disease. Darrieussecq, like Burroughs (and Céline), depicts humanity, disdainfully, as always already an altered state.[22]

In another ingenious vignette, the narrator confesses her habit of eating the bouquets of flowers given to her by her loyal clientele: "I'll have to get this out because I realize now that it was one of the symptoms . . . I used to eat those flowers. . . . It was their fragrance, probably. It went to my head, all that greenery, and the sight of so many colours. It was nature outside coming inside the boutique, and it stirred something in me" (25). Darrieussecq's prose moves seamlessly between different species of language. The episode bridges the ironic gap between the narrator's deficient (human) awareness and her acute (animal) sensitivity: from black comedy we are suddenly in the terrain of pastoral.

Pastoral, which Sontag sees as a "constructing or imaging of something inanimate, or of a portion of the world of nature," and which "entails an appropriate rescaling of the human" ("The Pornographic Imagination" 89), surfaces when the narrator is at her most pig to mitigate the blandness of the narrative voice: "I began to eat. There were acorns and horse chestnuts. . . . The acorns were especially delicious, with something like a faint flavour of virgin soil. They cracked between the teeth, the fibres softened in the saliva . . . I had a strong taste of earth and water in my mouth, the taste of forest, of dead leaves. There were lots of roots, too, smelling nicely of liquorice, witch hazel, gentian, and they slipped down my throat like a sweet dessert, festooning me with long strands of sugary drool. Belching gently, I stuck out my tongue and licked my chops" (*Pig Tales* 58). It is significantly in her pig-becoming that the narrator possesses this new language:

> I heard sparrows in the treetops, ruffling their feathers as they went early to bed, batting their eyelids silkily in a final reflex before sleep, and I felt their dreams glide across my skin with the last rays of the sunset. The dreams of birds were everywhere in the warm shadows of the trees, and the dreams of pipistrelles were everywhere in the sky, because pipistrelles dream even when awake. They were so moving, all these dreams. A dog trotted towards me to pee and I sensed that he wanted to talk to me, so to speak, and then he changed his mind and prudently rejoined his master. In the core of my being, I felt a violent, terrifying, delicious sense of solitude—all in the same moment.   (68)

As Deleuze and Guattari famously insist, therefore, writing and the discovery of a new language pass through the animal and through the woman; that is, they literally entail a re- or disfiguring of the human. For it is the pig, not the human, who becomes a *voracious* reader: "I found books everywhere. . . . I tried to eat them, at first, but they were way too dry. . . . I began reading all the books I kept finding, it . . . helped me forget my hunger" (*Pig Tales* 84–85).[23] And a little later, becoming-human is again literalized as the pig-woman "could speak again, probably from having read all those words in those books" (87). When she is discovered reading in the attic by a pack of cannibalistic human inmates, led by another former client from Perfumes Plus, known as the "religious fanatic" (85), it is the confusing spectacle of a literate pig that saves her: "it was while I was reading one evening that they tried to catch me. There wasn't anything at all to eat in the asylum any more, so naturally, by comparison, I must have still seemed rather appetizing. They hesitated when they found me sitting in the attic reading" (85).

Darrieussecq's generic medley of the pastoral, science fiction, and pornography draws on a long and heterogeneous tradition of antiliberal, antihumanist French writing, from Sade, Bataille, or *Story of O* to, say, Blaise Cendrars's *Moravagine*, and the critiques of Deleuze and Foucault.[24] These texts (whether from left or right, or—more explosively—from neither) commonly refuse the very idea of rational human progress, the sine qua non of liberal humanism. And sex is the arena most averse to humanist taming. Sontag's pornographic imagination is born of the need to articulate this impossible taming and is posited against the liberal quest to demystify—and control—sexuality. Jack Abecassis agrees. "Liberal logic," he explains in his incisive discussion of Houellebecq, "is not transferable to sexuality": "Whereas a democratic conception of liberty in almost all other domains would be compatible with the 'knowing-seizing-controlling' model of knowledge, with sexuality . . . the idea of complete freedom based on knowledge and dominion is illusory. . . . Sexuality can never be mastered. Its boundaries may be mapped, its possibilities enumerated, its field, as it were, outlined, but never shall it escape the gravitational pull of human constraints—hierarchies, domination, submission, violent differentiation, symbolic negotiations" (Abecassis 814–815). So, in Bataille's short story "My Mother," a human pig inhabits those regions immune to the topography and temporality of humanism: "Terror unendingly renews with advancing age. Without end, it returns us to the beginning. The beginning that I glimpse on the edge of the grave is the *pig* in me which neither death nor insult can kill. Terror on the edge of the grave is divine and I sink into the terror whose child I am" (Bataille 25). Sontag explains how alongside the *nouveau roman* (an important influence on Darrieussecq), pornographic literature too is "about" the "agonized re-appraisal of the nature of literature" ("The Pornographic Imagination" 91). Pornography and pastoral (and Sontag adds also science fiction) are antirealist and antipsychological: they lack characters as psychologically accessible subjects and place form over content. Their motioning away from the human is necessitated by the dark truths of sexuality, which I have tried to show *Pig Tales* literalizes through the metamorphic device and the thematics of species. Since writing *Pig Tales,* Darrieussecq has continued her dissociation from conventional humanistic writing by drawing on a number of materialist discourses, especially cognitive science. Darrieussecq's interest in materiality also borrows from the richly poetic language of physics.

In her 2003 novel *White*, for example, Darrieussecq takes the idea of physical transformation to the cellular and molecular levels, and finally also to the level of the fundamentals of matter. Using the clean white slate of Antarctica as setting, *White* follows Peter and Edmée (eventually referred to simply as P and E—chemical elements, or variables in a mathematical equation), members of the White Project research team. Their initial encounter becomes in Darrieussecq a neurological "bio-drama": "Whether Peter keeps on his dark glasses or not . . . Whether the particles of light that convey Edmée's stare have to cross that barrier or not . . . All the photons emitted by Edmée's shell shoot in a straight line on to Peter's retinas in order to reconstruct an image of Edmée, with the memory of light. And with just as much infallibility, her optic nerves inverse the image, left to right, and the lobes of her brain put it back the right way, *zig zag*, and here he is, Peter" (*White* 49). In "Darrieussecq's Mind," Simon Kemp argues that the "neurological discourses" in this passage are "used both to defamiliarize and to demystify mental events that are commonplaces of literature" (Kemp 430). Darrieussecq's "method . . . involves 'physicalizing' the self, not only through the brain, but through the body more generally" (Kemp 431). Darrieussecq's "facetious physicalism" (Kemp 432) utilizes the discourses of cognitive science and neurobiology (as well as physics) as a literary, lyrical resource. Without overstating the continuity between *Pig Tales* and the subsequent novels, Darrieussecq's work overall is committed to material surfaces.

Scientific language is stretched to its materialist limits by Darrie-ussecq's choice of phantom narrators. *White* is narrated by a phan-tom chorus made up of the heroes of polar exploration (Shackleton, Amundsen, and Scott, their crews, dogs, ponies, even an errant fly that accidentally found its way into the cargo). The phantoms take on the sense of an utterly abstracted geography, geography that has become imperceptible. Here is how, rather drolly, the narrators explain who or what they might be:

> Several mythologies situate us here: sometimes we are the dead, or those who are still moving. Above all, we avoid being counted. Of course, we can drift up to the surface of the planet, like an atmo-spheric phenomenon, El Niño or La Niña, but if the Earth holds us, then Antarctica is our . . . what? Our anchorage? Leave that to the sailors. Our territory? Leave that to the animals, the seals, whales and penguins. Our field? For the gardeners. Our empire, our realm? For others still. Our country? What a joke. Marshland is for the will-o'-the-wisp, lava for trolls, forests for elves; but the South Pole is our identity, like the sea for the melancholic, the *chaise-longue* for the consumptive, or an empty room for the amne-siac. And if precision were compatible with our nature, we would say this: Antarctica is our geographical equivalent. We would set down this equation: that Antarctica is to Geography what our bodies are to History.
> (*White* 34–35)

A tour de force of "spectralization," the passage uses recurring rhetori-cal figures and mock-equations to precisely convey the dissolution of space, time, and, indeed, matter. Do phantoms, a device that returns in a number of Darrieussecq's novels, run counter to the materialist bent of her fiction? For Kemp, ghosts do "not necessarily raise a con-tradiction with the materialist view of mind, since Darrieussecq's many ghosts may be interpreted as mental projections of the bereaved" (434). Yet it is possible, I think, to see the operation of ghosts more radically still, and more materialistically, as something other than mental or imaginary projections that conform to Darrieussecq's overall understanding of brain function. "We, the ghosts of Edmée and of Peter, are like mercury. Our fragments join up, gravity unites us; then we scatter" (*White* 116). Phantoms both belong to and transcend the individual mind. In *White* they seem to belong to the universe as much as to the characters. In this sense, ghosts are the highpoint of Darrieussecq's nonanthropocentric literature of becoming, the crystallization of the transformations or metamorphoses that her prose so keenly explores. Beyond bodies, beyond molecules even, these ghosts are abstracted antimatter, "indifference made non-flesh" (*White* 119). Phantoms can be thought to emerge at the point at which matter and what is called "spirit" collapse and fold into one another in the quantum mechanical conception of waves. Indeed, the phantoms' movements weave waveform patterns of "reinforcement," "cancellation," "interference," or "dispersion" across the text:

> We mingle together and centrifuge one another, how to distinguish among us between those who have lived, and those who have remained in limbo? Between those who know something, and those who know nothing? Our disguises and appearances cut out shapes from the atmosphere, but the slightest breath undoes us, the wind mixes us up again, we shuffle our cards and swap our images, but they are all just as good, *hop hop* . . . Here, where the winds are born, in the southern eye of the planet, here where we rest. Around Edmée, we rest. Around Peter, we rest. Around the building site, we rest. Around the wind turbine, *chip chip*, that harvests the slightest puff of wind, watt by watt building up the small amount of energy required if there is a breakdown, and a Mayday must be broadcast, before everything cracks, breaks open, all data are lost. . . We blow, kindly. It does not cost us much. Ships sink at sea. Wars break out. Families murder one another. But our weather, so far as we know, is random. (*White* 120)

Darrieussecq's passing through different material orders of transformations, from the transformation of bodily form (*Pig Tales*) through molecules, particles (*Breathing Under Water*) to waves (*White*), maintains the framework whose focus is the material surface of people and things, not psychology. Exteriority is Darrieussecq's inexhaustible well of creative transformations.

Écriture de cochon and the Bad Faith of Humanism

The question of species and writing (and of the writing of species), what Darrieussecq at the outset introduces as écriture de cochon (the writing by and for pigs), is Pig Tales's central theme. Écriture de cochon takes up Sontag's question about the nature of literary representation and alludes to Roland Barthes's Writing Degree Zero (Le Degré zéro de L'Ecriture). One can equally see in this piggish writing an allusion to Derrida, whose own notion of écriture designated the internal differentiation and foreignness of language—its inhumanity.[25] But the becoming-human or animal of literature is not only an aesthetic matter. It is also a historical and political one, and, although Darrieussecq is less systematic than Houellebecq in her political critique, Pig Tales is partly a wicked millennial satire, partly a post-Holocaust text.

From a historical perspective, pig writing reworks a fundamental question of the modern West: How to write after the Holocaust? If the relation between these two questions may at first feel a little tenuous, they are nonetheless one and the same. Both take up the problematic of the human, a problematic made visible and urgent by the Holocaust's radical unraveling of human identity. As discussed earlier in the book, the genocidal (or sacrificial) economy of human identity was exemplified in the Nazi project, whose goal was the construction of an apparatus for the production of a coherent humanity. The ascent of man is not only synonymous with a disavowal of one's own animality; it entails the serial sacrificing of all of those deemed "animal."

Though no "Holocaust text" as such, Pig Tales summons the ghosts of National Socialism in the references to Knut Hamsun (1859–1952), the Norwegian novelist and 1920 Nobel Prize winner whose Nazi sympathies during and after the German occupation consigned him to postwar obscurity of, at best, cultish repute.[26] I have not come across commentaries that unpack Hamsun's role in this novel (he also makes a brief appearance in *White*, where a copy of his best known novel *Hunger* [1890] is found aboard the ship carrying Edmée to Antarctica). Hamsun is both within and without the narrative. A passage from his 1908 novel *Benoni* is *Pig Tales*'s epigraph. It describes the "great pig-killing day" in a remote Norwegian village: "Then the knife plunges in. The farmhand gives it two little shoves to push it through the thick skin, after which the long blade seems to melt through the neck fat as it sinks in up to the hilt. At first the boar doesn't understand a thing, he remains stretched out for a few seconds, thinking about it. Aha! Then he realizes he is being killed and utters strangled cries until he can scream no more." The rawness of description and rural setting bring to mind the memorable pig-killing scene in Hardy's *Jude the Obscure* (1895), another, if less immediate, "pigscript" precursor of *Pig Tales*.

Hamsun returns later in the novel, when the porcine heroine comes across Hamsun's book and delivers it to the censorship bureau as potentially "subversive" (*Pig Tales* 88). Ironically, it is the discovery of Hamsun's Nobel Prize that earns him the ban. The layered ironies here are difficult to disentangle: where do we locate Hamsun—and Darrieussecq—in this interweaving of the (meta-) fictional and the historical? How to balance the truisms of Europe's historical past with our interpretation of the novel's fictional-political allegory? Where does Hamsun's reactionary ideology fit in with Darrieussecq's dystopian vision of a totalitarian, brutalized, and regressive future?

First, to read the regime in *Pig Tales* as simply "fascist" (or Nazi-like) is misleading, since it defuses the novel's contemporary political and cultural implications. The debauched neoauthoritarianism of Social Free Progressionism reads more as an extension of late-capitalism (a mutation whose early flowering is arguably detectable in several of our Western democracies) than as a return to reactionary (sentimentalist, aestheticized, antimodern) ideology.

As I have already argued at length in chapter 1, whereas Auschwitz made plain the contingency of humanity, post-Holocaust discourse has committed itself to the opposite task: the rehabilitation and reassertion of human dignity. Like several other writers of her generation (Houellebecq again), Darrieussecq audaciously stages the *in*dignities of humanity.

In *Pig Tales* and beyond, therefore, Darrieussecq is concerned with the limits of language as the limits of species. The novel lays bare the drama of species as the drama of writing. Metamorphosis reflects, metafictionally, literature's (fictional) production of the human and also—through an insistent ploughing of materiality—the literary transcending of the human. This is why the concrete (nonmetaphorical) animal is crucial to this text. Only as nonsymbolic does the animal inhabit and reshape the human. If Darrieussecq avoids explicitly affirming, under the auspices of universal humanism, women's dignity and agency, this is because she is out to contest the very inventory of humanism: dignity, autonomy, subjectivity, rationality, morality, and language. At the threshold of species, *écriture de cochon* recasts humanity along other lines: corporeal, nomadic, and debased. Writing, like vision, enacts the becoming-human, and, like Agamben's optical machine, writing must transcribe its own otherness in order to become human.

Pig Tales ends with a last transformation that inverts the archetypal werewolf myth in a final affirmation of hybridity. The pig looks up at the moon in memory of her dead wolf-lover Yvan, not in order to become wolf, but to become human again: "The mood comes over me when the Moon rises, and I reread my notebook in its cold light. I try to do what Yvan taught me, but for the opposite reason: when I crane my neck towards the Moon, it's to show, once again, a human face" (135). The pain of this closing scene is neither experienced nor delivered as the interiority of emotion. Language remains committed to the surface of the body and the exteriority of form. Darrieussecq paints even grief not as psychology, but as anatomy.

2 THE INHUMANITY OF FILM

4 Cine-Zoos

The essence of cinema becomes a story about animals.

> —Serge Daney, "The Screen of Fantasy (Bazin and Animals)"

Zoo: Seeing, Not Seeing

Published in 1980, John Berger's "Why Look at Animals?" remains a landmark essay on modernity's relationship to animals and the vicissitudes of their cultural visibility. An elegy for lost encounters between man and animal, Berger's is one of the most moving and most influential pieces to be written on the subject of animals in the field of vision. The central thesis of "Why Look at Animals?" concerns the gradual fading of the modern animal from everyday life. The disappearance of animals takes several forms, some of them paradoxically those of enhanced visibility. Animals appear as pets, as endeared subjects of live action or animated film, as stuffed toys, and, most significantly for Berger, in the zoo: "Zoos, realistic animal toys and the widespread commercial diffusion of animal imagery, all began as animals started to be withdrawn from daily life" (Berger 26). In place of an exchange with animals—as fellows, adversaries, or magical ciphers on the continuum of creation—animals have become, to borrow Laura Mulvey's phrase, the "bearers of the human look." This look is prurient and savvy. It masters what it simply calls the animal as its object of study: "animals are always the observed. The fact that they can observe us has lost all significance. They are the objects of our ever-extending knowledge. What we know about them is an index of our power, and thus an index of what separates us from them. The more we know, the further away we are" (Berger 16).

Relations to animals, which in premodern societies comprised both likeness and mystery, have gradually shifted into the arena of facts and the abstract order of data. Animals' alluring animality (along with our own) has been removed from the everyday, replaced by nostalgia, anguish, and (though Berger does not mention it) aggression. Animals, says Berger, presently appear as our lost objects. "One could suppose," Berger argues, that innovative visualizations of animals, "were compensatory. Yet in reality the innovations themselves belonged to the same remorseless movement as was dispersing the animals" (26). The disappearance of animals from daily life that renders them utterly visible—that re-presents them—as objects of mastery and knowledge has only intensified under the conditions of endangerment. With a hint of titillation, endangerment lends new legitimacy to zoos as engines of species "conservation." Conservation is only the latest in a list of justifications—in the name of public enlightenment—to prop up the practices of what Acampora called "extinction by exhibition." Echoing Berger, Acampora argues that "the contemporary zoo has become a scientific park and aesthetic site, and its meaning is redemptive; it stands as an emblem of conservation policy, projecting a religious image of man-the-messiah—the new Noah: savior of species, the beasts' benign despot" ("Extinction by Exhibition" 1). Conservation—as deployed by the institutions that incarcerate and exhibit animals—plays an increasingly ambiguous role in animals' final disappearance. Zoos will never be able to offer a solution to the problem of the disappearance of animals, because from their very inception and in their very being they are part of the problem. Even in its new conservationist guise the zoo is a forlorn place. Its gloominess and poverty derive from the fact that the zoo categorically fails to transform the mode of relation to animals, which has led to their demise and the demise of their habitats.[1] Instead, zoos draw a new benevolence from an improved and sanitized discourse: enriched enclosures (not cages), provision of "real" contact between humans (mostly children) and wild animals via interactive or "immersive" experiences, and specimens (not trophies) of endangered species.

For Berger zoos remain a salient form of the marginalization of animals, places characterized by apathy and boredom on both sides of the cage (unlike Heidegger, Berger insists that animals can and do become bored—perhaps because in the zoo animals are no longer themselves or maybe because Heidegger did not really *see* animals). Now, more than ever before, zoos converge with and complement a plethora of media platforms of wildlife exhibits, primarily in film and television.[2] In terms of the institution of looks, zoos are unable to cut loose of their colonial roots. As emblems of colonialism, they exemplify particular constellations of "powered looking": the ethnographic and the pornographic gaze. In the variety of critiques after Berger, the zoo as a visual space remains emblematic.[3] It is difficult, moreover, to ignore the inverse relation between diminishing wildlife and animals' enhanced visual presence. Fussed over, tagged, screened, projected, and surveyed, exhibited, simulated, incarcerated, conserved, even manufactured and invented, nature and animals are gaining an exclusive kind of cultural visibility.

Despite its pessimism, Berger's thesis of disappearance and loss remains compelling and has set the tone for subsequent theories on animals in cinema and the visual arts. In the first part of this chapter I follow developments of Berger's thinking by Akira Mizuta Lippit and Steve Baker and the corrective to them offered by Jonathan Burt. While Lippit and Baker begin from Berger's notion of animal absence, Burt rejects the overemphasis on disappearance and lack as the exclusive modes of modernity's relation to animals. From a host of cinematic examples, Burt tries to retrieve animals as a thorny but potentially transformative cultural presence.

Burt's complex relation to the cinematic animal as acutely suspended between reality and artifice suggests some fascinating correlations with classic realist film theory, especially the work of André Bazin. Bazin's thinking on cinema will serve as the link from the actual zoo as a place of impoverished encounters to the cinematic zoo (films that display animals) and finally to *cinema as a zoo*: cinema as a zoomorphic stage that transforms all living beings—including humans—into creatures.

It is Bazin's special appreciation of cinematic animals that provides the transition from the Berger approach, via Burt, to my principal argument of the "cine-zoo." But the argument cuts both ways: looking back at Bazin from, as it were, the space of the screen animal also exposes "the virtues and limitations" of Bazinian humanism. To follow through Bazin's realism to its logical conclusion, therefore, effectively means abandoning the distinctions of—and more importantly the narrative conventions attached to—the identity and hierarchy of species. The result is the absorption of the human figure within the leveled plain of the photographed world. I therefore want to propose a fully "realist" reading of cinema that necessarily surpasses the specificities of species identity to which Bazin was still attached. To do so, I look at several examples, all of which include documentary elements, not as a claim to authenticity or unity of form but as a mark of cinema's immediacy and materiality—its corporeal zoomorphic quality or creatureliness. But I begin with recent theorizations of the visual animal as the basis for thinking up such a creaturely cinema.

Visual Animals

Steve Baker's work on "postmodern animal art" ("You Kill Things" 75) looks at ways in which contemporary artists incorporate animals (or animal parts) into their artworks. Baker calls this "botched taxidermy" (*Postmodern Animal* 75), described as "a kind of *fluid sub-ethical practice*" ("You Kill Things" 75).[4] The postmodern animal appears as an image that has been intentionally "de-formed," and Baker wants to argue that "its botchedness or gone-wrongness is deliberate and has its own integrity" ("You Kill Things" 76).[5] The integrity of art that features killed, wrong(ed) animals resides in the potential for "reframing human thinking about that killing" (80). Baker relishes rather than denies the moral ambiguities inherent in the "sub-ethical practice" of using dead animal parts to reflect on the act of killing:

"There is troublingly little physically to differentiate the animal skins used in a fur coat, a hunting trophy head, or an artwork that 'reworks' the trophy theme. The remainder of this essay therefore tries to offer a preliminary assessment of this kind of art's political efficacy in questioning the anthropocentric values that continue to tolerate the human killing of animals" ("You Kill Things" 80). The postmodern works Baker discusses—including Damien Hirst's pickled, sliced cows and pigs (*Mother and Child Divided; This little piggy went to market, this little piggy stayed at home*), Angela Singer's *deer-atize, sore (flay) and wild-deerness (Kill Joy)*, or Jordan Baseman's "empty trophies"—are subversions of trophy kills, though the precise nature of their interventions is difficult to qualify. Baker clearly finds in these works something thoughtful and positively unsettling. He concludes that "the dead animal of botched taxidermy is not the dead animal of the hunting trophy, though each might be said to haunt the other. . . . What is at stake here is an intense and inventive looking, a rigorousness of investigation, which has to be coldly unapologetic in its attitude to the looked-at being. . . . Killing is addressed by investigating the looking. In this sense, far from being sensationalist, these works do indeed constitute what Lapointe calls 'a place for the spectator to think'" ("You Kill Things" 92).

Contemporary art rejects the nostalgic and the mournful in favor of a supposed willingness to, as it were, look the subject (the killed subject, the subject of killing, and the looking subject) in the eye. Baker sees postmodern artists addressing head on the reality of animal death and in so doing opening up a genuine space for self-reflection. I remain unconvinced. Far from using the literal as an assault on the viewer's resistance, rigorous literalism in some of these works acts as a justification of cruelty; it speaks of complicity without responsibility—a most pernicious kind of violence.[6]

Akira Lippit's *Electric Animal* professes its debt to Berger in its opening sentence: "Everywhere animals disappear" (1). But if the notion that "animals now inspire a sense of panic for the earth's dwindling resources" constitutes a kind of "cliché of modernity" (1), *Electric Animal*'s poststructuralist reworking of Berger's thesis lies in animals' "state of *perpetual* vanishing"(1). Animals dwell in the spectral state of an active disappearance. The cinematic importance of animals derives from the (Western) conception of their "undeadness"—the "paradox of animal death (animals die but are incapable of death)" (Lippit, "The Death of an Animal" 12). Animals cannot die because they do not possess language and therefore cannot know or name their death. The animal's inability to die is reflected in cinema's essential feature, its *reanimating* function, cinema as "spectral loop" ("The Death of an Animal" 12) whose central figure is the animal.

While acknowledging that "Berger and Lippit have plenty of grounds for pessimism given the recent history of human-animal relations that the rapid rates of species extinction and widespread animal cruelty reveals" (Burt 27), Jonathan Burt's *Animals in Film* argues for a more nuanced theorization of the visual animal. For Burt, "the theory that the animal is becoming increasingly virtual, that its fate is to disappear into technological reproduction to become nothing more than imagery, would make sense were it not for the fact that this imagery is not uniform but unavoidably fragmented, both in terms of the technical variety of its reproduction and in terms of the various conflicts around the image itself" (87). By emphasizing the existence of a variety of (at times contrasting) constellations of looks between humans and animals, and of different regimes of visibility for the animal in the modern public space, Burt wants to reclaim the visual animal as a potentially positive presence.

Lippit's analysis of the strain in Western thought that sees animals as incapable of death shows the animal persisting as specter and trace in the body of cinematic technology. *Electric Animal*, claims Burt, tends to regard the animal as a "pure sign" (Burt 29), which, in turn, "*reinforces* at a conceptual level the effacement of the animal that is perceived to have taken place in reality even whilst criticizing that process" (29). Thus "theories of loss . . . in fact turn out to be another version of the flight from the animal" (30). Burt's claim is reminiscent of Diamond and Cavell's criticism of Derrida's general economy, which I looked at in the introduction.

Burt provides several correctives to the spectral economy of the (post)modern animal. First, he asserts the *agency* of the cinematic animal (30–31), not in the more problematic sense of animal subjectivity, but in terms of the animal's affective power vis-à-vis the human observer: "much of the power of the film animal derives from the fact that in film human-animal relations are possible through the play of agency regardless of the nature of animal interiority, subjectivity or communication" (31). The second qualification touches on the nature of modernity itself, which Burt sees as exhibiting more complex attitudes to animals. Citing the work of historian Hilda Kean on the emergence in the nineteenth century of animal welfare legislation, Burt insists that the link between vision and animals should not be reduced to the backward glance of nostalgia, but also acknowledged as "forward-looking"(Burt 35).[7] This too ascribes a kind of agency to animals whose very visibility catalyzes social and legislative reform. Beyond disagreements on which forms of visibility are humane, "the fact that the legislation places so much emphasis on seeing gives the animal . . . a significant normative dimension in the visual public domain" (38).

Shifting "ideas about appropriate and inappropriate seeing" (40) render the animal a unique cinematic subject. More than a spectral and passive object of the human look, the animal embodies the "extreme collapse between the figural and the real" (44). The animal in film solicits rather than defers questions of reality, since (as Lippit has shown) the animal is both central to the development of film technology and the subject of "the unresolvable dialectic between humane and cruel attitudes to animals that governs their history in modern culture" (85). Questions about the cinematic animal arise at the point at which "fiction and reality collapse into one another" (161). This is not because "animals are, in essence, like photographs" (*Electric Animal* 176), an ontological lack. The history of the visual animal attests to plenitude as well as spectrality signaled by the animal image. Plenitude resides, however, not in the debates over subjectivity (or its absence), but in the connection between cinema and the corporeal.[8]

Cinematic Realism and the Creaturely

> Whenever it is possible to enclose two heterogeneous objects in the same frame, editing is prohibited. In that sense, we shall see that the essence of cinema becomes a story about animals.
>
> —Serge Daney, "The Screen of Fantasy"

"The idea that animals represent an insertion of the real or the natural into film is crucial to the question of violence" (Burt 136). With this Burt comes close to articulating the preoccupations of classic realist film theory, to which the animal, perhaps more than any other cinematic subject, is key. It is no accident that the real asserts itself through the issue of violence, and, as we shall see shortly, death. That realist film theory grants animals a special place is evident from the writings of André Bazin, for whom animals are purveyors not so much of the "thing in itself" as the markers of film's representational limits: death, contingency, and temporality.

Despite Burt's affirmative mission to supplant the negative inscriptions of the animal as specter, abstraction, or loss, Bazin's omission from *Animals in Film* restricts its understanding of the cinematic animal. Bazin is incredibly suggestive not only when it comes to the animal as a peculiarly *cinematic* being, but to the being of cinema as peculiarly *animal*. Serge Daney goes as far as stating that for Bazin "the essence of cinema becomes a story about animals" (but the question immediately arises: does Daney mean that *only* nonhuman animals reveal the essence of cinema? Or could it be, once more, the other way around: that cinema thought to its photographic realist conclusion wants nothing more to do with the particularities of species, be they human or animal?).

Bazin's "The Virtues and Limitations of Montage" arrives at the question of animals via the children's film. Bazin is interested in the genre's use of animals in terms of what he describes as the "comparative possibilities of anthropomorphism and montage" ("Virtues" 44). What does Bazin mean by this? The films of Jean Tourane, for example, use heavily edited animal footage in fablelike narratives with animal narrators (Bazin calls this "Disney pictures with live animals" [43]).

Tourane's editing anthropomorphizes animals in the negative sense of the word, removing what is animal about them and obscuring their nature (Bazin is not opposed to anthropomorphism as such, and his brief remarks are extremely pertinent to contemporary discussions on the topic). Tourane's animal protagonists are only required to stay still, their actions and emotions created by editing (and humanizing props like hats or bowties). This means that "the apparent action and the meaning we attribute to it do not exist, to all intents and purposes, prior to the assembling of the film, not even in the form of fragmented scenes out of which the set-ups are generally composed" (44). Montage becomes "that abstract creator of meaning, which preserves the state of unreality demanded by the spectacle" (45).

In this case editing interferes with the continuity of space and time and masks rather than reveals reality. We observe little about the animals, because their movements and relations are constructed (animated) through editing. On the whole, therefore, "essential cinema, seen for once in its pure state . . . is to be found in straightforward photographic respect for the unity of space" ("Virtues" 46). Bazin's prohibition on editing is stated as an aesthetic law: "'When the essence of a scene demands the simultaneous presence of two or more factors in the action, montage is ruled out.' It can reclaim its right to be used, however, whenever the import of the action no longer depends on physical contiguity even though this may be implied" ("Virtues" 50).

Daney shows how Bazin illustrates this rule primarily through scenes involving animals, either in the presence of other animals or with human beings. In an exploration film called L'Afrique vous parle, "a Negro gets eaten by a crocodile. In Trader Horn another Negro is charged by a rhinoceros" (Bazin, "Cinema and Exploration" 155). Another example is slapstick, what Bazin calls a "comedy of space" ("Virtues" 52), which equally requires the unity of place for the gags to be believable, that is, funny. The gags comprise a relationship between people and things and would not work unless people and things were contained in the same space in a single shot. One of the reasons why slapstick is moving as well as funny is due to the way it emphasizes the awkwardness of our presence in space. Comical mismatches between bodies, objects, and spaces arise at the point in which gravity is most obviously at work (think of Laurel and Hardy's Sisyphean short *The Music Box* [1932], in which the pair struggle to carry a piano up a steep set of steps). Slapstick is thus the most "scientific" and most philosophical of all cinematic genres (its direct opposite are the zero gravity scenes of, say, *2001: A Space Odyssey*). Slapstick exploits spatial contiguity to bring out the existential dimensions of our physical being in the world. Keaton and Chaplin illustrate how essential for the comedy is the integrity of space, but here too Bazin returns to animals: Chaplin's *The Circus*, in which "Chaplin is truly in the lion's cage and both are enclosed within the framework of the screen" ("Virtues" 52).

It is the precariousness inherent in the cohabitation of heterogeneous elements that Daney sees as fully expressed in the withholding of the edit: "the status of the protagonists (in this case men and animals) who are forced to share the screen, sometimes at the risk of their lives. The ban on editing is a function of that risk" ("The Screen of Fantasy" 33). Discontinuity (the mixed, fragmented, disjointed nature of reality) is not to be achieved through editing (a mere staging of discontinuity), but, on the contrary, through patient observation that reveals the fissures in reality's continuum. "Risk" can mean any number of things, but in *The Circus* it is the mortal danger of sharing space with a wild animal.

"Death," Bazin writes in "Death Every Afternoon," on Pierre Braunberger's 1951 film *The Bullfight* (*La Course de taureaux*), "is surely one of those rare events that justifies the term . . . *cinematic specificity*" (30). "Before cinema there was only the profanation of corpses and the desecration of tombs. Thanks to film, nowadays we can desecrate and show at will the only one of our possessions that is temporally inalienable: dead without a requiem, the eternal dead-again of the cinema!" (31). Bazin is fascinated by cinematic death, but also by death's affiliates, temporality, contingency, and love: "Like death, love must be experienced and cannot be represented (it is not called the little death for nothing) without violating its nature. This violation is called obscenity. The representation of a real death is also an obscenity, no longer a moral one, as in love, but metaphysical. We do not die twice" ("Death" 30).

In "'We Do Not Die Twice': Realism and Cinema," George Kouvaros explains that realist cinema is not "an attempt to show 'things as they are,' but rather grounded in moments of sensory experience in which the contingency and finitude of everyday life is brought to the fore" (Kouvaros 377). Thus Bazinian realism pertains to the "capacity of the cinematic image not simply to represent a sense of material contingency, but to make it present on screen" (381). In Ivone Margulies's words, "what interests Bazin are precisely the rough edges of representation, the moment of encounter and productive maladjustment between representation and the actuality of filmmaking" (Margulies 4). Death as the ultimate contingency marks the limit of cinematic representation, capturing a reality that escapes representation, which acts both as a remedy to the contingency of death and yet also heightens and intensifies it. Mary Anne Doane pointed out that "the cinema made achievable duration itself. In that sense, it was perceived as a prophylactic against death, ensuring the ability to 'see one's loved ones' gesture and smile long after their deaths" (Doane qtd. in Kouvaros 381). But this means that the passing of time in film is not overcome but rather enhanced: "the indexical nature of film reaffirms a notion of time as fleeting and non-essential" (Kouvaros 381).

Bazin happily admits that cinema's desire to represent the singular and irreplaceable moment of death constitutes a "metaphysical obscenity," replaying and repeating that which can happen only once. "For Bazin," writes Margulies in "Bodies Too Much," "nothing better illustrates the radical breach between the transience of existence and mechanical reproduction, which transcends it so obliviously, than a never to be repeated spectacle in flesh and blood" (5).

On the filming of executions Bazin remarks that

in the spring of 1949, you may have seen a haunting documentary about the anti-Communist crackdown in Shanghai in which Red "spies" were executed with a revolver on the public square. At each screening, at the flick of a switch, these men came to life again and then the jerk of the same bullet jolted their necks. *I imagine the supreme cinematic perversion would be the projection of an execution backward* like those comic newsreels in which the diver jumps up from the water back onto his diving board.

("Death" 30–31; my emphasis)

What has happened to Daney's cinema of animals? Bazin has moved seamlessly from the mortality of animals (the bull) to the mortality of humans (the executed men). Bazin's "frenzy for the visible," to quote Linda Williams, is equal in both cases. There is, moreover, the suggestion of the "supreme cinematic perversion" of a reversed human execution. Bazin has not outgrown the original cinematic pleasure of the Lumières' *Demolition of a Wall* (1895), regularly screened backward, delighting audiences by magically reconstituting the wall they had just seen destroyed. But what is the meaningful difference between a wall and a man from the point of view of cinema?

In many of Bazin's examples, it is true, the dying men are non-European (African, Chinese). The hungry gaze is surely also an exoticizing one. But Bazin seems far more interested in the general capacity of cinema to transcend (or debase) the human: to *show* the susceptibility of material beings and things to natural forces and events.[9] The idea of animals' inability to die seems wide of the mark in this context. For in Bazin, realism's encounter with death ultimately dehumanizes all who come under its technological spell. The sight of death, Roland Barthes's photographic *punctum*, pierces not because it confirms what in *Camera Lucida* Barthes called "absolute subjectivity" (our singularity and individuality, our place in the ontological realm of being) but precisely because it exhibits mortality as unindividuated and impersonal. Photography decrees an equality of finitude, regardless of the photographed subject. What is photographed (or filmed) touches on the general conditions of material being. Viewing the dead depersonalizes them by reminding us that they (and by extension we) are subject to exposure, the transience and finitude of matter. A photograph's subject, whether human or not (and perhaps also buildings and landscapes), is subsumed by exposure. Clinging to the machinations of subjectivity, we resist what photographs also show: not just the undeadness of the spectral subject but also the materiality and contingency—the anonymity—of the pictured subject. Rather than highly personalized, the portrait form in fact dramatizes time's corrosive impersonality.

Impersonality also applies to Bazin's understanding of film acting. Acting is not "simply the simulations of feelings and identities" but the "presentation of states of being" (Kouvaros 385). The actor's proper role is as a "temporal avatar" because, rather than acting classically (expressing an inner meaning), the performer in realist cinema is an aging being: "in a genuinely realist cinema the work of acting would be judged not by its capacity to re-create character, but in terms of its ability to transpose affective states and durations fundamentally different from those which characterize classic acting, in other words, affective states and durations that highlight the contingency and finitude of human existence. Again, death enters Bazin's discussions of cinema's essential qualities as both an ever-present lure and the thing that marks the limits of what it can show" (Kouvaros 386). But how should one take the qualification *human* existence, which points to a certain subjectivity and interiority, even though these are unrelated to the temporal process cinema is attuned to in its unique way? Would not a fully blown realist cinema do away with the artificial constructions of species in the pursuit of what Derrida called the "living in general"? Film's realism is its inhumanity.[10]

Two examples illustrate this point. Bazin singles out Vittorio De Sica and Robert Bresson as filmmakers loyal to the truths of realism (Bazin died before Bresson's *Au hasard Balthazar* and *Mouchette*, two masterpieces of his middle period that only strengthen Bazin's view). Of De Sica's *Umberto D*, Bazin tells us, "I have no hesitation in stating that the cinema has rarely gone such a long way toward making us aware of what it is to be a man. (And also, for that matter, of what it is to be a dog)" ("De Sica" 78). Again, equality between man and animal derives from fidelity to reality, in this case achieved through the cinema of pure duration: "the sequence of events which De Sica reports obeys a necessity that has nothing to do with dramatic structure" ("*Umberto D*" 80). De Sica makes no concessions to "classical dramaturgy." He allows his camera to capture time as it passes, subjecting the "plot" of *Umberto D* to the plotlessness of everyday life: duration. The profilmic "event" of De Sica's neorealist films is thus time itself. The ruptures, discontinuities—what in narrative terms is called drama—are identical to the actual passing of time. Bazin calls this "making 'life time'" ("De Sica" 76).

Weil's aesthetics of vulnerability, the guiding thread of this study, correspond to Bazin's understanding of cinematic realism. It is tempting to draw parallels between Weil and Bazin, both of whom pursued reality in the encounter between materiality and the sacred, revealed through the mechanical (in Weil's case, the mechanism of nature, in Bazin's case the photographic apparatus). Their (loosely Catholic) ideas may have been informed by their physical frailty, and both died unusually young. In critical terms, both have been viewed with suspicion (or scorn) by a predominantly secular scholarship and both are enjoying critical revaluation that reintroduces a theological grammar—not solely but significantly also into the study of film. Weil and Bazin's understanding of realism commonly has its roots in ideas of necessity and the body. For both, "taking hold" of necessity—by either capturing it in film or by submitting to it via a process of attention—is very nearly synonymous with love. This accounts for the hint of perversity that permeates Bazin and Weil's writings—their commitment to naked, unedited, reality and to contingency (Weil's *Gravity and Grace* hails as salutary the meditation on chance with the same anti-dramaturgical fervor that Bazin calls for the camera to simply observe what chances before it). The creaturely is an invocation of this sort of encounter because it rejects in the name of realism the editorial constructions of humanism.[11]

The recent return to realism that Kouvaros carefully analyzes has special resonance for the study of the cinematic animal, which, as Burt insists, emerges on the borderline between technological artifice and corporeal reality. No wonder, then, that for Bazin animals simultaneously embody the indexical nature of cinema—the primary connection between the image and its referent—and the threat of the image's obfuscatory nature.[12] As Kouvaros notes, it is wrong to align Bazin with the classic realist style when, as is clear from reading him, his choice of films was so diverse. In keeping with Bazin, "realism" in my discussion acts as an arc for a range of aesthetic forms, genres, and themes.

It is not limited to any particular cinematic practice but emerges out of a work's manner of picturing the material conditions of life cinematically. What I call a creaturely cinema corresponds to no particular style. The adherence to realism consists in these films' contestation of the mythologies of speciation.

To explore creaturely cinema, I turn to three examples: Vladimir Tyulkin's *About Love* (*Pro Iyubov*, 2005) and *Lord of the Flies* (*Povelitel Much*, 1991), Kira Muratova's *Asthenic Syndrome* (*Astenichesky Sindrom*, 1989), and Artur Aristakisyan's *Palms* (*Ladoni*, 1993). Serge Daney remarked that "when André Bazin is asking questions about cinema, he often finds his answers in marginal films" ("The Screen of Fantasy" 32). The films I discuss by Tyulkin, Muratova, and Aristakisyan, all made in the period just preceding or following the end of the Soviet Union, can be considered marginal in four ways: in terms of their commercial appeal; in their location away from the Muscovite center of Russian cinematic culture (in Kazakhstan, Ukraine, and Moldova respectively); in terms of their narrative structures and formal devices; and, finally, also thematically, in that all of them explore the idea of marginality itself.

Vladimir Tyulkin's *About Love*, and *Lord of the Flies*

A woman's face in close-up. She shuts her eyes in concentration, occasionally straining toward something invisible, internal. The image is one of devotion. Classical music dominates the soundtrack, and it is possible that the silver-haired woman is moved by the beauty of the piece. A cut follows the beginnings of a tear, just forming in the woman's right eye. Whereupon it is all dogs, dozens and dozens of mongrels crowding the frame, drowning out the music with dog-sound. *About Love* deals with devotion, music, and animal sound. It is a film about *vocare*: vocation and voice. The woman weeps for Dyuma. From a box she removes the twisted body of a small dog, matter-of-factly rolls it in newspaper, and puts it in a plastic bag for disposal. We cut back to the image of the woman in deep concentration, and she explains: "People won't understand this. They say I'm crazy. How can I cry about the dog. But it's not just a dog. Dyuma . . . and the night goes without sleeping. I dream of her through the nights. It feels like she's behind me . . . I feel this till now. Nobody can be replaced by anybody, of course everything is going to be dulled somehow. But something very bright and kind has gone. I'll be different. Something has died inside of me."

Screened at the 2005 Oberhausen film festival, *About Love* is the portrait of Nina Perebeyeva, who cares for more than one hundred abandoned dogs in her small house.[13] Perebeyeva's living space has given way to a dog's life and needs. Eating, sleeping, toilet space, and recreation are shared between Perebeyeva, her elderly mother, and the dog pack. The film explores proximity pushed to its limit: domestic space is transformed into dog space, cheerfully ruled by the animal pack. Perebeyeva's dogs are not wild, but neither are they housetrained. *About Love* makes a mockery of the idea of the domestic pet, which Deleuze and Guattari describe as "the little cat or dog owned by an elderly woman who honours and cherishes it" (*A Thousand Plateaus* 269). Here, life spills forth in wolfish torrents. Tyulkin occasionally switches from color to black and white and a low-angle shot from a dog's point of view. His accomplice is a wiry terrier with piercing eyes: "wherever there is multiplicity, you will also find an exceptional individual, and it is with that individual that an alliance must be made in order to become-animal" (*A Thousand Plateaus* 268).

A cross-dissolve from the dog-crammed interiors of the flat to a busy church Perebeyeva and her mother attend establishes the parity between human and dog space. The motley human crowd—Slavic, Asiatic, old and poor, worn faces, mongrel faces, washed up from the Soviet project—queue to kiss the priest's hand. People and dogs are shown in their impinging physicality; both clamor for protection and love.

Little is said in the film. Action takes place against the deafening backdrop of barks and growls that drown out human language. But like space, human and animal sound are also paralleled. Tyulkin cuts between the singing of church hymns, and the wailing of the dogs. One by one, as a chorus of mourners, the dogs raise their heads and howl. Human and canine voices mingle and mix. The living voice is instinctively directed upward. Something needy and mammalian calls out. Survival and salvation are equaled in these moments of creaturely longing.

Animals are also consoling. In one scene, we find Perebeyeva in a room stacked high with papers. She sits at a dusty piano, but the keys no longer work and her fingers run nimbly along the bar to an inaudible score. Her arms drop in resignation and a small dog pops its head on her lap. Perebeyeva strokes its chin: "Knopa. Knopa." Nothing is known of Perebeyeva's past, save from old photographs where she is recognizable as a girl with a dog, very nearly a lady with a lapdog. Of this Chekhovian heritage only the ruined piano and photographs remain. Tyulkin does not portray love as a humanitarian gesture. *About Love* is excremental and snarling, shocking to the conventional and well-off dog lover. While claustrophobically intimate, the film contains clues (the piano, the photographs) of a larger story about Soviet demise and a neglected post-Soviet backwater.

Tyulkin's earlier *Lord of the Flies* explores a similarly confined universe scandalously divvied between man and beast. If Perebeyeva is submerged in her small empire, Kirill Ignatyevich Schpak is the self-appointed sovereign of a kingdom devoted to the gruesome breeding and extermination of flies. Tyulkin's mad master describes himself as a typical product of Soviet brutalism. Born in Georgia, Schpak lost his father to Stalin's gulags and was sent as a farmer to Kazakhstan. Schpak considers himself an inventor of sorts. Slicing through animal remains, he explains his scheme of producing a fly "lure" made of dead flesh to yield larvae, which he feeds back to his chickens. The self-sustaining farmyard is not only a life-size model of the world of Hieronymus Bosch but a miniature Soviet empire ruled with an iron fist. Schpak's obsessions mimic the maneuvers of a doomed empire generating its own foes in order to destroy them. The political, then, looms large in Tyulkin's film. Shot during perestroika, *Lord of the Flies* is a record of imperial disintegration and displacement, poking the cadaverous remains of a decaying order. Granddad Kirill, as he is affectionately known (with a wink and a nod to Stalin's Uncle Joe), has some words of advice for Mikhail Gorbachev: "Stop visiting kings and stay home more. If you have to go on visits, don't be so pompous."

Both of Tyulkin's films bear what Russian film scholar Nancy Condee has called the "imperial trace": films that strive against "an imaginary of belonging" (Condee 115) in the irreconcilable tensions between Russian nationhood and empire. "The year 1913," Condee explains, "marked the three-hundredth anniversary of the Romanov dynasty. Within four years it would be destroyed, together with the dynasty's empire. But unlike much of Europe in the course of the twentieth century, Russia in 1917 did not undergo the transition from empire to nation-state. Instead, it gradually replaced its dynastic empire with a socialist one enduring three-quarters of a century, until 1991" (5). In a range of post-Soviet films animals appear as emblems of displacement and the inassimilable, exploding the pretensions of the old and new Russia alike to deliver coherence and order. Tyulkin is not alone. Sergei Dvortsevoy's documentary studies of post-Soviet life, *Bread Day* (1998), *Highway* (1999), and *In the Dark* (2004) display a similar "imperial haunting" (Condee 46). *In the Dark* distills the essence the new Russia from the daily routines of a St. Petersburg apartment that a blind man (the director's uncle) shares with his cat. Loneliness and isolation similarly dominate Cristi Puiu's post-Ceauşescu feature *The Death of Mr Lazarescu* (*Moartea domnului Lazarescu*, 2005), whose protagonist's only companions are cats. Animals and animality communicate the exhaustion of both the Soviet and the neoliberal project and return the human to the zoological fold. It is no surprise therefore that Condee's chapter on Russian auteur Kira Muratova should focus on what Condee rather beautifully terms Muratova's "zoological imperium."

Kira Muratova's *Asthenic Syndrome*

> I can love a concrete man, not "people." ... There is the concept of "humanity" but not of "dogdom," "cathood," or "birdkind," which are much closer to me and to whom I feel much more responsible. ... I understand my responsibility for my own children and grandchildren, and also for animals, which mankind has domesticated. As for "the people" [*narod*] ... I don't owe it anything, and it doesn't owe me.
>
> —Kira Muratova

Asthenic Syndrome is the last film to be censored by the Soviet authorities (Taubman 46; Condee 133). In the late 1980s, Muratova's films toured the Western festival circuit (*Créteil* held a Muratova retrospective in 1988; in 1990 *Asthenic Syndrome* premiered in Berlin where it won the Silver Bear). A year after its Western release, *Asthenic Syndrome* opened domestically to critical acclaim and limited commercial success.

Ruslan Janumyan called *Asthenic Syndrome* a "demented master-piece."[14] Jane Taubman described it as a "Soviet apocalypse," "seemingly unstructured . . . built from a series of episodes involving and observed by . . . two main characters, which add up to a portrait of the era" (Taubman 46). The film is a culmination of Muratova's evolving styles, from her early poetic realism through to surrealism and hyper-realism, all of which retain an interest in "the *realia* of everyday life" (Taubman 5). Muratova's theatricality, her use of repetition, and love of eccentrics have led to comparisons with Fellini, though in her irrev-erence and black humor she reminds one also of Marco Ferreri.

Asthenic Syndrome has two parts. In the first, black-and-white seg-ment, Natasha (Olga Antonova), a doctor, abruptly leaves her hus-band's funeral. Grief-stricken, she argues with passersby, fights, shouts, and cries. She picks up a street drunk for sex then throws him out. The film's second, longer part is shot in color. It centers on the high school English teacher Nikolai (Sergei Popov), whose unstable nerves lead to narcoleptic spells. Natasha and Nikolai suffer from asthenia, which Muratova defines as "a condition of nervous exhaus-tion, resulting in inappropriate behaviour or lack of affect" (Mura-tova qtd. in Taubman 45). The film's two parts are linked formally. The Natasha segment is revealed as a film screening within the sec-ond Nikolai segment. As the lights come on in a large auditorium, the audience rushes out amidst scraps and squabbles, leaving Niko-lai asleep in his seat. Displays of aggression and vigor contrast with scenes of exhaustion and lethargy. At a fishmonger's, people shove and shout, while, in the underground, swarms of commuters dose off in carriages or on the escalators. *Asthenic Syndrome* owes its idiosyn-crasies to the attention it pays to daily detail. Places and events are invested with what Muratova calls "ornamentalism" (Taubman 5). This includes an eye for the artful playfulness of cruelty involving both humans and animals.[15]

The film opens with a surrealist shot of found objects: a doll, flowers, a garment or old cloth. Soap bubbles blow across the frame. The camera pulls back to a full view of the discarded heap, with an upturned pram or cart, a clock with no dials. In the next shot, a chorus of three old women recites: "In my childhood, in my early youth, I thought it was enough for everyone to read carefully through the work of Lev Nikolaevich Tolstoy and everyone would understand absolutely everything. And everyone would become kind and intelligent." Soap bubbles continue to float. Next, we discover the source of the bubbles, a boy by a large open window. The soundtrack plays Schubert and the boy continues to blow bubbles. From the window Muratova cuts to a construction site, where three men in a shallow pit are tying a can to a cat's tail with a string. Two other men watch and laugh from above. Classical music continues to play. These three sequences precede the first Natasha segment. From the cat episode, Muratova cuts to the cemetery where a number of funerals are underway (we see men digging a pit) and Natasha is burying her husband. The repetition of elements (number three, bubbles, the pit, the theme of play) illustrates that "Muratova's work overall is less accessible through its plots than through its recurrent patterns (Condee 119). The opening sequences establish Muratova's antihumanist cinema as a "negative edifice" and "private zoo" (Condee 136). She does not single out humanity from the world's other things. The mystery of man is but the mystery of the universe, which man foolishly claims as his own.

Both Taubman and Condee point out the intertextual importance of the boy blowing bubbles (Condee notes a reference to Grigorii Chukhrai's *Ballad of a Soldier* [1959], and Taubman to Tengiz Abuladze' *Repentance* [1987]), but Condee suggests that the boy's innocent play is repeated, not contrasted, in the grown men's abuse of the cat. Cruelty and play are closely and amorally linked. The motif of "unreflective play" (Condee 121) is rehearsed throughout the film, as when two girls amuse themselves by abusing Misha, a mentally handicapped youth.

The spectacles of ordinary cruelty committed by children, animals, or adults are levelers. Muratova "replaces the humanist query (What does it mean to be human?)"—a question that for all his commitment to realism still underscores Bazin's understanding of cinema—"with her own: What use, in the first place, is this distinction?" (Condee 122). For Muratova there is no essential moral difference between humans and other animals. The focus on actions (rather than interiority) shows humans as mammals who live through the playful exercising of force. In Muratova's biopolitical anarchism,

> "lofty citizenship," vitiated of its disciplinary authority, is more akin to human despotism, an unjust tyranny by *Homo sapiens*. The social is reduced to biological struggle without moral exemption for the human. Predatory human consciousness is pitched in a losing battle with its own predatory rule of law. Insofar as no moral difference exists between discipliners and disciplined, all legal and civic projects inevitably turn to brawling. *Asthenic Syndrome* provides a cascade of examples: the school principal Irina Pavlovna attacks her colleague, Nikolai, who in turn attacks his student, Sitnikov, who in turn brawls with a passerby. . . . The pet bird is chased by the pet cat, chased by the father, chased by his daughter. The film returns to Nikolai, eventually hospitalized in a psychiatric institution where the staff pummel each other in the exercise yard. The school, the street, the family home, and the psychiatric hospital are *linked in a visual continuum as common sites for an ongoing discharge of aggression*.
>
> (Condee 122–123; my emphasis)

The idea of an "ongoing discharge of aggression," it should already be clear, is central to my readings in *Creaturely Poetics*, and corresponds to Weil's notion of gravitational force. Humans are distinguished from other animals not through their particular qualities but via the intensity of pressure they exert on their environment.

Muratova's characters' go about their day eating, shopping, talking, or fighting. Repetitive action patterns override moral qualms the characters may have of their survival at the expense of the less fortunate.

Tolstoy used a similar method of repetition to illustrate the dulling of the ethical by routine. "Look at my life," Tolstoy urged in *What Is to be Done?*: "I eat, talk, listen; then I eat, write or read, which are only talking and listening in another form. I eat again and play. Then eat, talk, and listen, and finally eat and go to sleep. This is my entire life" (Tolstoy 140). Mankind's self-proclaimed greatness is misplaced, since, if anything, man is better equipped for the practice of aggression than most other creatures. Muratova counters the moralist's illusion that makes humanity a privileged moral agent. "We shake our heads and wonder at the barbarism of our forefathers," writes Tolstoy, "from the height of greatness, we are dumbfounded at their inhumanity. Why aren't we dumbfounded by our own?" Humans tend to project evil outside, and regard themselves as a source of the good: "we are so self-assured that the good tree bearing good fruit is we ourselves, and that these words [of the Gospels] apply to others, not to us. We gloss over these words and feel quite assured that this terrible thing has not happened to us, but to some other people. But it is for this very reason we do not see that this happened to us and is taking place in our midst. We do not hear, we do not see, and we do not understand with our heart" (Tolstoy 138). *Asthenic Syndrome* mirrors Tolstoy's critique most clearly in the film's toughest sequence in the dog pound.

Four women go to the pound to look for a lost dog. They are cheery enough when they enter, but as they peek inside they begin to cry. A long take follows in which the camera patiently tracks the filthy cages crammed with dogs so dejected that they no longer bark (the difference between this scene and Perebeyeva's home in *About Love* is especially chilling). As the camera moves along the room, dogs whimper and reach through the bars, others stare into the camera with downcast eyes. The dogs' responsiveness discloses the presence of the camera crew and, by extension, our presence as viewers. The dogs' instinctive desire for human company becomes a self-reflexive device. The disclosure is indicting and shaming. Muratova ends the scene with a Tolstoyan intertitle:

People don't want to look at this.
People don't want to think about this.
This should have nothing to do with
conversations about good and evil.

Here, again, a difficult reality renders moralism—conversations about the meaning of good and evil—null and void. To illustrate the use of morality to avoid painful contact with reality, Muratova inserts a second controversial scene in which a woman in a subway carriage emits a random string of profanities. "These key scenes in the pound and the metro . . . are set off against each other so as to raise questions about what we take for granted and what shocks us" (Condee 135). Placed as censor's bait—pure excess and artifice—the metro scene exposed the state's empty moralism, which initially shelved *Asthenic Syndrome* for obscenity. The voices of propriety and the public good (in Russia and elsewhere) are more easily shocked by the performance of bad language than by the unperformed reality of abandoned, dispensable pets.

But Muratova's insistence on showing human beings as "carbon-based life forms, periodically requiring a warm body to discharge accumulated energy" (Condee 138) is not simply admonishing. Human restlessness is also creative. Thus Muratova's "regressive logic captures, a consciousness charming in its raw exchange of impulses that sustain biological existence" (Condee 138). The Tolstoyan references in *Asthenic Syndrome* suggest reflexivity and vigilance as ethical responses to the conditions of all life, human, animal, or inert. Muratova expands on Weil's vulnerability of precious things by theatrically tracking the gravitations of power between living bodies. Though she avoids a sacrificial economy of suffering (common in her compatriot Andrei Tarkovsky), Muratova is nonetheless alive to the pain of creatures. From Natasha's explosive, inarticulate animal grief to Nikolai's chronic escapism or the beseeching faces of the condemned dogs, the artist's role is to show without concealment, for the sake of opening, or, as Artur Aristakisyan describes it, *polishing* our eyes.

"A String of Prayer Beads for the Eyes": Artur Arystakisyan's *Palms*

> "The film was shot like a string of prayer beads for the eyes. When we watch a film with our eyes, we sift through those beads. The figures of those poor people in the film polish up our vision . . . each frame of this film should polish the eyes of the person watching the film."
>
> —Artur Aristakisyan

Palms is an extreme and extremist film. Its gospel is uncompromising, its visual lyricism harsh. The film stages a return to cinematic realism, with conscious nods to Bazin and Bresson, but on a scale and in a style that are truly original. *Palms*, Aristakisyan's diploma film at the VGIK (the Moscow Film School that Muratova also attended), is patched together from footage of vagabonds living on the fringes of the Moldovan capital Kishinev, where Aristakisyan grew up and where he says he feels most at home.

Shot in black and white on 16mm and later blown up to 35mm, the film bears the grainy, aging scars of the transfer. The first images are indeed archival, taken from an unknown Italian silent film about the persecution of Christians in Nero's Rome. An intertitle reads: "Rome. Year 28 after the Crucifixion of Jesus." In Bazinian fashion, the film shows animals and humans in perilous proximity: lions and Christians thrown together in a Roman amphitheater. A woman tries to escape by climbing a piece of cloth lowered from the seats, but is snatched back by the animals, and devoured. A second intertitle: "Kishinev. Year 1991 after the birth of Christ." A beggar sits on the ground on a busy street. Passersby toss coins his way. A male voiceover speaks: "He said he was not going to move from this place until the coming of the Kingdom of God." The camera pulls up to the beggar's hand. A fistful of coins slips into the overcoat pocket. This is the first of the film's many hands. Hands, not faces, are the central image in *Palms*.

The two scraps of footage and the two periods look identical. This is a world in which the persecution of outsiders continues across epochs in essentially similar ways. Aristakisyan is expressing something about time, but more so about film as registering what he calls "flat snippets of time." Cinema, he says in the revealing interview included in Second Run's DVD edition of *Palms*, is a "light-bearing substance." *Palms* is committed to the medium of film as a light-bearing substance, not to the discovery of new images: "something new was what I least wanted to do." Why beggars and outsiders, then? The downtrodden allow one "to see the film itself, if you can put it that way"; they "serve to reveal the film's density." Throughout *Palms* the materiality of bodies enters and exposes the materiality of the film itself. This is the only properly "documentary" dimension of an otherwise poetic and allegorical film.

The voiceover (spoken by Aristakisyan) is of a beggar addressing his unborn son. "Your mother is not my wife, and it's possible that very soon you'll be scraped out of her womb. Piece by piece. Never mind. Can you hear me?" Though the foetus will be aborted, the father is grateful because "nothing will ever change the fact that today you exist. And I, your father, can talk to you." The father's monologue weaves a tapestry of paupers' tales. Each is an allegory that accompanies the visual prayer beads: Yazundokta, an old homeless woman dragging a trunk containing the head of her jailor turned lover. Srulik, a camp survivor who lives with doves. A blind begging boy whose blind parents, escapees from a mental institution, protect him by telling him that everyone in the world is also blind. A man with two round stumps for hands that other beggars refer to as "candles," who grieves for a woman by moving on his knees. A haunted widow, deserted bride, prisoners, madmen, the lobotomized; these outcasts are the only ones who live truly beyond the multifarious constellations of power known as the "system." Seeking nothing from it, the beggars evade the system's soul-corroding influence.

In "The Opened Hand: Reflections on Artur Aristakisyan's *Palms*," the essay accompanying the DVD edition, Graeme Hobbs explains that "the 'system' outside of which the beggars live remains undefined. This is unimportant; political system, social system, system of mercantile totalitarianism, whatever name you care to supply makes no difference. When you are outside of it, the terms are meaningless. The only thing worth knowing is the essential fact that power, wherever it is found, 'starts to ferment, like wine.' Always." *Palms* is about dissidence in its total and totalizing sense. Neither revolution nor democracy, social security, charity, philanthropy, or human rights; *Palms* is quietly contemptuous of humanitarianism. It is indifferent to all politics in the face of the demands of salvation. To resist power one has to become utterly powerless. So the father urges his son to save his soul by being poor: "There is something humiliating about people hurrying to work. You should try not to go to work. Don't do work useful for society. It's better to be a beggar. You see, people need guarantees. That's why they go to work. They are paid not for their work, but for having rejected the path of destitution. . . . I believe only those who beg earn their daily bread through their own labour. Follow the poor . . . become poor."

The pure possessions in life are poverty and virginity. The father says: "Destitution will protect you from the system, and virginity from fornications with the system." *Palms* replaces the social and sexual body with the naked body, or bare life. It is easy to see this veneration of destitution as exploitative. The hostility the film occasionally met with (Aristakisyan mentions one unsympathetic screening in London) is actively courted when in his interview Aristakisyan admits that no closeness arose between the filmmaker and his subjects: "there was no common human tie." These people existed solely as what Aristakisyan (echoing Bresson) calls "models." He shirks the social responsibility of the documentary filmmaker: "I was the artist and they were the models."

Palms also refuses the documentary ethics of "informed consent." Consent is not what is sought here from either subject or spectator. The people Aristakisyan films rarely return his gaze. The beggars do not make contact with the camera, and it seems that returning the gaze as a gesture of subjecthood and empowerment does not interest them. (This is another way of reducing the cinematic importance of the human face. Again like Bresson, Aristakisyan prefers hands and feet). Thus *Palms* paradoxically establishes absolute distance from its subjects as a means of proximity. The distancing is threefold: between the subjects and the filmmaker, between the subjects and us, and between the filmmaker and us. There is simply no contract and no communicative bond. This film is not intended for us and so grants us no favors. Its mode of presenting is as big a slur on the liberal principle of mutuality as it is on the postmodern lauding of otherness. Instead of reciprocity, there is physicality. *Palms*'s radicalism is born of the sheer persistence of bodies. As Hobbs explains: "there is no doubt that in *Palms* we are in the company of solid bodies, maimed and damaged bodies even, not seeking our attention or intervention, utterly indifferent to us at our safe distance, yet completely present. They feed no appetite, create no wealth, yet still they stubbornly exist, heavy with the affront of parasitic life."

Aristakisyan's marginal humans reveal what the father tells his unborn child, that "everything is divine in nature." These words are spoken against a high-contrast black and white image of a woman. Wrinkles plough deep ravines across her face, etching her body onto the filmstrip. The cumulative effect of these material images is to usher the cinematic toward the realm of the sacred. Despite denying that he has made a religious film, Aristakisyan suffuses *Palms* throughout with divine and devout language. In creating a space whose woundedness and poverty are neither hidden or pliant nor curable, *Palms* presents a defiantly Christian universe.

"One beggar said that Christians are creatures mad with love." To the extent that "human" is part of the system, the beggars are not quite human. *Palms* is rooted in a tradition of Christian radicalism—St. Francis of Assisi, Tolstoy, Simone Weil—that places salvation at the foot of the destitute and scorns social welfarism.

My little son,
beware of learned books,
beware of laws, any laws.
Because for the system we are not people.
It has established an order of things in which neither you nor I exit.
There is no one.
There's only the law which exists for us,
the law of blood, of fine matter.
Our blood, yours and mine,
is the sacred axis of the whole system.

The laws of dialectics deal with it.

The laws of dialectics are the laws of the system.

They work only within the system.

They are tested, logical and, of course, false.

According to these laws, the system is a great biomass,

and a human being is the number of its chances.

It's possible to take these chances away, or to leave them.

This is the foundation of everything.

These are the laws of dialectics,

For this reason they are immune from morality . . .

. . . immune from good and evil.

With all this in mind, it is getting ever harder to discuss whether we are human at all, or not.

This is *Palms*'s most powerful articulation of the system's dehumanizations, its abstractions of the human being into "chances" the system can uphold or withdraw. The words are spoken against close-ups of partially covered legs and feet, leathery weathered hands, open, begging, receiving a handful of biscuits or motionless. Frayed bandages reveal a scarred wrist. Grigory, who has lost both his hands, smokes a cigarette expertly between his two stumps. Salvation too is a kind of dehumanization, but different than the system's. The coming of Christ will erase all distinctions, between inside and outside, high and low, past and future, but the inhumanity of salvation is born of the paring of flesh and blood, not the system's cold calculations.

Palms offers its religious allegory as a provocation. It is the attachment to real bodies that ironically allows Aristakisyan to transcend reality allegorically. Under Aristakisyan's gaze, cinema becomes what the filmmaker Nathaniel Dorsky called a "devotional" practice, attuned to the material and temporal existence of its cinematographic "models."

5 Scientific Surrealism in the Films of Georges Franju and Frederic Wiseman

I shall strike you without anger
And without hate, like a butcher   —Baudelaire, *The Flowers of Evil*

Dadaism and surrealism are extreme cases; they represented the intoxication of total license. . . . The surrealists have set up non-oriented thought as a model; they have chosen the total absence of value as their supreme value.   —Simone Weil

The two documentaries I discuss in this chapter—Georges Franju's *Le Sang des bêtes* (*Blood of the Beasts*; 1949) and Frederick Wiseman's *Primate* (1974)—revolve around Simone Weil's conceptual relay between vulnerability, existence, and beauty as the threshold of a creaturely aesthetic. I have been arguing that the relationship between vulnerability, existence, and beauty cuts across the confines of the human, the illuminated zone in which Cartesian man basks in the glory of his own consciousness and self-knowing.

Franju and Wiseman's films address a common theme—the institutionalized violence against animals—in the contexts of the slaughterhouse and the research laboratory. These institutional sites perhaps more than any other disclose the fusion of rationality and violence as paradigmatically modern. In their visual economies, Franju and Wiseman's films also expose the distinctly aesthetic dimension of the institutions they study. The abattoir and laboratory are not simply observed by Franju and Wiseman in a manner that transforms them into a cinematic spectacle. They are treated as places that creatively produce their own visual codes inspired by what the film scholar Raymond Durgnat described as the "surrealism of science" (Durgnat 27), an aesthetic that strongly contrasts with the creaturely poetics I have been pursuing through Weil's work.

Sang des bêtes and Primate deal with institutions whose activities may literally be described as the controlling and processing of animal bodies. Sang des bêtes is a twenty-two minute short depicting the work at a Paris slaughterhouse (Franju filmed in three separate sites in Paris, but the distinctions in the film are between the different kinds of slaughtered animals—a horse, cows, calves, and sheep—not the locations of the slaughterhouses). Wiseman's feature-length Primate (105 minutes long) follows the experimental routines at the Yerkes Primate Research Center at Emory University, Atlanta. Both films are forensic in their theme and in their form, and I argue that both are also reflections on modern instrumentalism and technoscience as forms of surrealist art.

Le Sang des bêtes

Sang des bêtes, Franju's first important short (the format he was to excel in) is also the first in his series of films that deal directly with animals. This is the film to which most if not all subsequent cinematic images of the abattoir (very nearly a minigenre in its own right)—from Frederick Wiseman's Meat (1976) to Nikolaus Geyrhalter's Our Daily Bread (2005) or Richard Linklater's Fast Food Nation (2006)—look back. In the history of cinema, Sang des bêtes holds a special, iconic, status.[1]

Franju is first and foremost a director of setting and shape, and the abattoir presented him with some truly exciting visual possibilities. In 1929 Georges Bataille's surrealist magazine Documents published a series of photographs by Eli Lotar of the same La Villette slaughterhouse where Franju would later shoot his film. Lotar's photographs reveal surrealism's affinity with violent imagery.[2] Sang des bêtes captures the dismembered, grotesque figures of animal carcasses in a similar way to its companion documentary *Hôtel des invalides* (1951), which dwells on the disfigured faces of world war veterans.[3] The severed human and animal bodies in Franju's work function as a common mise-en-scène, and it is at this formal level that Franju's intersecting between cinema, science, and surrealism is at its most arresting. Franju's mixture of surrealism's fantastical, isolated objects and shapes with science's surgical graphics prompted Durgnat, in his important book on Franju, to discuss his visual style as scientifically surreal: "after all, what is more Surrealist than those scientific films which translate into visually perceptible forms the sectors, levels or patterns of reality which, with authority, undermine the frameworks constructed by our socially-conditioned perceptions, usually miscalled 'realism'?" (28–29). Moreover, Franju's surrealism does not hinge on a simple jolting juxtaposition of objects, whose point of reference is internal and psychic rather than worldly. "The mere 'colliding' of objects can, of course, rapidly become a cliché," Durgnat writes. "In Franju," on the contrary, "the reference is constantly to the objective world in which we do all move, and at which our eyes unseeingly stare. Far from cutting out the real world, his vision lets it in" (19). Scientific surrealism is thus "realistic" in the manner developed in the previous chapter, as a mode of attending to the condition of living exposure. Despite its unflinching show of violence, therefore, Franju's cinema does not preclude what Durgnat calls the "potentialities of tenderness" (27).

The first sequences of *Sang des bêtes* establishes the film's general pattern of alternating between a poetic surrealism (designated by a female voiceover) and a violent realism (designated by a male voiceover). Following the credits, a crane shot of the Paris outskirts carries the title *Aux portes de Paris*. We are coming into yet also looking out of the City of Light (the views are reminiscent of Céline's piercingly honest depictions of suburban Paris in *Journey to the End of the Night*). A woman enters the frame from the right, her back half turned. The female voiceover accompanies the images of an urban wasteland with its scattered treasures and found objects: household oddities, scraps, an armless mannequin. In the background, trains move horizontally across the frame. The camera closes in on an anonymous painting; children dance in a circle. An old man sits alone at a round table in the barren field. The sequence ends formally with the opening and closing of a fan that wipes to the next image of a couple kissing. The kiss is followed by the (recurring) image of trains, only this time more prominently occupying the frame. The trains become trucks in the next shot, as we arrive to the slaughterhouses of Vaugirard. Before the first violent sequence of the killing of a white horse, the killing tools are laid out and presented by the male voiceover. Only then does the camera cut to the horse led forward and stunned by the "Behr gun" introduced in the earlier sequence. The horse's throat is slit, and blood is drained from the body. The camera follows the swift skinning and segmentation of the horse.

The abattoir workers' movements are smooth and professional. The camera does not shy away from depicting the violent act in all its minute detail. There is obvious tension in these scenes between the first sequence, with its array of found "outmoded" objects on the outskirts of the Parisian metropolis, and the shock of the subsequent spectacle, reminiscent of Artaud's Theater of Cruelty "in which violent physical images crush and hypnotize the sensibility of the spectator" (Artaud qtd. in Sloniowski 171). The divisions are initially stable and clear: the dreaminess of the opening sequence leaves one unprepared for the violence unleashed in the next sequence of the killing of the white horse. But this is not quite how things work, for there is in the slaughter sequences, terrifying as they are, a muted quality, something akin to a banality of violence. Banality is signaled first by the male voiceover that presents the killing tools and explains the procedures with cool precision. The effect of such standardized violence is disquieting, and, more important, already questions the shock tactics of surrealism, as if exceeding (and critiquing) surrealism through banality itself. Violence, in short, is simultaneously surprising and utterly mundane: this type of violence is not merely the city's subterranean flipside or dark unconscious; it is the very paradigm of civilized urban modernity. What is disquieting here is not so much the goriness of slaughter as the shock of its banality—its extreme yet wholly quotidian occurrence.

Shot in 1948, a mere three years after Liberation and a short while before the arrival of the vast industrialized meat packing plants, *Sang des bêtes* is mired in the intense banality of the modern killing machine that so successfully merged the brutality of killing with the docility and asceticism of rational thought. Indeed, *Sang des bêtes* contains clear allusions to the Holocaust, both in the recurring shots of trains, in the final sequences depicting the killing of sheep, their "tricking" onto the kill floor by what the narrator calls the Judas sheep, and the last, ruminating shots (accompanied by a mournful female voiceover) of the remaining victims locked in an overnight pen, awaiting their fate the following morning. Jeannette Sloniowski notes the influence of *Sang des bêtes* on Alain Resnais's seminal Holocaust documentary *Nuit et brouillard* (*Night and Fog*, 1956) (Sloniowski 177). The Holocaust will return again in Franju's 1955 short *Mon chien* (*My Dog*), on abandoned dogs in Paris who end up in the municipality's gas chambers, and in *Les Yeux sans visage* (*Eyes Without a Face*, 1959), Franju's best-known (most commercially successful) horror film, in which the Mengele-like scientist/vivisectionist Dr. Genessier (Pierre Brasseur) kidnaps young women in order to steal their faces and graft them onto the ruined face of his daughter (played by Franju's regular actress Edith Scob). But how should one approach Franju's many references to the Holocaust?

A fair amount of scholarship on Franju and the Holocaust is still debating the significance of its many citations in Franju's ambiguous body of work. Adam Lowenstein's *Shocking Representation*, for instance, makes a detailed case for the historical relevance of *Sang des bêtes* as a postwar film. In his opening chapter, "History Without a Face: Surrealism, Modernity, and the Holocaust in the Cinema of Georges Franju," Lowenstein reads *Sang des bêtes* as historical allegory and its method as a powerful way of awakening the viewer—through shock—to France's recent historical trauma.[4] Franju's film, says Lowenstein, is "profoundly Benjaminian in its dialectical goal of imbricating perceptions of the familiar with those of the unfamiliar, even in the process of audience reception of documentary 'reality'" (Lowenstein 25). In the context of postwar France, *Sang des bêtes* functions as "an allegorical illumination of the ghosts of Occupation and the Holocaust" (Lowenstein 27).

Yet despite—or precisely because of—the persuasive appeal to Benjamin's critique of the "continuum of history" (Lowenstein 14), reducing the animal presence in Franju to the allegorical and the symbolic leaves interpretation with a questionable notion of history and historicity: still a firmly human and humanist understanding of the historical as a coherent if not teleological narrative at the center of which operate privileged human subjects. As I argued extensively in chapter 2, through the work of Hanssen and Santner, Benjamin's analysis of the creaturely and natural history undermines the humanity of the traditional historical subject. Franju's repeated return to animals in his films, precisely in the context of historical trauma, is thus visibly critical of a humanist understanding of history. Franju is therefore Benjaminian not only in resisting what Benjamin called historicism's "empty time" but to the extent that both read history nonanthropocentrically. Franju's insistence that "his interest is in the victim, that he is on the side of the victim, whether it's a white horse in a slaughterhouse, a salmon with the hook tearing at its mouth, a war cripple with shrapnel-twisted lips, or a mental patient staring at the wall" (Durgnat 31) addresses the workings of power in a nonanthropocentric way. Animals as cryptic signifiers complicate rather than facilitate a symbolic reading of Franju's animal films, not because animals are infinitely other but precisely because seeing animals as mere foils for humanity denies the shared physicality of human and animal life—and what Benjamin saw as the ahuman physicality of history itself. Can we really confine Franju's depiction of slaughter in *Sang des bêtes* to an allegorical reconnecting with—or the traumatic replaying of—human history?

If history penetrates Franju's films through what Lowenstein reads as the sensitizing gestures of extreme violence, or through what Franju called the "homeopathic" administering of horror, this is not only by way of an awakening to the realities of pre- and postwar France but more broadly and reflexively as a critique of modernity and its coupling between extreme violence and, as it were, extreme rationality. The killing in *Sang des bêtes* is already highly systematic, rationalized, and professionalized. The combination between the seemingly incommensurate elements of rationality and violence as one hallmark of modernity,

Franju seems to be suggesting, is formally surreal. Rather than channeling an alternative to modern rationalism (exemplified in the relentless rise of empirical science and the military-industrial complex), therefore, surrealism may be seen to merge with it. In the shadow of the two world wars, Franju's scientific surrealism invokes modern technoscience's cool monotony of violence whose effect is, oddly enough, to expose a certain "datedness" of surrealist art.[5]

Anyone who watches Franju's films is quick to note that his work stands apart from his contemporaries of the French New Wave. In her book *Georges Franju*, Kate Ince provides some illuminating comments on Franju's attitude toward the *nouvelle vague*: "In Franju's view the *nouvelle vague* was a movement without substance, little more than 'un "remous" publicitaire' created by certain directors in favour of their own films, and mounted with the aid of journalists whose job was to 'discover' new values (Vialle 1968: 92). A real 'wave' . . . had to be international, have a social dimension, and endure (92), and while German expressionism and Italian neo-realism met these criteria, the *nouvelle vague* did not" (Ince 7–8). *Sang des bêtes* and *Les yeux sans visage*, Lowenstein points out, are more fittingly thought as precursors of the slasher movie, bestowing on this often misunderstood subgenre a seriousness and depth: "Franju's films remind us that splatter does not preclude (and may sometimes even encourage) an allegorical confrontation with the historical trauma of modernity" (Lowenstein 53). In these two films, I would add, Franju anticipated the creeping (and creepy) merger between science and art, one of the most salient features not only of the horror film but of a wide range of contemporary visual culture.

Franju appreciated scientific cinema as an avant-garde art form. In 1945 he took over from the scientific cinematographer Jean Painlevé as the director of the Institute of Scientific Cinematography (he remained in this position until 1953). Both Franju and Painlevé had loose ties with the surrealist movement. Painlevé's famous scientific films, like *The Vampire* (1945), which studies the life of the South American blood-sucking bat accompanied by a Duke Ellington jazz score, are prime examples of the sort of scientific surrealism that Bataille's surrealist wing was engaged in. The "extreme reality" (André Bazin's *éblouissante vérité*, literally "dazzling truth") that scientific cinema was capable of delivering (including surgery, radiography, and other micro-cinematography films) attracted a great deal of artistic attention in the first two decades of the twentieth century. Ince writes that "this tendency of the scientific film to attract attention more for its aesthetic interest than for its content is a constant in the cinema of science in France up to and beyond Franju" (108). Bazin wrote about the so-called overtaking of surrealism by scientific cinematography. He went "so far as to estimate the surgical cinema of Thierry de Martel 'beyond' surrealism" and as encapsulating "film's purest aesthetic" (qtd. in Ince 110). Bazin is well nigh mystical about the cinematic purity of scientific imagery: "for this is the miracle, the inexhaustible paradox of scientific cinema: it is at the extreme of goal-oriented, utilitarian research, when aesthetic intentions as such have been absolutely ruled out, that cinematic beauty develops, excessively, like supernatural grace" (qtd. in Ince 110). Beauty for Bazin (emphatically not in the sense of "pretty" imagery) emerges just at the point when aestheticism has been purposefully abandoned. But beauty is not merely a by-product of a cinema that seeks reality through and as scientific endeavor; it is scientific cinema's excessive and abundant effect.

Far from "just a phase," we should, I think, take the seemingly unintended aestheticism and hypersurrealism of scientific cinema as the forerunner of our present, highly conscious fascination with scientific "bio arts," from the Welcome Trust's visual collections, exhibitions, and displays, to brain imaging, the body art of Orlan, Günther Von Hagens's *Bodies* and *Body Worlds*, the sliced cows and dying flies of Brit art entrepreneur Damien Hirst, the transgenic bunnies of the American artist Eduardo Kac, or Karl Grimes's animal embryos and fetuses in his Future Nature exhibition.[6] Reality television programs like *Live Autopsy* and extreme makeover shows such as *Plastic Surgery Live* or *The Swan* are throwbacks to nineteenth-century displays of anatomical models for the purpose of education and public entertainment alike. The molecular spectacles and cellular blowups of the television franchise *CSI*, in which an observable world—conceived in its entirety as a "crime scene"—becomes the dissectible object of scientific violence and the site for the corroboration of reactionary morals is perhaps the most popular example of this forensic fetishism. These examples illustrate just how interchangeable art and science were, and increasingly are, in the arenas of popular culture. This is the cultural and aesthetic mutation that I refer to as scientific surrealism.

Traces of the science film in *Sang des bêtes* do not reside in the visuals alone but also in the (male) commentary, written by Painlevé. Apart from the introduction of the professional killing tools at the beginning of the film, the narrator later recites two lines from Baudelaire's *The Flowers of Evil*:

> *I shall strike you without anger*
> *And without hate, like a butcher.*[7]

What is this violence that kills without hatred and without emotion? And what, if we were to take Baudelaire's lines at face value, could possibly be more terrifying than precisely this sort of violence? During a sequence about the slaughtering of cows, Franju shows a cow's severed head being smashed; we watch the face, that crucible of personhood, destroyed by repeated blows from an axe.

"I shall strike you without anger / And without hate, like a butcher." Deliciously ironic, Baudelaire's description of dispassionate killing is interesting precisely because we sense it is false. Despite being a truism of modernity, dispassionate killing is an odd and displaced notion. The belief that one can kill without hate, is, I suggest, more than just a modern fantasy about the complete rationalization of the biological processes of life and death; it is, in effect, a modern performance, modernity's peculiar and morbid ritual. Is it true that those who kill do so without anger, hate, or desire? The question is not meant psychologically but culturally. For a culture that holds that it is possible to slay without hate is one that believes the opposite is equally true: provision and imparting of justice are possible without love. Indeed, these twin assumptions furnish the dominant liberal theories that "ration" justice according to certain attributable qualities and speak of "moral subjects" or "agents" as possessors of ascertainable rights.

Baudelaire's nightmarish vision of the strictly professional act, of execution efficiently devoid of emotive expression, calls to mind not only the modern mechanization of slaughter but also its supporting discourses of welfarism and bioethics. What are we to make of this sort of mission, this professionalism, that goes by the name of animal welfare? Baudelairian irony may be said to expose the automated poetry of the mechanical itself and the cruelty (yes, hatred) inherent in the purely utilitarian act. Such cold lyricism is what I take to be at stake in Geyrhalter's documentary *Our Daily Bread*, in which various mechanized procedures in food production take on a peculiar mesmeric quality. *Our Daily Bread* invokes the poetry of agribusiness, whose hypnotic rhythms are freed from the quirky humanity of a voiceover. To what extent Geyrhalter is critiquing the global food machine depends on how susceptible one is to the undulations of his hypnotist's pendulum. *Our Daily Bread*'s aestheticism is the effect of rational excess, the point at which reason no longer pertains to or addresses the world. No film that I have seen makes visible the insanity (and comedy) of the rational—a distinctly modern achievement—more explicitly or painstakingly than Frederick Wiseman's *Primate*.

Primate

Made in 1974, *Primate* is one of the most striking of Wiseman's series of institutional portraits, begun in 1967 with *Titicut Follies* about life at Bridgewater, a Massachusetts state institution for the criminally insane. *Titicut Follies* and *Primate* are, in fact, close companions (the caged human inmates at Bridgewater are frequently naked, literally "naked apes"), with a number of scenes directly mirroring each other from film to film. Both focus on vulnerable and exposed bodies under the surveillance and control of a specialized institution and both exemplify Wiseman's longstanding interest in the mechanisms of institutional life and their impact upon the individuals within them. There is, therefore, a strong Foucauldian element to all of Wiseman's work. The focus on institutions (be they hospitals, schools, military bases, meatpacking plants, theater companies, or medical research facilities) rather than individuals renders the question of species almost redundant. What is common to *Titicut Follies* and *Primate* is the formative presence of the institution and the malleability of the institutionalized (both inmates and staff), regardless of their species.

Wiseman's unique style developed alongside the Direct Cinema movement in American documentary, though Wiseman differs from it in several ways. The divergence from the edicts of Direct Cinema is most apparent at the level of editing. Wiseman uses a mosaic rather than a linear or chronological structure. After shooting on location between four and six weeks and collecting many (often hundreds) hours of footage, the finished film is created at the editing stage, a process that in *Documenting the Documentary* Barry Keith Grant called "second order looking" (Grant 240). This means that the documentary we watch is a highly and consciously constructed artifact, a carefully ordered and condensed montage. Not only is *Primate* no exception to this, it contains a particularly high number of shots.[8]

The nonhuman primates at Yerkes are subject to a total management of their biological life functions. This includes a prurient interest in their sexual behavior. In the film's second scene, a primatologist says (referring to gorillas): "we don't want them doing anything sexually when we're not in a position to see it." On the wall beside him is a photo of two gorillas copulating. As the film progresses the procedures of sexual-behavioral research become increasingly intensive and intrusive. Some of the most disturbing scenes are those in which researchers forcibly masturbate apes (to extract semen for artificial inseminations) or experiments in which scientists literally switch monkeys on and off using different frequencies of electric brain stimulation, to induce and observe sexual and aggressive behavior ("electro-ejaculation" and brain localization experiments). In one experiment a monkey in a restraining device receives repeated brain stimulation via electrodes inserted into his skull and has his erections measured.[9]

Yerkes emerges in these episodes as an intricate biopolitical institution whose overall project is definable as the ceaseless production of a clear differentiation of species. It exemplifies, in accurate Foucauldian fashion, the convergence between knowledge and power: the absolute control over nonhuman bodies merges and overlaps with the production of expert scientific knowledge. Here again is a version of Agamben's "anthropological machine," which rigorously differentiates between "bare" life functions and those allegedly peculiar to human life. Struggles over the corporeal, Agamben shows, strive to maintain a clear cartography of species by isolating what is human and mastering and purging all that is not. But as already shown, Agamben is less interested in the place of actual animals in contemporary biopolitical institutions such as Yerkes or the slaughterhouse. His focus is on the internal management of the animality of man. *Primate* challenges Agamben's residual anthropocentrism, which overlooks the paramount place of animals in the Western humanist machine: real animals (not just conceptual animality) are the raw materials upon which depends the daily upkeep of human identity. This upkeep, *Primate* suggests, is indistinguishable from objective, scientific truths whose discovery is the official function of a center like Yerkes.

As in Wiseman's other films, *Primate* is strictly observational, with no voiceover or interviews. We watch complex and baffling scientific procedures without explanation. This strategy is central to *Primate* and has some far-reaching consequences. On its first airing on PBS, the Yerkes scientists reacted with anger. They complained that Wiseman unfairly denied them the opportunity to clarify and justify their actions. Without reasoned explanations, the experiments we see appear capricious, grotesque, or downright insane. In the absence of a scientific register, other discourses invariably suggest themselves: loaded (and topical) terms like torture, abuse, and detention begin to echo in the void.

Scholarly debates on the subject of animals are occasionally tinged with a theoretical density that serves as a rhetorical smoke screen, a way of circumventing the direct ethical appeal communicated by the sort of troubling content, the difficulty of reality, shown in *Primate*. On first watching *Primate* (and on subsequent, reluctant viewings of this painful and frightening film for the sober purposes of teaching and research), it is hard to hold back the visceral sense that here, truly, is a vision of hell. Is this the result of the lack of information on the purpose of the experiments?

In its missing or silenced voiceover commentary, *Primate* poses an opposite problem to the one raised by so-called traumatic material (for example, texts dealing with the Holocaust, genocide, or sexual abuse). Traumatic representation seeks words to express the inexpressible, the infernal, in the knowledge that words fail. Yet *Primate*, which contains the elements of trauma's catalogue of horrors (extreme violence, sexual exploitation, incomprehensible suffering), has not been discussed in traumatic terms. The reason for this is obvious: though unspoken, the horrors here are *speakable* because they pertain to nonhumans. Trauma's language of unspeakability is the sole preserve of the human because only those who can speak may be said to experience the unspeakable. And yet what is most significant (and brilliant) about Wiseman's documentary is that it *refuses to speak*: with no voiceover or interviews— neither a defense nor an assault on the subject of vivisection—*Primate* is the traumatic text par excellence and so belongs, in all its inarticulacy and silence, to the realm of *witnessing*.

How, then, to communicate in words and concepts what Wiseman's film communicates almost exclusively through pictures? *Primate* shows without telling, so that much of what is seen remains scientifically opaque. Yet this is precisely what makes *Primate* a unique intervention into the discourse of bioethics. Thomas W. Benson has suggested that it is mistaken to read *Primate* as "a rhetorical act in the narrowest sense—as persuasive discourse in the forensic and deliberative modes, accusing a group of particular scientists of cruelty to animals, and attacking the policy of public support for animal research" (Benson 192). Through its visual and narrative strategies, *Primate* renders difficult the common discursive moral frameworks for discussing vivisection. Criticisms of the film as unfair on science or as scoring cheap antivivisectionist points serve to reveal the discursive boundaries that govern how we do, and do not, talk about animal experiments. When considering the use of animals in research, the question asked—in classic liberal and utilitarian fashion—is whether the benefits of the research outweigh the costs. This line of questioning has definite limits and limitations. It revolves around matters of utility, policy, and practicality at the heart of which is a consensus about maximizing animal welfare and minimizing "unnecessary suffering." Much can be said about this way of framing the discussion, not least that it fails to question the moral grounds of our use of animals as a resource for human purposes and focuses instead on the manner in which animals are treated when used.[10]

Primate refuses to engage with the issue of animal experiments from the welfarist position just described. The film invites one to ask not how animals should be treated in vital medical research but, as Benson puts it, "whether any verbal justification is relevant to what we have seen" (198). At this point *Primate* ups the ethical stakes in ways some may find alarming. The film's real concerns, Benson writes, are "not merely forensic or deliberative"; they are "existential" (193). This is not a "problem film" anticipating some "easy liberal solution" (196), nor a shocking exposé of a rogue institution. Rather, *Primate* is "about something that is much more indivisible from our everyday lives, and about institutions that—even when they have some modifiable policies—are never going to be able to resolve the paradoxes they were set up to deal with. Problem films are most always optimistic, in that every problem implies a solution. *Wiseman's films do not imply any solution to the enterprise of being human*" (196; my emphasis).

While the Yerkes scientists criticized Wiseman's method for manipulating the material in such a way that it obscures the rationale of the experiments, *Primate* suggests, conversely, that rationalism and scientific discourse are themselves a sophisticated form of manipulation. What these discourses deflect and distort is the fact of animal powerlessness and the assumption of ethical difference that follows (rather than precedes) this fact, an assumption on which an institution like Yerkes is founded, and which it must tirelessly labor to perpetuate. In so doing, Yerkes utilizes the discourse and methodologies of science to narrow down the possible meanings of the word *life*—the *bio* of ethics—and reduce it to a set of predictable biological procedures.[11]

By, as it were, muting narration, Wiseman "dumbs down" the language of science, disclosing its contours, exposing its limitations and its peculiar constructions of the object of life. In this way *Primate* raises the ultimate (bio)ethical questions: Could *any* explanation, however rational, or any amount of information justify the activities at Yerkes? Can—or should—there be any reason for using animals in this way, and can we not identify here a profound overlooking of the state of creaturely vulnerability and, by extension, also an overlooking of the very same vulnerability humans share with other living beings? Wiseman does not venture to answer these questions (he claims to hold no position in the vivisection debate). *Primate* raises these questions instead to make clear the limits and lacks of our way of addressing the issue.

An expanded notion of life—around the shared creatureliness of vulnerable bodies—is apparent in the film's glimpses of the so-called extracurricular activities of animals as they play together in their cages, care for their infants, sit pensively in their cells, cling to, show affection for, or actively resist their human captors. *Primate* flatly refuses to cast such gestures as anthropomorphic. The film (and ironically also the scientists) reads these living gestures without scientific prejudice, as coherent and transparent. It is at once curious and telling that at no point in the film does anyone behave as if it were impossible to decipher what an animal thinks or feels. One of *Primate*'s greatest merits, then, is to not follow the skeptical path by making the otherness of animals a serious issue. *Primate*'s wit and originality lie in shifting attention from the alterity of animals to their institutionalized disempowerment. Otherness in this film is not an attribute of animality but of the discourse of science and the odd way it prefigures and orients the bioethical conversation. The proper "other" in this film is finally instrumental rationality itself, exposed as profoundly and precisely *irrational*.

Baudelaire's chilling couplet on modern butchery—calculated, unemotional, reasoned—is equally important in *Primate*. Hate, anger, and rage have not been superseded; they have merely been abstracted and displaced. In her novel *Good Morning, Midnight*, Jean Rhys—another important writer of exposure—called this predicament humanity's "cold insanity" (Rhys 145), by which she means the cruelty and irrationality inherent in reason itself. To counteract this cold insanity, *Primate* replaces positivist scientific observation with an ethics of vision: our observation of scientific observation yields incomprehension. We cannot understand what the scientists are looking at, but we *do* see something they remain blind to. Scientific opacity enables ethical transparency. Wiseman makes viewers attentive to the fragility of those who are mere stuff at the hands of the powerful. By resisting the cool seductions of scientific rationalism, *Primate* institutes an alternative quizzical space in which questions about human domination over nonhuman bodies cannot be repressed and are considered without recourse to scientific objectives. As with *Titicut Follies*, where criminology and psychiatry are bracketed off and lose their purchasing power, so in *Primate*, scientific currency deflates by being linked not to truth but to the exercising of power. Whatever else it may produce, research at Yerkes primarily transforms living bodies into mastered and dispensable stuff and into sets of abstract scientific calculations.

In "Question Concerning Technology," Heidegger describes the essence of modern technology not as a means or an instrument but as "a way of revealing" (Heidegger 39). What is revealed in this way is not a particular use of nature, but rather a "challenging [*Herausfordern*], which puts to nature the unreasonable demand that it supply energy that can be extracted and stored as such" (40). Yerkes is a classic example of the "challenging forth" of nature and its transformation into an energetic "standing reserve," which Heidegger regards as the essence of modern technology. The repeated "milking" for semen and the artificial inseminations at Yerkes, for instance, disclose the status of the animals less as mere objects and more as a resource—Heidegger's "standing reserve"—for the potentially endless extraction of energy or, in this case, the (re)production of further resources. Heidegger's point about modern technology, it is important to stress, is not that it objectifies but, on the contrary, that it annihilates objects. Interestingly, the common opposition to vivisection that rejects its reduction of sentient beings into things is only a preliminary stage in Yerkes' activities. Following Heidegger's logic, the essence of Yerkes is more radical still: animals are not simply objectified but ultimately *disappear* as objects. This aesthetics of disappearance, to borrow Paul Virilio's phrase, is at its clearest in the film's most unsettling sequence, which follows the procedure of the killing, decapitation, and brain dissection of a squirrel monkey: the animal is transformed from a body into a thing, and finally into a microscopic, abstracted representation of a brain. The sequence is the film's violent coda and brings together the various motifs of power, instrumental rationality, and the visual codes of scientific surrealism.

Yerkes does not merely produce what, in *Primate Visions,* Donna Haraway describes as the "achievement of 'man's' humanist goals of self-knowledge in science and technology" (117). There is also an important aesthetic dimension to the place.[12] Wiseman's film is scientifically surreal. Its "look" is deliberate: the interiors of labs with their futuristic paraphernalia are the visual embodiment of the fantasy of rationalism. Wiseman heightens this by the use of dense montage and by occasionally zooming in on the technology itself—revolving machines, a flickering monitor, test tubes arranged in geometric rows, the view through the lens of a microscope, or the film's science fiction finale in which a rhesus monkey is launched into space. We are finally in Kubrick territory with its clinical decors and hushed white corridors. Surrealism's chimeric aesthetic is also present in the subtle insinuations of bestiality: images of the sexual exploitation of animals or the nursery scene early on in the film, in which newborn chimpanzees are gently cuddled and bottle-fed by women in surgical masks. The rows of cells in which the animals are kept between experiments cannot but recall the efficient architecture of indefinite detention, from Auschwitz to Guantánamo Bay.

Hate Machine

Whereas in *Sang des bêtes* violence and poetry reanimate one another through tension and contrast, in *Primate* they can no longer be told apart. *Primate* displays the muted affectations of the scientific machine becoming their own poetic-artistic expression. We can think here again of surrealism's attachment to the irrational, the fantastic, and the bizarre as lending a visual, aesthetic dimension to science. *Primate* can be seen, in the most polemical terms possible, as an extended exposition, not just of the banality (or rationality) of evil but of the *aesthetics of evil.*

I should like in closing to return to Simone Weil's notion of beauty entailing an apprehension of vulnerability with which this chapter began. At the end of the long dissection sequence, the two scientists examine the sections of the squirrel monkey's brain through a microscope and converse excitedly:

"Oh, here's a whole cluster of them. Here, look at this."
"Yeah. My gosh, that is beautiful"
"By golly, and see how localized. No fuzzing out . . . "

We can now more clearly conceive two different notions of beauty. In this sequence the beauty of science refers first and foremost to technical and technological prowess—the power to observe *beyond*—to take apart, scrutinize, disassemble, penetrate, quantify, and calculate—the integral objects of the world. This is the very same beauty that fired the mind of Dziga Vertov, Soviet cinema's avant-garde pioneer and inventor of the kino-eye, the rational enhancement of the human eye by cinematic technology, an early example of cyborg vision that hoped to fulfill the Communist dream. The vulnerability of living beings is for the rationalist a condition to overcome and an opportunity for the creative powers of thought. But it is at the very same time, as Foucault realized, an invitation to dominion and mastery. Only in these terms, which conflate beauty and power, could the sectioned brain of an animal be deemed beautiful.

No notion of beauty could differ more profoundly or more essentially from the kind of aesthetic appreciation Weil's work espouses, an appreciation whose proper object is not the fragmented and abstracted body but its opposite: the beauty inherent in the perilous integrity of living things. The first, scientific beauty, revels in taking apart and looking in; the second, vulnerable beauty, is a pained response to the ease with which living bodies may be taken apart. Both are commonly rooted in natural law—in the materiality and finitude of living bodies—but whereas Weil's notion of beauty is mournful, scientific beauty is morbid.[13]

In *Screening the Body* Lisa Cartwright explores the historically close alliance between science, cinematic technology and popular visual culture. Film was organically suited to the study of physiology, but its object lay beyond the mere understanding of motion: "The film body of the motion study . . . is a symptomatic site, a region invested with fantasies about what constituted 'life' for scientists and the lay public in the early twentieth century, and anxieties about whether the 'life' scientists studied in the laboratory was something that could be seen, imaged, and ultimately controlled (whether by prolonging it, as Lumière wished to do, or by having the authority to determine the moment of death)" (4). In *Primate* the medical gaze penetrates the body at the microscopic level in a bid to magnify, resolve, and finally "possess" the object of life. Visuality and aesthetics emerge as inseparable from both the microscopic apparatus and from what Cartwright describes as the "unmanageability of the object" (86) under inspection. "The unseen 'promicroscopic world,'" Cartwright explains, "exists only in part as a phantasm of the Western viewing subject. It exists more significantly as a subjugated institutional history, a history of the agency of the object of the gaze, the subjective being represented in the bodily fragment posed on the microscopic stage" (88). Anxiety and uncertainty over the elusive nature of the researchers' objects of study underlie *Primate*'s portrait of Yerkes.

The microscopic representation of the monkey's brain fragment in *Primate* is one example of Cartwright's Foucauldian reading of the "surveillant gaze" (13) of science. In designating the visual code of this and other images in both *Primate* and *Sang des bêtes* "scientific surrealism," I am suggesting a final twist to Foucault's famous dictum "knowledge is power/ power is knowledge." For, in Franju and Wiseman's films, power is no longer just knowledge; power is beauty. Virilio's "A Pitiless Art" sums up in blunt capitals the stakes of the overlap: "*Ethics or aesthetics?* That is indeed the question at the dawn of the new millennium. If freedom of SCIENTIFIC expression now actually has no more limits than freedom of ARTISTIC expression, where will *inhumanity* end in future?" (61).

Scientific surrealism's prurient gaze unites the experimentalism of science with the experimentalism of art in pursuit of a radical (if always resistant) object of vision. Scientific surrealism returns to

Benjamin's famous (and erroneous) singling out of fascism as a form of aestheticized politics. Today's onslaught of prescribed freedoms, of the market, of science, of industry and art, Virilio suggests, is hell-bent on producing an extreme biopolitics, whose evil eye yields a new kind of beauty.

6 Werner Herzog's Creaturely Poetics

The universe sees itself through our eyes.
—*Encounters at the End of the World*

Herzog and the Tragic

This chapter looks at Werner Herzog's relationship to the nonhuman—both nature and animals—with a view to revising (as well as bringing into sharper focus) certain accepted wisdoms about Herzog's representations and conception of humanness. By rethinking the ways in which "man" appears—and disappears—in Herzog's oeuvre, I wish to trace several artistic and intellectual trajectories that have thus far shaped the reception of his films. My argument is, first, that the recent cycle of nonfictions set in remote wildernesses cements Herzog's interest not just in landscape but in nature and, second, that Herzog's films in general communicate an ambiguity about the meaning and place of human beings vis-à-vis the natural and material order. The ambiguities pertaining to the human as well as those that underscore the central relationship in Herzog between nature and history reveal the importance of what I have been calling the creaturely.

Herzog's 2005 releases, *Grizzly Man* and *Wild Blue Yonder*, and 2007's *Encounters at the End of the World* by no means for the first time in Herzog's career, though far more explicitly, interrogate the place of the human in nature. These films overturn the conventions of the increasingly pervasive genres of the wildlife documentary and natural history film. That little has been written specifically about Herzog's understanding of nature and animals is due partly to the misconception that "Herzog has little regard for the natural world."[1] Not only does Herzog consistently regard the natural world, but exchanges between nature, the human, and the ultra- or supernatural may be said to be at the heart of his work. Two interrelated limits underlying Herzog's oeuvre and its reception concern me: the limits of (liberal) humanist discourse that commonly frames critical writing on Herzog and the limits of species—of the human itself—as the crepuscular zone in which so many of Herzog's protagonists dwell.

Herzog is not easily contained by a single tradition or school. In his introduction to the collection *The Films of Werner Herzog: Between Mirage and History*, Timothy Corrigan calls him a "romantic artist" ("Producing Herzog" 4), only to then describe him (as Herzog often describes himself) in the opposite terms as "medieval artisan" (5). In "Comprehending Appearances: Werner Herzog's Ironic Sublime," Alan Singer reads Herzog against the backdrop of German idealism and the Romantic sublime in order to rehistoricize him. Elsewhere Singer applied the Kantian notions of effort and "purposiveness" to the seemingly futile pursuits of the community in crisis in *Heart of Glass*.[2] More recently, Brad Prager's *The Cinema of Werner Herzog: Aesthetic Ecstasy and Truth* strikes a fine balance between Herzog's crypto-Romanticism and his anti-Romantic predilections. As discerning and diverse as these readings are, they move in the orbit of classical humanism. I wish to challenge some of the claims that these readings make as well as the broader assumptions they depend on. This chapter turns to Nietzsche, whose proximity to Herzog has not been widely discussed, yet who from the outset serves to redirect debates on Herzog's cinema away from the humanistic terrain of Romanticism toward the transhuman domain of the tragic.

Many if not all of Herzog's films confront one with limit situations (in subtle distinction from what Gertrude Koch in her important essay on Herzog's relationship to the aesthetic avant-garde has called "extreme situations" [Koch 76]), situations beyond which the human slowly erodes until it ceases to be intelligible. The human in Herzog is not so much rejected as caught in mid-unraveling, a process simultaneously heroic and self-destructive. In Herzog's nonfictions the human being is thrown into situations of harsh necessity. In the course of these ordeals, traditional human markers (reason, language, free will, and morality) gradually give way to the tragic and the creaturely.

The transition from human to creature is directly explored in Herzog's two "survival tales": *Little Dieter Needs to Fly* (1997) and *Wings of Hope* (1998), set against the humanist convention of survival as the triumph of will over necessity.[3] Herzog's creaturely repertoire extends to his cast of disabled or "damaged" humans: the sadistic dwarfs in *Even Dwarfs Started Small* (1970), the deaf-blind of *Land of Silence and Darkness* (1971), or Bruno S. as the *enfant sauvage* in *The Enigma of Kaspar Hauser* (1974). The creaturely plays a part in Herzog's nonfictions with a religious theme, *Bells from the Deep* (1993) and *Pilgrimage* (2001), which feature humans stooped and crawling on all fours like animals. The creaturely can even be extraterrestrial, as in Herzog's "natural history" films: the aliens in the opening of *Lessons of Darkness* (1992) or the narrator from planet Andromeda in *Wild Blue Yonder*.

Of Herzog's characters whose humanity is in some way contested, it is the slick brutality of Klaus Kinski that is most philosophically resonant, modeled as it seems to me with uncanny precision on Nietzsche's "beasts of prey" (*das Raubthier*) from *The Genealogy of Morals* (1887). The *Genealogy* is an anthropological fantasy on human evolution from its beginnings as amoral, joyous, and beastly to its subsequent domestication by a meek and degenerate priestly class. This later phase, culminating in Christianity, is marked for Nietzsche by asceticism and internalization, a repression of human animality, and the onset of "bad conscience." Read today, not only is the *Genealogy* a remarkably *cinematic* text, but, in keeping with Herzog's poetic license with regard to historical truths, also intensely speculative and fictional.

From *Aguirre, Wrath of God* (1972) to *Cobra Verde* (1987), Kinski may be said to embody that most notorious of the *Genealogy*'s prehistoric predators: the "blond beast" (*blond Bestie*). Daniel W. Conway explains that

> Nietzsche treats the "blond beast" as a particular expression or instance of what he more regularly calls a "beast of prey." Like the blond beast, the beast of prey is not so much an animal as it is a *biomorphism*, i.e., a human/hominid type described in terms pertaining more conventionally to non-human animal species. As such, the beast of prey designates any human (or proto-human) being who acts like a wild predator toward other human (or proto-human) beings. . . . It is well known that Nietzsche takes as his task the "translation" of the human being "back into nature" . . . . It is also well known that he attempts to accomplish this task by placing the human being on an organic continuum with all other animal species. He consequently locates the human being squarely within the amoral environs of the animal kingdom. (Conway 158)

Nietzsche's retranslation of man into nature is, however, far from a sentimentalist retort against the perversions of civilization. Nietzsche's nature should not be conceived as prelapsarian or romantic. Instead, Nietzsche sought to elaborate a new *cultural* relationship with nature. He wished to reclaim the material, nonhuman, and amoral phenomena of life by bringing them into the cultural fold. At the end of this reanimation and reanimalization of civilization, Nietzsche envisioned the being he called (though only once) the *übermensch*. Kinski's wild-eyed antiheroes (as well as his petulant off-screen persona) could be regarded as aspiring Nietzschean "overmen," trying (and failing) to mend the modern rift between man and nature, resituating the human within the material order, and rekindling the tragic sensibility that for Nietzsche—and I would argue also for Herzog—had once allowed human beings to cope with the random suffering of earthly life.

The association between Nietzsche and Herzog is an important one. Whereas Herzog is often mentioned in relation to Wagner and thus in the context of Romanticism, his proximity to Nietzsche (a passionate champion of Wagner who later denounced him precisely for his Romanticism) complicates the Romantic resonances in his films. I end the chapter with the affinities between Nietzsche and Herzog, most suggestive in Herzog's use of music not as soundtrack but in terms of the fundamental musicality of film. A Nietzschean (rather than Wagnerian) framework reveals Herzog as an essentially tragic-musical artist.

The creaturely as the point of encounter between human and animal underlies Herzog's *Grizzly Man*. This film, I will show, revisits Nietzschean territory by staging its own powerful reenactment of Greek tragedy. Timothy Treadwell, the film's ill-fated protagonist is himself an American (Whitmanian) version of the Germanic blond beast. I discuss this multilayered film in the fourth section of this chapter. But I begin with an exploration of the creaturely in a much earlier film, *Land of Silence and Darkness*.

Blank Gaze

In "Blindness as Insight: Visions of the Unseen in *Land of Silence and Darkness*," Gertrude Koch is critical of Herzog's formulation of the relationship between the human and the material. For Koch, the film's "move toward transfiguration, the affirmative celebration of alleged proximity to death, sheds light on Herzog's relationship to inner and outer nature. For him nature is a frontier: the mountain, the jungle, the desert, the river, the island, the volcano, the bare rocks, the by-nature-limited body of the disabled" (83). Yet the extreme situations that this Herzog film and others at first seem to celebrate are couched in a style Koch calls "paralyzed pathos": "the coldness in Herzog's films, this paralyzed pathos that contradicts its own longings for extreme experiences, keeps its nature (human) pictures from slipping into the idyllic lowlands of a *locus amoenus*, of a neo-romantic Biedermeier" (84). The tension between the conventionally Romantic pursuit of sublime experiences via extreme situations and even death and the quality of "blankness," "mutedness," or "asceticism" (Koch 78) that freezes and arrests Herzog's human figures not only makes the depiction and potential of humanness unsystematic but renders them ethically problematic: "in view of the tendency toward re-sacralization and affirmative transfiguration already apparent in *Land of Silence and Darkness*, and more so in his recent films, I, at any rate, find a reading of the film as an example of the humane representation of our fellow (human) beings unsatisfying and negligent of its aporias. The stylistic intent that subjugates human beings and situations to the role of material and not the aesthetic construction remains, at its core, pre-modern" (Koch 84). The distinction between premodern and Romantic sensibility corresponds to the division between the material and the aesthetic. Thus material nature, animals, or the corporeal are conceivable as boundaries and frontiers to be crossed, trespassed, or transcended at one's peril. Moreover, to depict a person "humanely" for Koch means to deliver them from the constraints of materiality, be they the "by-nature-limited body of the disabled" or the vast expanses of the South Pole. Koch rightly warns against dismissing the aporias in Herzog's depiction of humans. Yet her implicit understanding of what it means to be human is synonymous with a release from what modernity and liberal humanism deem inhuman: the mineral, vegetative, or animal life functions—the material limits to man's (if less so woman's) freedom. While Koch's observations on the inherent tensions in Herzog's work between a premodern materialism and a more modernist aestheticism are illuminating, I find problematic her assertion that the subjugations of the human to material necessity are ethically—rather than literally—"inhumane."

I wish to reassess the encounters between human (and aesthetic) freedom and material necessity in Herzog in the hope of addressing the aporias Koch highlights. The creaturely neither reduces nor simply restores man to nature. It signals Herzog's peculiar attentiveness to the material and the animal that pass through the human. The embeddedness of the human in the material order seems to me implicit in Herzog's cinematic treatments of human individuals in limit situations.

One device that powerfully expresses the creatureliness of Herzog's humans is the blank gaze, one of the moments of "paralyzed pathos" that most trouble Koch. The blank gaze—inscrutable and opaque—is one of Herzog's signature gestures.[4] He achieves this by momentarily disrupting narrative flow and fixing his subject in the gaze of the camera, usually in medium shot. The subject looks into the camera, but the gaze bypasses us without endorsing the communicability between spectator and subject. One can describe this gaze as "indifferent," a term Herzog often uses to describe nature.

In *The World Viewed* Stanley Cavell points out that the inscrutability of the cinema actor betrays "a tendency of film as such," an indication that all films are somehow about "unknowness" (181). Cavell writes of the *Passion of Saint Joan* (1928): "Dreyer's film above all declares at once the power of the camera to interrogate its subjects and, for all its capacity for pitilessness, its final impotence to penetrate the mystery of the individual human face" (181). But the point is not to affirm (or celebrate) the untold riches of the human soul, which the camera intimates without disclosing. Cavell explains that cinema tends "to discover at any moment the endless contingency of the individual human's placement in the world" (181). In Herzog contingency is present through the *mis*placement of persons in unexpected or "inappropriate" settings (the sites of plane crashes, colonized territories, jungles, deserts, the Alaskan wilderness, Antarctica, and even the back roads of America).

The blank gaze appears memorably in a couple of forms in *Land of Silence of Darkness*. Koch discusses a scene in which Herzog visits a mental hospital with the deaf-blind Else Fehrer (80–81). For Koch, the exchange of sightless gazes in this sequence forms a kind of blind montage. It tells of the so-called intensity of inner sight and the "private spiritualism behind the documentary material" (81). This quest is, finally, Herzog's own and it recasts the artist as "not at all a radical subjectivist, but a privileged interpreter" (81–82), a guide and prophet on the path to ecstatic, "higher truths." Koch's reading is subtle and powerful, but her double bind to an economics of the gaze and to a wider humanist aesthetic prevents her from recognizing in these scenes another possibility of art and of the artist.

It is the very blankness of the gazes of the deaf-blind that Koch sees as, as it were, hijacked by Herzog for his own ends. Koch draws here on Benjamin's concept of aura to explain Herzog's negative or, in Koch's terms, regressive "re-sacralization of the aesthetic sphere, the transformation of artist as prophet" (75). The problem lies in the almost unbearable vulnerability of these gazes that Herzog suggests can "see without seeing."

Yet if this is indeed Herzog's co-opting of the blind gaze as the gateway to some higher truth—the higher truth of the artist—I do not recognize in these captured looks a contrived "transfiguration of mortal fear into existential experience of human existence" (Koch 82). In their blankness, these looks seem to lead precisely away from the sphere of sharable human experience. Herzog's crude portrayals of the "bodily stigmatized: dwarfs, the deaf-blind, and the retarded" (75–76) creates a space in which art brushes against the limits of human subjectivity and form.

This is undoubtedly an uncomfortable space, since it reappraises art's attachment to ideas of humanity and inhumanity. In this context it is perfectly telling that Koch, along with Herzog's other commentators, questions the use of the "bodily stigmatized" dwarfs in *Even Dwarfs Started Small* while remaining oblivious to the film's systematic violence against animals whose very visibility (and subjectivity) is canceled out by the same gesture of bodily stigmatizing that Koch reviles.

Koch's critique, in other words, relies on the familiar definition of humanness, which Herzog's portrayals of those whose humanity is somehow at stake inevitably complicate. The question of how we might relate to the severely disabled deaf-blind (and apparently "retarded") youth Vladimir in *Land of Silence and Darkness* is not raised by Koch. And yet those who encounter Vladimir in the film tiptoe nervously around the question of species. Vladimir's humanity, from a Cartesian perspective, remains undetermined. The question arising from the long sequence in which the camera films Vladimir's repetitive gestures and facial ticks (during what may or may not be his playing with a radio set) is whether it is Vladimir's *humanity* that needs ascertaining as a precondition for his visibility and personhood.

Blank gazes recur in *Little Dieter Needs to Fly*, *Wings of Hope*, *Grizzly Man*, and *Wild Blue Yonder*. The camera's capturing of arrested, sightless looks frustrates the humanist mantra that eyes are windows to the soul. The blank gaze in Herzog's films is opaque and inaccessible. It opens up within the human the zones of passivity and stillness associated with inert matter. The arrest may be momentary, but its effect is enduring: interrupting the flow of subjectivity and agency, which in turn also unsettles spectators' relation to the characters.

What is at stake in the flashing of the inanimate within the animate? If Herzog's still lives that halt the "animatedness" of narrative trouble us, this is because they disclose the strange pull of gravity (stillness and inertia) that haunts the human from within.[5] As the camera captures and holds Juliane, Dieter, or the deaf-blind who stare at us without seeing, it is their humanity itself that is suspended. Humanness becomes unfamiliar because it is no longer (literally) motioning or motivated, transparent and readable. These frozen moments in Herzog are, as Koch suggested, dehumanizing. But they also (positively) awaken viewers to human uncanniness and raise the question of the visual hermeneutics that produces the human in cinematic narrative.

Humanity and personhood in film are partly constituted via the economy of returned looks between subject and object, self and other. The sealed-off gaze, the gaze that *refuses to see us* (as in the case of the beggars in *Palms*) duly becomes the symptom of a jettisoned or absent interiority. An oddly narcissistic (quietly ruthless) economics of the gaze underpins the humanist regime of visibility: if the other does not look at me, personhood and kinship are withheld. One must not mistake the need to *be seen* by another for reciprocity. The demand (to rephrase Mulvey) "to-be-looked-back-at" belongs to the network of visual commerce by which the self replenishes its powers through another's look. A range of cultural, political, and ethical critiques—from feminism to postcolonialism and human rights as well as a significant body of film theory—take shape around this narcissistic economics of looking instead of revaluating the fundamental conditions of vision. In opposition to the humanist demand that the other look back at me as the condition for her claim to recognition and power, ethics perhaps begins with the blank gaze. For what is ethics if not my seeing without being seen—my unrequited attention?

One need distinguish here between voyeurism, as developed by feminist film theorists like Laura Mulvey and E. A. Kaplan, and what Weil called attention. What might it mean to speak about *cinematic attention*? Attention differs from the voyeuristic stipulation of looks. The attentive gaze cannot help being "innocent" to the extent that it sees while remaining unattached to (uninvested in) its object. Attentiveness is a mode of looking in the absence of reciprocity and recognition.[6] And so it is precisely outside the leveling symmetries of visual exchange that it becomes possible to speak of ethics. Attentiveness relieves the other of the tyranny of looking back and thus moves beyond the power play of subjectivity and personhood as the threshold of morality and representation.[7] More important, the absent gaze can sharpen other sensibilities that do not rely on the leveling of looks. This allows one to think of the nonhuman world as communicative. In Benjamin, for instance, the nonhuman world communicates without looking back, just as the human can sometimes give way to sightlessness and muteness and still speak.[8]

Another scene in *Land of Silence and Darkness* that troubles Koch is worth mentioning in this context. Again Koch returns to the question of the human:

> a deaf-blind farmer's son walks away from the conversation between the three women and into the garden where he tenderly embraces and touches a tree, as if it were human.
>
> The dimension of showing human bodies in front of and for the camera, bodies that in and of themselves are a piece of blind and deaf nature, and never letting this corporeality tend toward sensuality in the mise-en-scène, but only toward spiritualization, indicates that in Herzog's aesthetic cosmos nature itself has become the foil of the *deus absconditus*—its substance is coldness and absence. (83–84)

Just before this sequence, we learn that the farmer's son had for years shunned human company, preferring the company of cows. This is but one of several references to animals throughout the film: in the second sequence, the main protagonist Fini Straubinger and another deaf-blind woman tell of animals they know, and later on Fini's group visits a zoo (where they are shown handling a playful chimpanzee). In their sensory deprivation, the deaf-blind find themselves in a different relationship with the nonhuman world. As the film progresses, the parameters of humanness (rooted in vision and speech) are stretched to the limit, inviting the question of what forms of (human) life exist beyond seeing/looking and hearing/speaking. Herzog's "body pictures" (Koch 83) of the deaf-blind do indeed assert the harshness of blind nature, doubling as God's absence. Yet our recognition of the human subjugation to this blindness and absence can at the same time generate appreciation of the vulnerability of living bodies.

In his reading of Kafka and Leskov in "The Storyteller," Walter Benjamin attempts to articulate an ethics of storytelling to reengage the self-enclosed domain of art with the natural world. This engagement is crucially also a connection between the interiority of human experience and expression and the opaque, silent exteriority of nature. I have already suggested that this engagement rests on a two-way attentiveness, toward the innhuman within and without. If Herzog's extreme situations are also limit cases of humanity, they deliver art beyond the constrictions of a modernist-humanist aesthetic, face to face with the creaturely.

For Agamben, Benjamin evokes "an entirely different image of the relationship between man and nature and between nature and history" (The Open 81). Nature, Benjamin argued, need not be illuminated or mastered. Thought, language, and representation must not serve a redemptive economy that ascribes meaning to nature and forces open its secrets in pursuit of some lost paradise. Nature is neither the place of archaic harmony nor the destination of man's total management of life. Benjamin rejected both misconceptions as two sides of the same coin. Instead he envisioned a radically revalued relationship between man and nature, so that, "neither must man master nature nor nature man. Nor must both be surpassed in a third term that would represent their dialectical synthesis. Rather, according to the Benjaminian model of a *dialectic at a standstill*,' what is decisive here is only the 'between,' the interval or, we might say, the play between the two terms, their immediate constellation in a non-coincidence" (*The Open* 83; my emphasis). Benjamin conceived of a halted and nocturnal relationship between humanity and nature, which he called the "saved night": "a nature that awaits no day, and thus no Judgment Day... a nature that is neither the theater of history nor the dwelling place of man. The saved night" (Benjamin qtd. in *The Open* 81).

I am suggesting that Herzog's use of the blank gaze, which traps the human within material nature, does not point upward to the intensely spiritualized domain Koch rejects but rather to Benjamin's indeterminate space between nature and the human, which Agamben calls "the open." In these frozen moments, the human is stopped in its tracks, interrupting the dialectic which in its hopeless bid against nature continues to pointlessly and painfully fabricate the human. The frozen intervals "gather creatural life not in order to reveal it, nor to open it to human language, but rather to give it back to its closedness and muteness" (*The Open* 81). The saved night to which Herzog's human figures are momentarily transported is a space of resignation where identity is suspended. This creaturely space signifies a kind of *sentient neutrality*. Benjamin's saved night locates salvation outside revelation: salvation as acceptance of the impossibility of salvation, an acceptance of nocturnal unknowability as the absence of mystery. In Herzog's parlance this is simply nature's "indifference," not a negative limit but "saved night."

In the edicts of physical necessity Koch rightly recognizes the absence of God. The radical absence of the divine from the world—Koch's invocation of Luther's *deus absconditus*—and the helpless creatureliness of a humanity thus abandoned led Simone Weil to state that "there is every degree of distance between the creature and God" (GG 79). This infinite distance between God and creation is the organizing principle of two of Herzog's religious nonfictions, *Pilgrimage* and *Bells from the Deep*.

Quadrupeds

> Wherever it is certain that something indispensable for salvation is
> impossible, it is certain that there really exists a supernatural possibility.
> —Simone Weil, "Theory of the Sacraments"

In her "Spiritual Autobiography" Weil writes about one of "three contacts with Catholicism that really counted" (25), experiences that led to her (unofficial) conversion to Christianity: "It was the evening and there was a full moon over the sea. The wives of the fishermen were, in procession, making a tour of all the ships, carrying candles and singing what must certainly be very ancient hymns of a heart-rending sadness. Nothing can give any idea of it. . . . There the conviction was suddenly borne in upon me that Christianity is pre-eminently the religion of slaves, that slaves cannot help belonging to it, and I among others" (26). In her realization that Christianity was essentially a slave religion, Weil keeps company with Nietzsche, that other great diagnostician of human servitude. In contrast to Nietzsche, however, Weil embraces the state she calls slavery. This negative gesture profoundly marks Weil's theological reflections. Her idiosyncratic take on Christianity also helps to shed light on Herzog's cinematic depictions of faith.

The poor women Weil witnessed singing hymns recall the wretched vocals in *Pilgrimage*, Herzog's film of a religious procession, whose looped choral score (composed by John Tavener) is of a similar "heart-rending sadness." In the course of observing what is most unique to humans—their spirituality—the humans of *Pilgrimage* are depicted as creatures, proceeding on their knees along an apparently endless path. There is no Jerusalem and no Mecca, something that turns the linear-eschatological rationale on its head. The viewer's desire for resolution (revelation) gives way to movement and music and the agony and ecstasy on the pilgrims' faces.

The pilgrims move as if entranced, involuntarily committed to their dogged procession. The movement is "encased" by the music. Prager writes that *Pilgrimage* "represented another opportunity for Herzog to experiment with eliminating the boundary between music and cinema" (Prager 127). Music does not work to individuate particular pilgrims or "color" particular moments. It calls forth the Nietzschean "spirit of music"—life's undifferentiated flow in which human beings are engulfed.

Herzog's gaze in *Pilgrimage* is not Orientalist or exotic. The film eschews those colonial gestures of visualization and framing that allow for a gratifying construction of otherness. Dehumanization here is not a descent from humanity into otherness but a creaturely ecstasy. If humanity defines itself through ideas of autonomy and freedom, the pilgrims proceeding as if under a spell and beyond self-possession shows humanity as miraculously automated.

In addition to repetition and automation, the suffering and effort captured by the camera reinforce the sense of God's absence. God is present solely as abandonment and forsaking (*deus absconditus*). The pilgrims are creatures of the earth whose spiritual longing is expressed through their pained and exasperated bodies. God's absence from the world (and from this film world) ironically engenders devotion. While in one sense *about* spirituality, then, *Pilgrimage* is spiritually void. It is wrong, therefore, to read *Pilgrimage* as either celebrating or as mocking religion. The film suspends as irrelevant the question of Herzog's position on faith. As in the films of Tarkovsky, transcendence is paradoxically pictured as embodiment and a descending, downward movement. Transcendence is not "up there" but "down here" and Tarkovsky's characters at their most spiritual are frequently shown face down on the ground. Weil's epiphany of Christianity's slavishness realizes that "'Whosoever humbleth himself shall be exalted.' The upward movement in us is vain (and less than vain) if it does not come from a downward movement" (GG 93).

Herzog's earlier *Bells from the Deep: Faith and Superstition in Russia* takes a different look at religious instincts and the relation between humanity, nature, and the supernatural. The film engages the tensions inherent in Russian orthodoxy between monotheism and pantheism against the backdrop of collapsed Soviet rationalism. *Bells from the Deep* alludes to a tradition of films situated at the point of encounter between a totalizing Soviet project and the regional outposts resistant to its centralizing pressures. Among them one can count Mikhail Kalatozov's *Salt for Svaneti* (1930) and *Farewell* (1983; directed by Elem Klimov who took over the film after the death of his wife Larissa Shepitko on the first day of the shoot). A more recent example is Ilya Khrzhanovsky's dazzling post-Soviet fantasy *4* (*Chetyre*; 2005).

In *Farewell* a matriarchal community confronts the catastrophically misguided Soviet flooding project. The film depicts the days before the forced eviction of a Siberian village on the eve of its flooding. It contrasts urban progressivism with the villagers' rural attachment to their natural environment: to a tree that refuses to be cut down and to the rich muddy soil. Nature appears as a darkly enchanted dwelling place, not as a resource to plunder and tame. Yet one should also distinguish between the old women's witchy command over nature (their deeply lined faces are part of the natural topography of the film), and the protectionist impetus of much contemporary ecology. *Farewell*'s women are not stewards of but rather dwellers on the earth. Mainstream environmentalism sees nature as a resource irresponsibly tapped by a commercially driven civilization. In a different though no less humanistic vein, "new age" philosophy thinks nature as a redemptive prehuman Eden. Both these conceptions of nature are foreign to *Farewell*, which invokes the corporeal embeddedness of humans in their nonhuman surroundings.

Several memorable images in *Bells from the Deep* establish a similar creaturely embeddedness. In one (entirely staged) scene, human figures stretch out on a frozen lake and crawl about on their stomachs. They too are on a kind of pilgrimage, in search of the mythical lost city of Kitezh beneath the lake. In another part of the film, shot during the summer, an old man kneels down by the lake's edge, gently dipping his hand in the water, awaiting revelation. Later, an old peasant woman crawls on all fours into the woods to the site of a burnt shrub with magical qualities. Ancient pantheism clashes with the new boom in "healers" and miracle workers. An imploded Soviet ideology meets American prosthetic spiritualism with its mass revivals and televangelists.

Pilgrimage and *Bells from the Deep* "document" the continuum between the body and supernatural ecstasy. Herzog's understanding of religion (in this wider sense) recognizes spirituality itself as emanating from and extending to the material conditions of existence. But the path from human to creature, that unraveling of the human explored in chapter 1, is perhaps most striking in Herzog's twin tales of human survival.

Docile Matter

> In affliction the vital instinct survives all the attachments which have been torn away, and blindly fastens itself to everything which can provide it with support, like a plant fastens its tendrils. . . . Affliction, from this point of view, is hideous as life in its nakedness always is, like an amputated stump, like the swarming of insects. Life without form. Survival is then the only attachment. That is where extreme affliction begins—when all other attachments are replaced by that of survival. Attachment appears then in its nakedness without any other object but itself—Hell.
>
> —Simone Weil, *Gravity and Grace*

Little Dieter Needs to Fly and *Wings of Hope*—two nonfictional accounts of a plane crash and its incredible aftermath—sit uneasily within the genre of the survival story. Survival has in recent decades become a powerful cultural tag whose force lies in speaking the unspeakable, communicating from within the depths of trauma. Survival serves to rehumanize those occurrences whose sheer incomprehensibility and horror render them "beastly": war, (sexual) abuse, terminal illness. Survival is therefore always mental and moral as well as physical. The clichés of the "triumph of the human spirit" raise survival beyond biology and chance and give it meaning.

In Herzog's two films, however, survival returns to being, so to speak, a matter of matter: the quiet endurance of organic stuff. The films' protagonists, Juliane Köpcke and Dieter Dengler, speak of their miraculous survival in terms that belie the trusted formulae of survival stories. Neither regards their ordeal as heroic or edifying. Each speaks of the gradual undoing of their humanity and their becoming something other—not animals even, but things. Survival is impersonal and passive. It is only as aftereffect that personality sometimes recovers.

In "The Love of God and Affliction," discussed at some length in the first chapter, Weil likens the subjugation of the human to material necessity to "a stone that falls" ("Love of God" 75), Weil's determinism is not, however, purely materialist, but religious. She proceeds to translate the passivity of creatures and things into Godly "obedience." From a supernatural perspective, she says, "what seemed to be necessity becomes obedience" (76). The passages in which Weil discusses the docility of matter as a model for the human are nothing short of striking: "Matter is entirely passive and in consequence entirely obedient to God's will. It is a perfect model for us. . . . On account of its perfect obedience, matter deserves to be loved by those who love its Master, in the same way as a needle, handled by the beloved wife he has lost, is cherished by a lover. . . . In the beauty of the world brute necessity becomes an object of love. What is more beautiful than the action of gravity on the fugitive folds of the sea waves, or on the almost eternal folds of the mountains? . . . All the horrors produced in this world are like the folds imposed upon the waves by gravity" (76).[9]

After Dieter's escape from the prison camp and the death of his friend, he is left making his way blindly in the jungle. Gradually, Dieter's consciousness begins to dissolve. Beyond hope and dejection he becomes a creature without volition, abandoned to the laws of physical striving. Dieter claims he neither feared nor desired death. A state of barely sentient indifference engulfed him. For several days he noticed (without alarm) a bear that was tracking him. At this stage *Little Dieter Needs to Fly* assumes the air of myth so common in Herzog. The bear's mythical presence, however, does not work allegorically (ascribing symbolic meaning to the animal). Myth emerges instead from the materiality of both predator and prey. Not fearing death, Dieter miraculously befriends it: "at this stage, death became my only friend." Dieter's friendship with death in the shape of the bear is profoundly ambiguous of course. *Little Dieter*'s first-person testimony does not wholly free itself from the masculine heroics of the survival genre. Friendship with a bear—and perhaps also with death—returns in a more difficult form in Herzog's *Grizzly Man*.

A Diary for Timothy: Nature, Indifference, and Love

The friendly and flowing savage, who is he?

Is he waiting for civilization, or past it and mastering it?

—Walt Whitman, "Song of Myself"

As with ethnography before it, so today the nature film both charts and carries through the ultimate receding of nature. The wildlife film is fast becoming nature's final resting place, a repository of natural simulations that compactly ensconces all that has been bracketed off as nonhuman. The less of nature remains, the more its images cram our screens. Nature films (like so many contemporary zoos) now boast a conservationist ethos that mystifies their colonial impetus. In *Grizzly Man* Herzog radically revises the conventions of wildlife cinema. How does the film redress not only the conventions of the wildlife documentary but also those governing ideas about human-animal relations?

It may seem odd to arrive at a discussion of *Grizzly Man* by way of Michael Haneke's *Hidden* (*Caché*; 2005). The association is only partly fortuitous. Released in the UK in close proximity, both were reviewed side by side in the national press and in more specialist publications such as *Sight and Sound*.[10] While both films won critical acclaim, the furor of rave reviews occasioned by *Hidden* alone warrants comment. As critics stumbled hyperbolically about, armed with superlatives for *Hidden*, *Grizzly Man*, in an altogether more dignified fashion, was described as the tale of a man who mistook a bear for a friend.

Each film in its own way was commended for its disavowal of sentimentalism. That the reception of each was fairly uniform, that both issued a "standard reading," may at first seem surprising for films whose narrative structures and devices are blatantly noncommercial. *Hidden* confirmed the bourgeoisie's penchant for self-rebuke; it is a film that lubricates rather than cuts through *les bobos'* sentimental view of themselves. *Hidden*'s savvy reads as little more than the sentimentalized expression of middlebrow narcissism. In Herzog's case, critics enjoyed a self-congratulating sobriety: seeing through the misguided anthropomorphism that led to Timothy Treadwell's untimely death.

What connects *Hidden* and *Grizzly Man*, at least in terms of their critical reception is, then, their power to pierce through life's cozy facades and reveal the violence and terror that lie beneath.

Significantly, both films locate the animal at the point blank of authenticity: the animal marks a boundary as conceptual as it is cinematic, beyond which is glimpsed the blind mechanics of nonhuman life. Two parallel scenes in Haneke's film contrast a simulated, digital human world with the analogue reality of the animal: a lengthy sequence of the actual decapitation of a rooster, followed by the headless animal's involuntary throes, is later complemented by a man slitting his throat. The analogy seems to me deplorably crude, but more telling still is that Haneke's on-screen butchery unwittingly comments on *Hidden*'s own lack of authenticity, resorting to snuff to imbue the film with something "real."[11] This is not the first time that Haneke's examination of violence succumbs to the cinematics of slaughter in a manner that mimics the very tactics he is supposedly critiquing (e.g., 1992's *Benny's Video*). Each time the killing of an animal—carried out by a child in both *Benny's Video* and *Hidden*—is construed as a symbolic foreshadowing of the violence that threatens humans. While Haneke is worlds away from filming nature, the veritable trend in art-house productions to include the real slaughter of animals seems to me closely aligned to the remarkable flourishing, in quite other quarters, of the wildlife film. Each in its own way, then, *Hidden* and *Grizzly Man* are products of a nature-/animal-obsessed zeitgeist.[12]

I have argued that fear of sentimentalism drives the oversimplified readings of both *Hidden* and *Grizzly Man*. Oliver Burkeman of the *Guardian* sums up the standard reading of *Grizzly Man* and the position of its director: "Treadwell's fatal error, Herzog makes clear, was to believe in a Disneyfied version of nature: for all his talk of being killed, he saw the bears as fundamentally cute" (Burkeman 6). Certainly, *Grizzly Man* partly invites reading as a cautionary tale about the price of naïveté (Treadwell, after all, took his favorite teddy bear with him on his Alaskan expeditions). But there is much more in the film to complicate such a straightforward reading. A medley of cinematic materials (Treadwell's own footage, Herzog's interviews with Treadwell's family, friends, and lovers, and television excerpts of Treadwell on the Letterman show or in schools he lectured at for free), *Grizzly Man* is a complex and multilayered text. Its complexity challenges not only several of the film's testimonies that depict Treadwell as "goofy" and gooey eyed, but also Herzog's declarations about the essential hostility of nature.

The testimony of Sam Egli, the helicopter pilot who flew out to the scene of the attack, is indicative in this respect. With his back to the helicopter hanger, Egli gives his interpretation of the "Treadwell tragedy": "Treadwell was, I think, meaning well, trying to do things to help the resource of the bears but, to me, he was acting like a, like he was working with people wearing bear costumes out there instead of wild animals. Those bears are big and ferocious and they come equipped to kill you and eat you, and that's what he was asking for; he got what he deserved, in my opinion. The tragedy of it was taking the girl with him. I think the only reason that Treadwell lasted as long in the game as he did was that the bears probably thought there was something wrong with him, like he was mentally retarded or something." Over the first part of Egli's testimony, Herzog cuts to a still image of the culprit bear's disemboweled corpse, which Egli says "was full of people." This is the film's only image intimating Treadwell and his girlfriend Amie Huguenard's violent fate. The still can be read as the mark of retribution. Once the bodies were discovered, the bear (known only as "bear 141") was shot—executed—in an act of just revenge. In this bizarre meting out of interspecies justice, the "crime" committed is none other than the bear's natural omnivorousness. Bear diet notwithstanding, the hunters treat Treadwell's killing as somehow malignant and intentional. The conflicting reactions to Treadwell's death illustrate just how difficult it is to negotiate the seemingly clear-cut human/animal divide.

Egli's use of phrases like "the resource of the bears" sees the animals as an environmental asset, not as individuals. This starkly contrasts with his subsequent anthropomorphizing of the bears by attributing to them not only the ability to recognize humans but to comprehend (and respond to) human eccentricity. Certainly, Egli is projecting his own view of Treadwell as "mentally retarded" onto the bears. But his sense that the bears "can tell" ironically corroborates Treadwell's contention that he has found a way of living with, or alongside, these wild animals. Egli and the hunters are not the only ones who, while objecting to Treadwell's humanizing the bears, repeat his anthropomorphic gestures. Such inconsistencies run through the film's various testimonies and illustrate the false logic of anthropomorphism to sidestep the overlaps between human and animal life.

Herzog's spoken commentary, while sparse, ostensibly supports the view that Treadwell was misguided in his understanding of nature. Toward the end of the film Herzog spells out the conventional wisdom: "What haunts me is that in all the faces of all the bears that Treadwell ever filmed, I discovered no kinship, no understanding, no mercy. I see only the overwhelming indifference of nature. To me there is no such thing as a secret world of the bears, and this blank stare speaks only of a half bored interest in food. But for Timothy Treadwell this bear was a friend, a saviour." While Herzog says he has "set out to defend Timothy as a filmmaker," he does not share Treadwell's view of nature. "To me," Herzog proclaims, "nature is a place of violence, hostility, and murder." This rehearses Herzog's long-held view of nature in *Burden of Dreams* (1982), and in *My Best Fiend* (1999), in which Herzog mocks Kinski's view of the jungle as "erotic" by calling it "obscene." He speaks of the jungle as a place of constant struggle and death, terms that reverse Kinski's vulgar romanticism.[13] One might ask, however, whether nature's murderousness is not replicated in the murderousness of civilization and wonder (as Nietzsche had done) what is at stake in maintaining such an absolute division between nature and civilization.

And what of the "blank stare" and the "overwhelming indifference of nature" that Herzog sees in Treadwell's footage? As I have already suggested, blankness and indifference are recurring Herzogian motifs. The frozen portraits that arrest the character-viewer relation and deny mutuality belong also to Herzog's human protagonists.

Nor is the blank gaze more generally the property of strictly nonhuman environments. Alongside wild nature, the city is a prime location for this sort of blank looking. What do we find in the eyes of strangers as they momentarily meet our own in a crowded street? Can we really see something there beyond a blind, half-bored indifference? As humans we invest the gaze of our fellows with reciprocity and response, but the investment entails—always—a desire and a leap of faith, in other words, love. This gesture, by which humans presume in others a communicable interiority, is precisely anthropomorphic. As argued previously in the chapter on Marie Darrieussecq, humans make other animals "like us" only *after* making ourselves "like us."

This plea for reciprocity returns to the issue examined under the "economics of the gaze." In liberal humanist thought, ethics rests on the relationship of exchanged looks. The other gains entry into the moral fold by returning a look. This is a dynamic of power that yields to the power of looking (back). It is at bottom, I claimed, a narcissistic ethic that requires I be looked at, acknowledged by another who will then be deemed a "subject." The work of Weil and Benjamin (and I should add also Lévinas), used here to track a different trajectory of relations, suggests, conversely, that ethics takes place in the absence of the mutuality of looking. This logic of separation between subject and object locates compassion in the one who looks, precisely in the absence of a returned gaze, reminding us that ethics, not justice, is blind.

Perhaps ironically, *Grizzly Man* practices the very sort of one-way looking that acknowledges the other in his absence. Treadwell's absence eerily reverberates throughout *Grizzly Man*, which makes the film part chilling testimony, part moving tribute. On Lippit's own terms, moreover, it is Treadwell's ghostly presence—his inability to really die—that animates the film. Why should cinema as magnificent ghost train be restricted to the animal? The catacomblike nature of cinematic technology (in which animals are and are not dead) reveals human animality itself as incapable of death.

Having described some of the tensions that run through the body of *Grizzly Man* and undermine its standard reading, I now turn to the question of Treadwell's (and Herzog's) revision of the wildlife documentary form. The revision again concerns the stubborn tropes of sentimentalism and anthropomorphism. It leads back to where this chapter began: Herzog's tragic sensibility and Treadwell as a Nietzschean tragic hero.

When *Sight and Sound*'s editor Nick James points out the similarities between the real-life Treadwell and the fictional Ann Darrow (Naomi Watts) in Peter Jackson's 2005 *King Kong*, he bemoans Darrow's offloading of human characteristics onto wild animals. Saved rather than devoured by the oversized primate, Darrow "teaches Kong to communicate the concept of beauty. This fantastic and sentimental approach to ferocious wild beasts is one that the fictional Darrow shares with Timothy Treadwell" (James 22). Having compared the nonfictional (male) Treadwell to the fictional (female) Darrow, James goes on to say that "Treadwell is an unusual protagonist for a Herzog film: he has a high, squeaky voice, a mildly effeminate manner and a stridently sentimental impulse towards animals" (24). In the appeal to (virile) "objective observation," possible connections between the human and animal worlds are rejected. The zeal of separating "us" from "them" avoids what a film like *King Kong* precisely asks us to take seriously: the possibility that Kong *does* genuinely respond to Darrow, that a relationship *is* formed between them, that, while nonverbal, involves mutual recognition and, dare we say it, love.

A similar uneasiness greeted another 2005 release, Judy Irving's *The Wild Parrots of Telegraph Hill*. Irving follows the relationship between the long-haired unemployed San Francisco musician Mark Bittner and a flock of Cherry-headed Conures. Like Treadwell, Bittner is an outsider and, like Treadwell, Bittner maintains that he has forged a personal friendship with the wild birds. Repeating the anthropomorphic caveat, Edward Lawrenson warns that "*Wild Parrots* will be a stretch for those unpersuaded by Bittner's arguments. Irving's watchful camera style captures the birds displaying high and complex levels of sociability, but to read in their behaviour expressions of friendship and love is a leap of faith. . . . Are such sequences [which "encourage us to invest the birds with a personality"] genuinely revealing or just a consequence of suggestive editing?" (Lawrenson 83). As just argued, the very same "suggestive editing" takes (and must take) place in all human interactions that presuppose access to another's interiority. In human communication, language serves as a leveler, bridging an abyss of inaccessibility under the guise of transparency. We are reminded of these leaps of faith, however, when communication breaks down: when our assumptions about others and their intentions have proved imaginary.

Lawrenson goes on to say that "an instinctive comparison can be made with Werner Herzog's . . . *Grizzly Man*" (83), then reiterates the standard reading: "Whereas Treadwell saw in his footage of these bears a sense of harmony and purity, Herzog uses it to ruminate on the cold predatory instinct in nature" (83). This reading indicates that sentimentalism (another word for anthropomorphism) has become a pervasive cliché in sober rejections of certain ways of representing animals, especially by those who say they love them.

But just how sentimental is Treadwell's view of nature? Contrary to most commentaries, in his self-shot footage Treadwell rarely portrays nature as harmonious. Indeed, he often speaks of the possibility of his own violent death in rather gruesome terms. Sentimentalism is thus less a matter of what Treadwell says than of the manner in which he says it. His baby talk and gushy outbursts are signs of uncontained emotion, evidence of the rage he feels (rightly or not) at the predicament of the bears. His "cute" bear names (like Mr. Chocolate) are, of course, grotesque, but they show that for Treadwell (as for Bittner) these animals are individuals, not merely a species. Moreover, it seems to me that critics confuse the different concepts of sentimentalism and love. For a deep love of animals (dangerous, all-engrossing, and just a little mad) is indeed at the heart of Treadwell's footage.

Treadwell's language, his childlike mannerisms, his insistence on individuating the bears, and the emotional pitch of his experiences with animals sharply contrasts with the park authorities' rational, scientific approach. One park official interviewed by Herzog refers to the acceptable amount of bear "harvesting" that would not be detrimental to "maintaining a healthy population." Conservationist lingo employs the notions of "culling" and "harvesting" as biopolitical euphemisms for the authorized killing of animals to suit a range of human purposes. But it is important to recognize that here are two competing species of rhetoric—each with its own displacements, its own concealments.

Treadwell's project, then, flies in the face of mainstream conservationism, environmentalism, and philosophy. His petitioning on behalf of the bears is not concerned with nor contained by the notion of rights. In this, Treadwell (perhaps surprisingly) resembles Coetzee's Elizabeth Costello. His actions and reactions are a visceral response to the difficulty of reality, not the difficulty of philosophy. His relationship to the animals is at once concrete (like Costello, Treadwell lectures on the subject of animals) and, as one interviewee puts it "religious," that is, based on love. Treadwell's activism discards the "love disclaimer" of animal scholarship (from Peter Singer to Cary Wolfe) that takes liking animals out of the ethical equation.[14]

I want to suggest that Treadwell's *amour fou*—especially in the absence of the sort of reciprocity we associate (and demand from) domestic animals or pets—is potentially subversive. Besides being gendered (Treadwell is routinely feminized), the sound-minded rejection of sentimentalism by Treadwell's critics is also, and more subtly, a matter of a deep-seated cultural hostility toward childhood and adolescence. Treadwell's childishness is embarrassing, out of time and place, mainly because in its uninhibited and passionate way it questions the very foundations of the "mature" systems that sanction human dominion.[15] Treadwell, Herzog tells us, had a natural affinity with children. The cultural dismissal of his childlike ways (like the common rebuke of adolescence, in defense of which Susan Sontag so eloquently wrote in her foreword to Witold Gombrowicz's ode to immaturity, *Ferdydurke*) undermines the well-documented kinship between children and animals.[16] At this point, the novelty of Treadwell's cinematic project, which so fascinates Herzog, comes into view. "There are similarities between Herzog and Treadwell" writes Prager, "the real overlap between the two has to do with their affinities as filmmakers" (89). In its layered entirety, *Grizzly Man* is based not on the principles of cool observation but on the messy asymmetries of love. Like Herzog, Treadwell rejects scientific or documentary *vérité* in favor of an immersive and physical experience of the filmed material.

Herzog's heroes (or hero-losers) act outside the confines of adult rationalism, which often means they find themselves at odds with the civilized (and civic) orders. At the height of their powers, they are strangely hypnotic. But in their downfall they become a public embarrassment, court jesters, shunned or mocked. Is not Treadwell a typical Herzog character after all? Treadwell is explicitly and implicitly connected to other Herzog protagonists, not least to the blond beast himself—Klaus Kinski. It is not far-fetched to see Kinski too, in a pathologically feminine light, as a hysterical figure. Commenting on Treadwell's foul-mouthed tirade against the park authorities, Herzog says: "I have seen this kind of outburst before on a film set." Though he does not mention Kinski by name, the reference is as clear as the physical resemblance between Kinski and Treadwell. Like Kinski, Treadwell's going wild partly escapes and partly pursues his own private demons.

Herzog's fascination with Treadwell is both personal and cinematic. Like Herzog, Treadwell is a self-made character. Treadwell too had changed his name, and, like Herzog, Treadwell's filmmaking in the raw signals a shift from documentary "fact" to "truth," bringing the physicalities of the world and the mechanics of the cinema together in new and startling ways.[17] Treadwell's affectations—his squeaky voice, tantrums, vulnerability, and candor—make him an unlikely spokesman for the animal cause. It is easy to pathologize Treadwell and leave it at that, and it is one of *Grizzly Man*'s virtues to, on the whole, avoid this. While frank about Treadwell's troubled past (as he himself is in his confessional video diaries), *Grizzly Man* allows Treadwell to speak beyond mere caricature.

As with Nietzsche's "philosophizing with a hammer," *tonality* is everything. Treadwell's manner—what Nietzsche called style— refuses the measured tenors of rationality and objectivity. Treadwell's carefully crafted, consciously displayed style (he had originally wanted to be a Hollywood actor) is not just a collection of behavioral "ticks." In his book *The Gay Science* Nietzsche explains the importance of personal style: "*One thing is needful.*—to 'give style' to one's character—a great and rare art! It is practiced by those who survey all the strength and weaknesses of their nature and then fit them into an artistic plan until every one of them appears as art and reason and even weaknesses delight the eye" (232). As Michael Tanner explains in his introduction to Nietzsche, "style" is "to be able to organize the 'chaos within us'"

(Tanner 49). Style is inseparable from Nietzsche's tragic vision since it involves being able to bestow the beauty of form on the inevitable and the determined. "I want," declares Nietzsche in a passage resembling Weil, "to learn more and more to *see as beautiful what is necessary* in things; then I shall be one of those who make things beautiful. *Amor fati* [Love of fate]: let that be my love henceforth!" (*The Gay Science* 223; my emphasis).

To be sure, there is bravado in Treadwell's frequent declarations that he would gladly die for his bears. But there is also in these words a properly tragic understanding of the realities of nature and a sacrificial embracing of those realities, in the course of a self-styling of a personality. For Treadwell (as for Nietzsche) the question of relations between humanity and animality is both fundamental and urgent. An air of acute desperation increasingly pervades the expression of Nietzsche and Treadwell; Treadwell's emotional breakdowns cannot but recall Nietzsche in Turin, weeping at the feet of a mistreated horse. Nietzsche's writings and Treadwell's footage are like an open nerve. If their style strikes us as awkward, the awkwardness is philosophically (cinematically) revealing.

In *The Birth of Tragedy* Nietzsche claimed that "it is only as *an aesthetic phenomenon* that existence and the world are eternally *justified*" (32).[18] It is possible to read Treadwell, aided by Herzog, as reenacting that primal tragic drama of Dionysian suffering, which significantly involves the destruction of individuation through dismemberment. Nietzsche's 1872 masterpiece is, in fact, an uncanny match to *Grizzly Man*. Nietzsche describes the state of Dionysian man as the experience of intoxication: "Singing and dancing, man expresses himself as a member of a higher community: he has forgotten how to walk and talk, and is about to fly dancing into the heavens. His gestures express enchantment. Just as the animals now speak, and the earth yields up milk and honey, he now gives voice to supernatural sounds: he feels like a god, he himself now walks about enraptured and elated as he saw the gods walk in dreams" (*BT* 17–18). This performance, faithfully reproduced in Treadwell's self-shot footage, is embarrassing to modern audiences who, according to Nietzsche, have broken ties with the Dionysian sources of tragedy.

But the upshot of this process is that "man is no longer an artist, he has become a work of art: the artistic power of the whole of nature reveals itself to the supreme gratification of the primal Oneness amidst the paroxysms of intoxication" (BT 18). Treadwell's footage suggests an awareness of his role as both artist and artwork in a brutal drama acted out for and upon him by an order in which he is only one compositional element amongst others.

Nietzsche's brilliance lies in his unashamed attributing of aesthetics—even an artistic drive—to nature itself, outside and beyond human consciousness. This sits uncomfortably with a culture that views art as intensely subjective, but Nietzsche insists that "this above all must be plain to us, to our humiliation *and* our enhancement, that the whole comedy of art is not at all performed for us, for our improvement or edification, any more than we are the actual creators of that art world"(BT 32). What is the role of the human being in this materialist drama? Again, Nietzsche's reply echoes throughout the body of *Grizzly Man*: "Only in so far as the genius is fused with the primal artist of the world in the act of artistic creation does he know anything of the eternal essence of art; for in that state he is wonderfully similar to the weird fairy-tale image of the creature that can turn its eyes around and look at itself; now he is at once subject and object, at once poet, actor and audience" (BT 32). Treadwell's filming of himself (including his own death), his creation of what I would call a natural theater where he is simultaneously subject, object, and spectator, mirrors Nietzsche's understanding of the relationship between the inhumanity of art and the human artist. Herzog enters this constellation as a third party, literally transforming Treadwell into a work of art. Herzog gives the work its final shape, an additional distance, which pays homage to Treadwell by telling his story but, in the act of telling, also rechannels (and tames) Treadwell's wild energy.

Is Treadwell finally condemned to humanity? I do not think so. It is a simplification to cast *Grizzly Man* as a drama about the failed conciliation between nature and man. *Grizzly Man* is situated on the cusp of an impossible transition between man and nature, human and animal, the

in-between of the encounter, whose sensibility is tragic in the Nietzs-
chean sense.

Lessons of Darkness and the Spirit of Music

> Imbued with music's power, the word, the image and the concept seek an
> expression analogous to music.   —Nietzsche, *The Birth of Tragedy*

I have been arguing that the figure of the creaturely belongs to the
realm of tragedy—a markedly anti-Romantic and antimodern view of
life reminiscent of Nietzsche. Nietzsche's "perspectivism" repositions
the human within the natural order. The extravagant opening of his
1873 essay "On Truth and Falsity in Their Ultramoral Sense" conveys
this radically altered perspective: "In some remote corner of the uni-
verse, effused into innumerable solar-systems, there was once a star
upon which clever animals invented cognition. It was the haughtiest,
most mendacious moment in the history of this world, but yet only a
moment. After Nature had taken a breath awhile the star congealed
and the clever animals had to die. —Someone might write a fable
after this style, and yet he would not have illustrated sufficiently, how
wretched, shadow-like, transitory, purposeless and fanciful the human
intellect appears in Nature" ("On Truth" 173). Someone *has* told this
Nietzschean fable. *Wild Blue Yonder* opens with uncanny similarity to
Nietzsche's piece, featuring an extraterrestrial narrator whose alien
perspective highlights humanity's blindness to its own self-destruc-
tiveness and ultimate insignificance.

In 1872, a year before the publication of "On Truth and Falsity in
Their Ultramoral Sense," Nietzsche published *The Birth of Tragedy: Out
of the Spirit of Music*. The text charts the rise and fall of Greek tragedy as a
form that simultaneously apprehends and redeems life's essential suf-
fering. For Nietzsche music is neither principally cultural nor historical.
Music reflects the ruthless and formless flow of life (the Dionysian),
which, paired with art's other half—its form-making and individuat-
ing capacity (the Apollonian)—produces tragedy. This positioning of
music prior to all symbols and concepts is most significant. Having

its source in music, tragedy remains true to the inhuman thrusts of being, something Nietzsche claims modern art (humanistic, subjective) sadly lost. Without a sense of existence's anonymous painflows, however, genuine happiness is impossible.[19] Music mimics the impersonal tides that threaten to subsume individual identity and will. It is in their mutual attention to this primordial operation of music that Nietzsche and Herzog come together.[20]

Music, then, is not simply a central feature of Herzog's cinema, but a fundamental one. Paul Cronin is aware of this when he asks Herzog: "what do you mean when you talk of 'transforming a whole world into music?'" (*Herzog on Herzog* 259). Music for Herzog is not used as a conventional soundtrack. While music usually functions as an accompaniment to the visuals, sound in Herzog is as important as the image. Music signifies the primordial life movements of which the visuals themselves are a belated translation. What precisely is the relationship between music and Herzog's tragic vision, and how does it make up what I have called Herzog's creaturely poetics? I want to conclude with a brief discussion of the essential musicality of *Lessons of Darkness*.

Roger Hillman's learned study *Unsettling Scores: German Film, Music, and Ideology* focuses on the function of music in the New German Cinema. Hillman takes Herzog as a "counterexample to the general thrust of this book" (139), since, unlike other New German directors, from Syberberg to Fassbinder, Herzog's use of preexisting music is fairly oblivious to the problems (even traumas) of modern German national identity (postwar and post-Wall). Herzog is not concerned with the ideological baggage that the use of, say, Wagner entails. Herzog's music veers away from the specificities of historical and cultural memory toward myth.[21] Hillman writes that, in *Lessons of Darkness*, music "captures images far more telling than the CNN footage sampled within the film, but transmutes those images into ahistorical myth (rather than virtual reality), not least through a prominent soundtrack, whose musical examples function narratively as a threnody for the West" (Hillman 147). *Lessons of Darkness* is a case in point for the amalgamation of nature and history (discussed in chapter 2), which neither treats history as a purely human domain nor nature as a blank slate upon which human actions unfold. *Lessons of Darkness* is at once a wildlife film and a film about the first gulf war. The musical scores "play a far more prominent role than spoken commentary, absent for over half the film, and in places yield only to the greater volume of 'natural' sound effects, such as jets of water in a fire-extinguishing operation" (Hillman 147). Thus music, not words or ideas, tells us something about the reality we are seeing: a political reality, but first and last a natural one; the earth's oil resources turned into infernal lakes of fire.[22] Hillman notes that nearly all the music in *Lessons of Darkness* is taken from the highly aestheticized and theatrical world of opera, "taken from operatic, sacred, or stage music or, with the Mahler example, a (vocal) symphonic rendering of a highly theatrical program. Their national provenance . . . seems secondary, and the prevailing sense is of spectacle, to match the slanting of the breathtaking images" (147–148). The synthesis here is threefold: between nature, the aesthetic, and the historical, with history, as Hillman implies, assuming the generic form of an elegy for civilization, a dirge for human folly and incompetence.

Lessons of Darkness achieves a striking cinematic rendering of opposites: it shows oil as water and water as fire. These are literally visions of the apocalypse, Milton's "darkness visible." In its breaching of contrasts between light and dark, water and fire, *Lessons of Darkness* harks back to Dionysian reality as formless and contradictory. Formlessness and contradiction are expressly *musical*. The aesthetic and artificial, epitomized by Wagner's music, which turns the Kuwaiti desert into a grand opera set, is thus neither a flight from nature into artifice, nor nature's Romantic idealization, but a recuperation of the primary aesthetics of nature.

What is the lesson of *Lessons of Darkness* in relation to the documentary form? By refusing to separate the historical from the natural, Herzog also refutes their generic separation. In terms of historical representation, Herzog is suggesting that a great distance separates "history" from "reality" and thus also reality from documentary observation. While the blazing oil fields are a historical fact, treating the conflict in the gulf in the restricted manner of political documentary tells us little about the nature of reality and the place of human history within it. In

Herzog's film the burning lakes signal beyond history, the political, and the human. They express the formlessness and inhumanity of nature of which, in Nietzsche's terms, history is but one kind of dream. One of the lessons in this film concerns the inadequacy (and unreality) of historical representation in capturing and communicating the real. To put this simply: history that does not include in its very foundations those natural, temporal processes (for Benjamin, as we have seen, these are the workings of transience and decay) remains fantastic. Historical documentation that treats nature as either a human resource or as a stage set fails to recognize in the very workings of historicity the susceptibility of the human to the mechanism of the world. Thus *there is no history that is not at the very same time natural history*, which makes *Lessons of Darkness*, which Herzog called "a requiem for an uninhabitable planet" (*Herzog on Herzog* 249), an environmental film par excellence.

We might grieve the disappearance and destruction of nature as our most prized possession (and here again, as Lippit reminds us, it is cinema that provides the space to mourn), but nature itself is unable to mourn. Benjamin's proposes the strange notion of "nature's mourning," which discovers in the silence and indifference of nature something expressive—not unlike the blank stare of Treadwell's bears. For Benjamin, the mutedness we often associate with nature is articulate, and in this articulate silence Benjamin hears nature's mournful appeal. Conventional environmentalism is still biblical in its conception of stewardship. Herzog's wildlife fantasies carve out spaces for the encounter between the natural and the human order outside this custodial logic. The revelation of the historicality of nature and the naturalness of history is the intersection that *Lessons of Darkness* embodies.

Moreover, is not the humanist understanding of history itself tragic? Closed in on itself, historical narrative is blind to its own illusory foundation (what Nietzsche would call history's origins in Apollonian dream state and the form-making capacity of the *principium individuationis*). Herzog's version of history, on the other hand, is cut to size: non-narrative and wordless, as in the scene with the Kuwaiti torture victim who has lost the capacity for speech and cannot tell her story. Here as in *Land of Silence and Darkness*, Herzog dehumanized his subjects.

It is not enough to dismiss such gestures as cruel when what they enact is also a retranslating of the human into the creaturely order, into the anonymity of perishable matter.

The inhuman condition and alien perspective are conveyed at the outset when Herzog's says, in voiceover, "The first creature we encountered tried to communicate something to us." *Lessons of Darkness*, Herzog explains, "progresses as if aliens have landed on an unnamed planet where the landscape has lost every single trace of its dignity, and—just like in *Fata Morgana* with the debris-strewn desert landscapes—these aliens see human beings for the first time" (*Herzog on Herzog* 249). This is the very same alien eye Nietzsche employs in the 1873 essay, performing the "rescaling of the human"—and of history—to the musical movements of a battered earth. In this tragic vision, man as the center of the universe is no more, and a new history, a musical and natural history—the natural history of creatures—is born.

CONCLUSION *Animal Saintliness*

Every worm is a martyr,
Every sparrow subject to injustice,
I said to my cat,
Since there was no one else around.

It's raining. In spite of their huge armies
What can ants do?
And the roach on the wall
Like a waiter in an empty restaurant?

I'm going in the cellar
To stroke the rat caught in a trap.
You watch the sky.
If it clears, scratch on the door.   —Charles Simic, "Explaining a Few Things"

This is one of quite a number of animal poems by Charles Simic in which he uncomplicatedly states a relationship to animals (as he sometimes does also to things) that is casually ethical—a plea that neither mentions the idea of rights nor entertains "pet" feelings for other creatures. Simic writes about cats and dogs, but also about cockroaches, flies, ants, or chickens—animals that are resolutely *not* our pets, who inhabit our domesticity in the form of a disturbance or as food. "Explaining a Few Things" presents a creaturely fellowship by default, self-evident and undeniable, in a world of imbalance and injustice.

The ordinariness of this poem captures a general truth: the martyrdom of animals is often noted, even by those who take no issue with eating, wearing, or testing on animals, as a fact of life. Somehow, at an unreflective and commonsense level, without having to be consequential about it, people seem to agree that animals pay the high price of human ascendancy.

Ordinariness and martyrdom are a startling combination, which I tried to argue characterizes—and quite uniquely so—the current predicament of animals. This marriage of orders, between the everyday and the extraordinary, is also reflective of my methodology. My point of departure has been, to borrow Stanley Cavell's phrase, "in quest of the ordinary," a way of illuminating the relations we currently have—and the ones I believe we ought to have—with the world around us, human, animal, and other. Clever deconstructions of the human are not exclusive to this task, partly because theoretical nuance is just that, theoretical, and partly because methodologically we are better off speaking about situations, persons, texts, and events and how theory comes to bear upon them, than thinking abstractly.

My use of *ordinary* might seem odd in the face of chapter 1 on the Holocaust. But the Holocaust too was ordinary, in the sense of an event that took place in recent history, not "banally," as is now customary to claim, but steadily, involving millions of people and complex industrial, military, and social apparatuses. A commitment to ordinary reality should make one think twice before promoting fake reverences in relation to history and to humanity. That was the cardinal point of my first chapter. The danger here is double: of falsifying what is truly extraordinary about the ordinary and, conversely, of squeezing out of life a sort of phony astonishment about the everyday. In both cases we risk missing the "difficulty of reality" and warping the proper task of criticism.

The crossing of ordinariness and extraordinariness also underpins the thought of Simone Weil, the theoretical backbone of this study. The natural and the supernatural in Weil appear respectively in the guise of *gravity* and *grace*. Siân Miles writes that Weil's "greatest influence has been in, as it were, demythologizing mysticism. She believed that the truths she glimpsed in her mystical experiences were simple truths, open to all, which had been deformed over time (since the thirteenth century in particular) by a certain patriotic and partisan spirit in the Church" (Miles 51). Weil uses seemingly contradictory discourses: unforgiving materialism on the one hand and a sacred vocabulary on the other. My analysis has centered on a similar conjunction between the material and mechanistic conditions of life and the wholly uncommon demands of the ethical. Articulating the encounter between these two incommensurable levels is the defining gesture of a creaturely poetics. The readings in the book hinge on Weil's idea of reality, recognizable in its "unbearableness." Wherever thought recoils or shrinks from the unbearable and inconsolable in the world, it is most likely encountering reality. Weil's rule of thumb was to counterintuitively force thinking into a painful contact with reality without seeking solace. Sharon Cameron captures the richness of this maneuver precisely when she explains that "the intrigue of Weil's formulations (speaking for myself personally) lies in the promise of an escape from the predictability of what is possible in the human world if comfort is not the driving factor. Thus Weil's writing offers an *idea* of what might be experienced if one had courage to perceive the body without consolatory illusions; if 'difficulty' were a joy" (*Impersonality* 137). Cora Diamond's "The Difficulty of Reality and the Difficulty of Philosophy" entertains a similar sense of Weil's unique contribution. Diamond knows that what might be called "comfort-thinking" (perceiving the body *with* consolatory illusions) can be very good thinking: carefully teased out philosophical arguments. But good thinking may still deflect from the truth, if by truth we understand not a terminus of thought or a resting place of concepts but the site of encounter with reality that rattles concepts and confounds thought. This confrontation with reality in response to the vulnerability of bodies in their affliction and exposure can be "turned equally toward splendor and toward horror" ("Difficulty" 61). That is to say, beauty can also present us with the difficulty of reality, can also be confounding, overwhelming, or unthinkable:

> In the case of our relationship with animals, a sense of the difficulty of reality may involve not only the kind of horror felt by Elizabeth Costello in Coetzee's lectures, but also and equally a sense of astonishment and incomprehension that there should be beings like us, so unlike us, so astonishingly capable of being companions of ours and so unfathomably distant. A sense of its being impossible that we should go and *eat* them may go with feeling how powerfully strange it is that they and we should share as much

as we do, and yet also not share; that they should be capable of incomparable beauty and delicacy and terrible ferocity; that some among them should be so mind-bogglingly weird or repulsive in their forms or in their lives. ("Difficulty" 60–61)

The pedestrian, whether splendid or dismaying, is, then, the foundation of the creaturely readings that center on those aspects of existence common to humans and animals whose source is the concrete, vulnerable materiality of life. This reality of a fellow animal in all its familiarity and distance, beauty and repulsion, comes alive with characteristic virtuosity near the end of Saul Bellow's *Henderson the Rain King*, in the protagonist's childhood memory of his experiences with an aging performing bear called Smolak:

This ditched old creature was almost green with time and down to his last teeth, like the pits of dates. . . . He had been trained to ride a bike, but now he was too old. Now he could feed from a dish with a rabbit; after which, in a cap and bib, he drank from a baby bottle while he stood on his hind legs. But there was one more thing, and this was where I came in. There was a month yet to the end of the season, and everyday of this month Smolak and I rode on a roller coaster together before large crowds. This poor broken ruined creature and I, alone, took the high rides twice a day. And while we climbed and dipped and swooped and swerved and rose again higher than the Ferris wheels and fell, we held on to each other. By a common bond of despair we embraced, cheek to cheek, as all support seemed to leave us and we started down the perpendicular drop. I was pressed into his long-suffering, age-worn, tragic, and discolord coat as he grunted and cried to me. At times the animal would wet himself. But he was apparently aware I was his friend and he did not claw me. I took a pistol with blanks in case of an assault; it never was needed. . . . So if corporeal things are an image of the spiritual and visible objects are renderings of invisible ones, and if Smolak and I were outcasts together, two humorists before the crowd, but brothers in our souls—I enbeared by him, and he probably humanized by me . . . Smolak (mossy like a forest elm) and I rode together, and as he cried out at the top, beginning the bottomless rush over those skimpy yellow supports . . . we hugged each other, the bear and I, with something greater than terror and flew in those gilded cars. I shut my eyes in his wretched, time-abused fur. He held me in his arms and gave me comfort. And the great thing is that he didn't blame me. He had seen too much of life, and somewhere in his huge head he had worked it out that for creatures there is nothing that ever runs unmingled. (Bellow 338–339)

Fellowship is ridiculous, ungainly, carnivalesque even—but solid and unquestioning. It is rooted in bodies exposed to time and (literally in the roller-coaster ride) at the mercy of gravity. Exposure, then, is the properly universal condition that underlies the ordinariness of all life, yet whose consequences for our thoughts on justice and for the possibilities of art are surely extraordinary.

In two films, *Au hasard Balthazar* (1966) and *Mouchette* (1967), Robert Bresson exemplifies a creaturely approach that places solid and exposed bodies, an animal's and a child's, at the center of reality. James Quandt summarizes the plots of these twin works succinctly as "rural dramas in which the eponymous innocents, a donkey and a girl, suffer a series of assaults and mortifications and then die" (Quandt 18). Bresson submits these films—everyone and everything within them— to the formal workings of material necessity and chance (*au hasard*, by chance). This logic is beautifully encapsulated in *Balthazar*, whose "most striking innovation is," according to Keith Reader, "the use of a donkey as the 'central character.'" Reader continues that "Bresson himself adopts an unabashedly anthropomorphic attitude towards the donkey, speaking of how 'l'âne a dans la vie les mêmes étapes que l'homme [the donkey goes through the same stages in life as man]'" (Reader 77). But the charge of anthropomorphism can only be amusing in a director whose human protagonists are so unrecognizably human. Bresson's humans, no more and no less than Balthazar, resemble marionettes rather than fully blown characters. If Bresson sought to "reduce acting to physiology" (Schrader 66), this was because "psychological acting humanizes the spiritual" (65). Thus, even before *Balthazar*, Bresson's formalist approach to filmmaking was decidedly nonanthropocentric. Like Weil's rejection of "human personality" as the source of the sacred, Bresson pursues the divine outside of all identity, in a radically impersonal way.

In the essay "The Animals: Territory and Metamorphoses," Jean Baudrillard writes that animals at once generate and refute discourse. Once the uses of animals have been (discursively and nondiscursively) exhausted, there remains in them a stubborn resistance, which is turned back on the human and exposes its own discursive and conceptual vagrancy: "In all this—metaphor, guinea pig, model, allegory (without forgetting their alimentary 'use value')—animals maintain a compulsory discourse. Nowhere do they really speak, because they only furnish the responses one asks for. It is their way of sending the Human back to his circular codes, behind which their silence analyzes us" (Baudrillard 137–138). The silence of the animals in the face of all that is said and done to them returns to the idea of martyrdom or rather to the notion of the saint. A saint does not pontificate. He or she remain true to the reality that has been conferred without conforming to the demands of communication and persuasion. A saint reaches others not by canvassing but as embodied revelation. Suffering becomes saintly when its inarticulacy is revealed as a refusal to speak. Thus the powerlessness of those who do or cannot participate in a given discourse paradoxically carries its own inalienable force.

Balthazar's silence functions in precisely this way, which is not sentimental and does not rely on either the anthropomorphic or the "othered" animal to be read as saintly. Baptized by the children Jacques and Marie at the beginning of the film, Balthazar grows up to suffer in silence the hardships of work and the cruelty of humans. Handed from owner to owner, Balthazar is finally "borrowed" by the village thug Gérard to carry smuggled goods to the border. When shots are fired, Gérard and his friend flee, and the wounded Balthazar is left wandering the hills. Come morning, Balthazar, bleeding, reaches a field and sits amidst a flock of sheep. In the film's last shot, as the sheep scatter, Balthazar lies dead.

In his wordless suffering and his attentiveness to the human wickedness around him (Bresson repeatedly shows Balthazar's gaze and flinching ears as signs of witnessing), Balthazar is not silent. The film opens with a piano sonata, interrupted suddenly by donkey's brays. It is perhaps the braying rather than the music that signifies most immediately and unambiguously to viewers (including those familiar with Schubert's Sonata D959). Balthazar's silence is a special kind of saintly speech: neither arguing against nor consenting to the injustices he suffers. Silence in Bresson has an almost material quality, which makes God's presence felt through and as the vacuum of his absence.

It therefore seems to me mistaken to regard *Au hasard Balthazar* as a religious allegory, with the donkey as the innocent Christ figure. Although the film contains much allegorical paraphernalia, Balthazar does not stand in for anything or anyone.[1] He is quite literally the embodiment of creaturely suffering. A process of interpretation that replaces the donkey with the idea of a suffering humanity (or with Christ who suffers *for* humanity) with a view to a redemptive meaning of the animal's death at the end of the film does not do justice to Bresson's insistence on blind necessity and chance as the world's operative modes, nor to the bleakness with which he views humanity.

When, toward the end of the film, Marie's mother tries to dissuade Gérard from taking Balthazar, she tells him that the donkey is "a saint." Keith Reader is bemused by the proposition, and by his own reaction to it: "Why does this remark, to me at least, appear deeply moving rather than the theological absurdity it so patently is? (Reader 86). But is the notion of animal saintliness really so preposterous? Saintliness does not profess a "message," let alone a doctrine. That is the role of the priest, a figure that Bresson's film treats with considerable contempt. (We should not, however, take the priest as a representative of the Church per se, but as someone who debases religion by treating it as a source of comfort—and thus also as a source of social control. In this sense Bresson is less anticlerical than anti-Jesuit).[2] The saint, in contrast, can be thought as an embodiment of truth, a pure witness who precisely resists the corrosions of priesthood. Badiou locates the origin of saintliness in "the sudden eruption of chance, the event, the pure encounter. . . . Whenever the world of History tends to escape into mystery, abstraction, pure interrogation, it is the world of the divine (of saintliness)" (*Saint Paul* 37).

Chance (events unsupported by a narrative structure of cause and effect or by the characters' "motivation") creates the series of pure events that make up the body of *Balthazar*. At its center is the donkey, whose life as solid but mysterious determines the "difficult reality" we must contend with. Balthazar is thus a figure of what I discussed earlier as Weilian *affliction*. I see no reason for excluding this configuration from what we might think of as "saintly," even more so in light of the association Bresson makes between the saintly and the lowly or everyday.

The communication of the extraordinary through the ordinary is central in Bresson. Like Weil, Bresson employs a method of stripping away inessentials to create the possibility of a transcendent reality. Paul Schrader points out that the "everyday in films has precedents in religious art; it is what one Byzantine scholar calls 'surface-aesthetics'" (61). Bresson's meticulous surface, light on the cinematic ornaments of plot (causality), acting (psychology and personality), editing (for dramatic effect), camerawork (manipulation via angles and composition), and (with a few exceptions, including the Schubert score in *Balthazar*) nondiegetic sound, has the function of "seeing through the surface reality to the supernatural" (Schrader 64).

Joseph Cunneen agrees that Bresson's "sense of the sacred is primarily communicated in terms of a pared-down style; his rejection of what he called 'photographed theater' also meant an avoidance of cheap emotional effects" (Cunneen 37). Bresson told Schrader that "the more life is what it is—ordinary, simple—without pronouncing the word 'God,' the more I see the presence of God in that. I don't know how to quite explain that. I don't want to shoot something in which God would be too transparent" ("Bresson, Possibly" 27). This is particularly true of Bresson's middle to late so-called Jansenist phase, in which characters are thrown into a determinist universe whose God is hidden if not totally absent. Bresson is often compared here to Pascal, but this is also the point at which Bresson seems closest to Weil.

When the cinematic is disentangled from the ideological cues that render the filmic world "comfortable" for viewers, film yields both beauty and goodness and becomes devotional. "The word 'devotion,'" says Nathaniel Dorsky, "need not refer to the embodiment of a specific religious form. Rather, it is the opening or the interruption that allows us to experience what is hidden, and not to accept with our hearts our given situation. When film does this, when it subverts our absorption in the temporal and reveals the depths of our own reality, it opens us to a fuller sense of ourselves and our world. It is alive as a devotional form" (*Devotional Cinema* 16). Bresson's films are simultaneously sumptuous and flat, hypnotic and monotonous. Here, it seems to me, is a final point of contact between Bresson and Weil, known for the "inexorably monotonous voice" (Thibon, GG viii) with which she argued for extraordinary truths.

Watching *Balthazar* is a strangely fused experience. Bresson's style achieves a strong consonance between the filmic and profilmic worlds. There is the donkey "character," but also—and more intensely—the real animal in excess of the fictional diegesis. One worries about the actual tail Gérard sets on fire, the pulling, kicking and shoving, all of which make Balthazar cinema's own beast of burden. Balthazar turns cinema itself—its cost on living bodies—into a creaturely medium.

"We are both appreciators and victims of material existence," writes Dorsky (*Devotional Cinema* 17). A creaturely poetics begins from this simple truth. Each of the texts discussed in this book betrays a dual fascination: with physicality and with the transgressing of species identity. I focused on works that take up the body as a way of *attending* (seeing, hearing, articulating, and responding to) the inhuman within and without. A creaturely poetics is the sum of this attention: the literary and cinematic forms that challenge the defensive inventory of humanism (consciousness, language, morality, dignity) and the anthropocentric critical idioms it gives rise to. The study brought together two distinct but intimately related projects: the theoretical refutation of humanism and anthropocentrism as impoverished modes of confronting exposure and an attention to the reality of animal lives as the basis of cultural and ethical inquiry.

My readings drew closely on the ideas of Simone Weil (as well as on the temperament of those ideas). Weil's connections between vulnerability, beauty, and reality, with which this book began, illustrate that reading to a creaturely compass is not only aesthetic but also profoundly ethical. Though Weil herself did not recognize in the predicament of animals something ethically unique, I made the case for animal suffering—often seen as inarticulate, silent, banal—on Weil's own terms, as somehow approaching the conception of the saintly. I also showed how a "contracted" rather than expanded humanism is a gateway to a more inclusive engagement with other animals. Cora Diamond's adaptation of Weil's critique of rights to allow thinking about injustices done to animals suggests that the ethical premise has significantly shifted: we should no longer attempt to establish the framework and limits of the rights of animals but inquire instead about the conditions that affect the modes of our attentiveness to them. My contention more broadly has been that secular liberal morality remains blind to the workings and potential of attention as an orientation toward the sacred, and that in so doing it commits itself to an unduly narrow—and deeply deficient—notion of ethics. A creaturely ethics, on the other hand, does not depend on fulfilling any preliminary criteria of subjectivity and personhood. Its source lies in the recognition of the materiality and vulnerability of all living bodies, whether human or not, and in the absolute primacy of obligations over rights. A creaturely ethics, which recognizes in animals an exemplary case of worldly suffering, does not ask, What are the limits of rights? but, What are the limits of attention?

NOTES

INTRODUCTION: *Creaturely Bodies*

1. In "A Cyborg Manifesto" (1991) Donna Haraway suggested that clear distinctions between humans and animals were no longer scientifically or publicly viable. Assuming for the moment this were true, scientific and popular perceptions of the permeable human/nonhuman boundary have not translated into changed relations between humans and animals in terms of shared spaces/habitats and ethical inclusion. Use of animals as/for food and in scientific research has steadily grown since 1990. A UK Home Office report (available on the Home Office Web site) confirms a rise of 14 percent in scientific procedures using animals between 2007 and 2008. Increases are set to intensify in the coming years.

2. *Gravity and Grace* first appeared in French in 1947, hereafter cited as GG.

3. A creaturely poetics partly operates as a "dehumanizing" perspective. This no more than translates Viktor Shklovsky's famous notion of "defamiliarization"—art's making the common uncommon by way of an estranged eye—

into the terms of the discourse of species. See Viktor Shklovsky, "Art as Technique," in Julie Rivkin and Michael Ryan, eds., *Literary Theory: An Anthology*, 2d ed. (Oxford: Blackwell, 2004), pp. 15–22.

4. See for example, Mark S. Robert, *The Mark of the Beast: Animality and Human Oppression* (Indiana: Purdue University Press, 2008), which looks at the history of dehumanization and animalization of "inferiors," including slaves, Jews, and also animals. See as well Judith Butler's *Precarious Life: The Powerrs of Mourning and Violence* (London: Verso, 2004).

5. *Philosophy and Animal Life* includes essays by Cary Wolfe, Cora Diamond, Stanley Cavell, John McDowell, and Ian Hacking.

6. The "bodiliness" of *The Lives of Animals* is doubled by the fact that Coetzee first performed it as the Tanner Lectures. Laura Wright has written about the importance of performance in Coetzee as a form of interspecies ethical displacement:

> While Coetzee does not write drama, his writing does refuse a controlling narrative position and raises dialogic questions about *embodiment as a kind of performance*—acting as the other—that is potentially possible through imagined identification with the bodily suffering of the other. According to Coetzee, "in South Africa it is not possible to deny the authority of suffering and therefore the body" because "it is not that one *grants* the authority of the suffering body: the suffering body takes this authority: that is its power" (*Doubling* 248). . . . The bodies with which Coetzee's characters and audience are asked to engage in imagined physical dialogue not only consist of white women and racially designated others, but also of animals.

> Laura Wright, *Writing Out of All the Camps: J. M. Coetzee's Narratives of Displacement,* p. 13 (New York: Routledge, 2006; my emphasis).

7. J. M. Coetzee's *The Lives of Animals* (hereafter *TLOA*) was published with commentaries by Amy Gutmann, Marjorie Garber, Peter Singer, Wendy Doniger, and Barbara Smuts (Princeton: Princeton University Press, 1999).

8. Derrida, "The Animal That Therefore I Am," hereafter AIA.

9. I am thinking not just of Boethius's classical text, but more recently of appeals to the so-called therapeutic uses of philosophy, for example, Alain de Botton's best seller *The Consolations of Philosophy* (London: Pantheon, 2000).

10. On carnophallogocentrism see Derrida's interview with Elisabeth Roudinesco, "Violence Against Animals," in *For What Tomorrow . . . A Dialogue,* trans. Jeff Fort (Stanford: Stanford University Press, 2004). pp. 62–76. See also Calarco's *Zoographies* (131–32).

11. The quote is taken from an expanded version of "The Love of God and Affliction" reprinted in Springsted, *Simone Weil,* pp. 41–70. Springsted prefaces Weil's text by explaining that "this is one of the most important of all Weil's essays. It was originally published in a shorter form. However, additional pages were later discovered, and are included here" (*Simone Weil* 41). Other quotations from "The Love of God and Affliction" are taken from the shorter version published in *Waiting for God.*

12. Badiou makes this argument strongly in *Ethics.* See also Slavoj Žižek and Glyn Daly, *Conversations with Žižek* (London: Polity, 2004).

13. The quote is from Badiou's text (*Saint Paul* 46), modified slightly from the authorized version of *Corinthians.*

14. It may be premature—or undesirable—to speak of a "theological turn" in the humanities, but there is no doubt that religious discourse is being revaluated in traditionally secular, leftist, and progressive debates. Besides Žižek, Badiou, and Agamben, philosophers like Leszek Kolakowski and John Gray have insisted on the significance of religion in a seemingly increasingly secular world. Terry Eagleton's reengagement with Christianity in *Reason, Faith, and Revolution* (New Haven: Yale University Press, 2009), or *On Evil* (New Haven: Yale University Press, 2010) is also part of this shift.

1. Humanity Unraveled, Humanity Regained

1. Novick's is one of several critiques of the contemporary appropriations of Holocaust memory. See for example Norman G. Finkelstein, *The Holocaust Industry* (London: Verso, 2000); and Hilene Flanzbaum, ed., *The Americanization of the Holocaust* (Baltimore: Johns Hopkins University Press, 1999). The filmwork of Eyal Sivan is devoted to a similar critique of the "instrumentalization of memory." In films like *Yizkor, Slaves of Memory* (1990) and *The Specialist* (1999) Sivan is engaged instead in the creation of what he calls the "common archive," a new paradigm for recording and conceptualizing histories of conflict transcending the sectarian division between victims and perpetrators.

2. For other references to the *Muselmann*, see also Levi, *If This Is a Man,* pp. 94–96, 131, 134.

3. Druker's *Primo Levi and Humanism After Auschwitz* provides a nuanced reading of Levi's memoirs as the site of a struggle to sustain his secular humanism in the face of Auschwitz. Druker proposes—unsatisfactorily in my view—a Lévinasian model as a viable post-Holocaust ethics and a "new humanism" (133). See also Zygmunt Bauman's influential *Modernity and the Holocaust* (Ithaca: Cornell University Press, 1989); and Robert Eaglestone, *The Holocaust and the Postmodern*, especially chapter 12: "The Postmodern, the Holocaust, and the Limits of the Human," pp. 317–338 (Oxford: Oxford University Press, 2004); Bernstein's "Bare Life, Bearing Witness" is a highly critical response to Agamben.

4. Dalia Sachs explains that Levi's title is not only grammatically but also temporally inconclusive: "there is no mention of a specific historical moment that led to Levi's writing, nor does a second clause arrive with which we could situate the present tense use of the verb 'to be,' which instead remains unqualified and leaves the reader suspended in an inconclusive temporality, faced with an ambiguous challenge." Dalia Sachs, "The Language of Judgment: Primo Levi's *Se questo è un uomo*" *MLN* 110 (1995): 755–784, 758.

5. Céline's *Fable for Another Time* (1952) opens with the following dedication: "For animals, for the sick, for prisoners." Céline, *Fable for Another Time,* trans. Mary Hudson (Lincoln: University of Nebraska Press, 2003).

6. See Wyatt Mason's excellent "Uncovering Céline," *New York Review of Books,* January 14–February 10, 2010, pp. 16–18, in which Mason dismisses sidestepping the antisemitic trilogy and excusing Céline as a wild satirist: "to understand Céline, we must be ready to, and permitted to, read all that he wrote. Only in this way can we begin to understand what we are saying when we might think to class him as—of all things—a humorist" (18). In "The Art of Evil," Sylvere Lotringer writes of Artaud, Bataille, Céline, and Weil that "from the mid 1920s until well into the war their work seems to anticipate the Holocaust, responding to it from a distance, 'like victims signaling through the flames' (Artaud)"; *FAT* 1.1, http://www.thing.net/~fat/vol1no1/sylvere.htm.

7. "No English word exactly conveys the meaning of the French *malheur.* Our word *unhappiness* is a negative term and far too weak. Affliction is the nearest

equivalent but not quite satisfactory. *Malheur* has in it a sense of inevitability and doom." Emma Craufurd in a translator's note, "Love of God," p. 67.

8. Several scholars link affliction to the Holocaust, but they do so only tentatively. Commentaries focus mainly on Weil's difficult relationship to her own, repudiated Judaism. See, for example, Richard Bell, *Simone Weil: The Way of Justice and Compassion* (New York: Rowman and Littlefield, 1998), especially chapter 9: "Simone Weil, Post-Holocaust Judaism, and the Way of Compassion" (165–190). Bell places Lévinas and Weil at opposite ends ("Simone Weil you have never understood anything about the Torah!" [Lévinas qtd. in Bell 180]). Weil's *Letter to a Priest* contains one of her most fervent attacks on Judaism. Idolatry is an invention of "the cult of Jehovah," whose conception of God is inherently aggressive since it places power before goodness: "if some Hebrews of classical Jewry were to return to life and were to be provided with arms, they would exterminate the lot of us—men, women, and children, for the crime of idolatry. They would reproach us for worshipping Baal and Astarte, taking Christ for Baal and the Virgin for Astarte" (5). For Weil, Judaism itself is idolatrous because of the doctrine of chosenness: "the Hebrews took for their idol, not something made of metal or wood, but a race, a nation, something just as earthly. Their religion is essentially inseparable from such idolatry, because of the notion of the 'chosen people'" (6). The letter dates September 1942. Patrick Drevet asks whether Weil was irrationally blind to the suffering of her own people. "Puisqu'aucune déduction rationnelle ne parvient a rendre compréhensible (et encore moins acceptable) cet aveuglement, il faut bien chercher autre chose" ("Since no logical inference could render comprehensible [even less so acceptable] this blindness, one needs to look for something else"; Drevet 210; my translation). Drevet believes Weil could not acknowledge the victimization of the Jews because she refused to regard herself as a victim, member of a particular persecuted group, or someone deserving protection: "Simone Weil détestait l'idée de se défendre pour elle-même, de s'ériger en victime; il lui était dés lors impossible de regarder le groupe auquel on la sommait d'appartenir comme une victime particulière à plaindre ou à protéger" (210). Moreover, the alleged denial of Jewish victimhood was part of Weil's process of "decreation," which refused to identify her dual embodiment (as a woman and a Jew). The question she thus faced was "comment effacer ce corps de

Juive?"—How to erase this Jewish woman's body? Drevet wants to distinguish between Weil's theological objections to Judaism and her indifference to concrete Jewish suffering. As he puts it: "le problème ne tient pas dans son refus (tout à fait discutable) de la spiritualité juive, de nature religieuse, mais dans la violence et la mauvaise foi des arguments de Simone Weil pour alimenter ce refus" (210). Not the religious rejection of Judaism, but the violence and bad faith that feed and fuel this refusal are the issue. I would question several of Drevet's points, especially his turn to a psychopathological discourse to explain Weil's difficult position. Much more can and needs to be said here, but this is a task for a separate study, devoted solely to the problem of Simone Weil's anti-Judaism.

9. Alain Finkielkraut's *La mémoire vaine: Du crime contre l'humanité* was first published by Gallimard in 1989. It appeared in English as *Remembering in Vain* (New York: Columbia University Press, 1992).

10. For background on the trial see Alice Y. Kaplan's excellent introduction to the English edition of *Remembering in Vain*, "On Alain Finkielkraut's *Remembering in Vain*: The Klaus Barbie Trial and Crimes Against Humanity." The essay also appeared in *Critical Inquiry* 19 (1992): 70–86. My references in the chapter are to *Critical Inquiry*.

11. For the legal definition of war crimes and crimes against humanity see *Remembering in Vain,* pp. 76–77n6.

12. Finkielkraut believes that the case against Barbie (like that against Eichmann) was undermined by being handled locally, yet has little faith in the United Nations' ability to justly assess Nazi crime. Would the International Criminal Court (ICC), set up in 2002, have provided a better framework for the justice Finkielkraut seeks? A number of Western and non-Western states (including the U.S. and Israel) have not ratified the ICC's treaty, which significantly limits the court's efficacy as a properly universal institution of justice.

13. While the origins of French universalism are elusive, this much is certain: at the beginning French universalism derives from its relationship to the Church; it is, as it were, borrowed from Catholicism (from the Greek *Katholikos*, "universal"). Referred to since the Middle Ages as "the elder daughter of the Church," France drew from its privileged

relationship to the Church its founding reputation and mission as a disseminator of a universalist creed. Indeed, in a paradoxical fashion, the very event of the French Revolution, which did so much to destroy the power of the Gallican Church, by the same gesture enabled French universalism to perpetuate and propagate itself. The French Revolution, in this view, did not mark a rupture between a pre-universalist and a post-universalist France but rather drew on and gave new impetus to France's time honored civilizing mission. (Schor 43–44)

14. On Schmitt and the vicissitudes of the state of exception as a contemporary judicial and political paradigm, see Giorgio Agamben, *State of Exception*, trans. Kevin Attel (Chicago: University of Chicago Press, 2005).

15. See the criticism of Father Joseph-Marie Perrin in the chapter "Syncretism and Catholicity," in Perrin and Thibon, *Simone Weil as We Knew Her*, p. 53.

16. *Passenger* is split between past and present. Sequences set in the past were shot on location in Auschwitz, and the present was filmed on the luxury liner. But after Munk's accidental death in 1961 the film's future looked uncertain. Munk's collaborators and friends completed *Passenger* two years later. Extra scenes were shot in Auschwitz. For the contemporary portions existing stills were used and a voiceover commentary (written by Wiktor Woroszylski) was added. The final film is an assemblage of Munk's original footage, still photographs, and the voiceover commentary on both the plot and the complex process of the film's completion. This disjointed and self-reflexive form says much about the challenges of representing the Holocaust and of the deeply interpersonal nature of this challenge. For more on the film, see Ewa Mazierska, "Double Memory: the Holocaust in Polish Film," in Toby Haggith and Joanna Newman, eds., *Holocaust and the Moving Image: Representations in Film and Television Since 1933* (London: Wallflower, 2005), pp. 225–235.

17. In "The Love of God and Affliction" Weil asserts that the mechanism of the world—gravity—applies similarly to the workings of nature and human psychology: "The mechanism of necessity can be transposed to any level while still remaining true to itself. It is the same in the world of pure matter, in the animal world, among nations, and in souls" ("Love of God" 76).

18. Höss was involved with nationalist paramilitary organizations after WWI. In 1923 he was charged with murder, committed with other members of an

illegal *Freikorps* successor-organization in 1922. The group tortured and killed a schoolteacher named Kadow suspected (wrongly, as it happened) of being a communist infiltrator. Höss received a ten-year sentence but was released early in 1928. He joined the SS in 1934 and became commandant of Auschwitz in 1940. Hoess, *Commandant of Auschwitz,* pp. 43–45, 61, 64.

19. Singer himself had a complex relationship with Judaism. He called his position "private mysticism," which, not unlike Weil's, was based on the idea of God's hiddenness or absence.

20. On the importance of Singer's vegetarianism, see Qiao's *The Jewishness of Isaac Bashevis Singer*: "Singer's vegetarianism is crucial to his understanding of the evil deeply embedded in history and in nature itself" (17). Qiao also claims that vegetarianism is Singer's only "-ism" (132), a basic moral code and part of his revision of Judaism.

2. Neanderthal Poetics in William Golding's *The Inheritors*

1. In "New Models and Metaphors for the Neanderthal Debate" Paul Graves traces the shifts in archaeological and anthropological theories on the origins of "modern" Homo sapiens. Changes in scientific thinking were partly shaped by the wider cultural and political context of the time. "Paleontologists of the 19th and early 20th centuries tended to regard all fossil hominids as representatives of the 'true' human stock. . . . Moreover, this phylogenetic paradigm had, from its very beginnings, been extended to an essentially racist analysis of human types, representing non-Europeans (and sometimes women) as both separate and less evolved lineages." But in the second half of the twentieth century these propositions were reversed: "indigenous development may be seen as the predominant metaphor for a world reacting against imperialism and the Nazi terror and living through the upheavals of colonial independence and the civil rights movement." Graves sees Wells and Golding's texts as examples of the "the role of the Neanderthal debate as a literary metaphor" (514).

2. Raine cites Kipling's "The Knight of the Joyous Venture" as a specific precursor of *The Inheritors.* See "Belly Without Blemish."

3. See Helen Tiffin and Graham Huggan's *Postcolonial Ecocriticism: Literature, Animals, Environment* (New York: Routledge, 2010).

4. See for example, Peter S. Alterman, "Aliens in Golding's *The Inheritors,*" *Science Fiction Studies* 5.1 (1978): 3–10; and Jeanne Murray Walker, "Reciprocity and

Exchange in William Golding's *The Inheritors*," *Science Fiction Studies* 8.3 (1981): 297–310. See also Kinkead-Weekes and Gregor's seminal study *William Golding* (69). In "Utopias and Antiutopias," Golding himself discusses the aptitude of science fiction for describing his work. William Golding. *A Moving Target* (London: Faber and Faber, 1982), pp. 171–184.

5. In the essay "In My Ark," Golding reflects on humanity's place in the world, its relation to nature and to other species. He professes an indifference to animals: "the positive *love* of animals has always amazed me" (103). The amazement is due to the fact that (the English) affection for animals is too often possessive: "I would preserve a dinosaur in my ark if I could, but not out of affection. Our manipulation of the world has grown explosive. Animals are capital, but they are not ours. I do not know whose they are, nor whose we are, except that we do not belong to ourselves. Once in a way, I smell purpose in the world and guess it may include not only Adam but also the delectable lamb and the loathsome spider" (103).

   The mysteries of the world call for an attitude very different to the Victorian "lassoing phenomena with Latin names, listing, docketing and systematizing. Belsen and Hiroshima have gone some way towards teaching us humility" (105). At the end of the essay Golding sounds a little like Benjamin or W. G. Sebald when he says that "it is not the complete specimen for the collector's cabinet that excites us. It is the fragment, the hint. For the universe has blown wide open, is a door from which man does not know whether blessing or menace will come" (105).

6. See my discussion of Acampora's *Corporal Compassion* in the introduction.

7. Golding, *The Inheritors*, hereafter *TI*.

8. The "sadness of the creatures" is the second line of Auden's "Our Hunting Fathers," a poem that deals with the issue of human inheritance. For an interesting discussion of this poem in the wider context of Auden's anti-Romantic appropriation of nature, see Rainer Emig, "Auden and Ecology," in Stan Smith, ed., *The Cambridge Companion to W. H. Auden.* (Cambridge: Cambridge University Press, 2004), pp. 212–225.

9. Other films in the series include *I Dismember Mama* (2000) and *The Killer Inside Me* (2000). Grandin's status as a media darling was cemented by HBO's 2010 biopic *Temple Grandin*, with Claire Danes in the title role.

10. Grandin is included (twice) in Susan J. Armstrong and Richard G. Bot-
zler, eds., *The Animal Ethics Reader* (London: Routledge, 2003), pp. 184–186,
187–190. In "Deflections," his essay in *Philosophy and Animal Life*, Ian Hacking
writes: "laws have a moral stature not only because they create legal duties
and obligations but also because they are benchmarks from which to move
on. Grandin's norm for abattoirs has the same virtue" (163–164). Besides
the odd pairing of "abattoirs" and "virtue," there is much else here one can
find unnerving. Hacking writes that Grandin "changed the practices of most
American abattoirs and in so doing has made the animals' last walk down
the alley of death less horrible" (149); on the face of it the welfarist call for
improving conditions and reducing animal suffering. The serious difficulties
inherent in animal welfare notwithstanding, large-scale industrial slaughter
is surely a problem even for welfarists. Has Grandin become a sacred cow
for a movement too anxious to avoid seeming "radical"? Are the majority of
meat packing plants "less horrible" for the millions of animals who die there
or for the mainly poor, mainly nonwhite people who labor in them? For a
sober look at the state of modern U.S. abattoirs, see Gail A. Eisnitz, *Slaughter-
house* (New York: Prometheus, 1997). On the abolitionist position see Gary
Francione, *Rain Without Thunder: The Ideology of the Animals Rights Movement* (Phil-
adelphia: Temple University Press, 1996), and *Animals as Persons: Essays on the
Abolition of Animal Exploitation* (New York: Columbia University Press, 2008).

11. Toward the end of the book, Grandin says that she is often asked if she is
a vegetarian. Grandin almost addresses but finally dismisses the issue and
moves swiftly on. There are a number of missed opportunities in the book,
but it is the deflection itself that is telling (*Thinking* 235).

12. Köhler's *The Mentality of Apes*, published in 1925, dealt with the issue of "prob-
lem solving." Köhler showed that chimpanzees possessed the capacity (or
"insight") to resolve practical problems and proceed to carry out solutions.

13. The discrete religiosity of mechanical food production is the subject of
Nikolaus Geyrhalter's film *Our Daily Bread*, which I discuss in more detail in
chapter 5.

14. In 1940 Benjamin declared that historical materialism alone has the poten-
tial to "seize hold of a memory as it flashes up at a moment of danger" (the-
sis 6, "Theses" 247). Benjamin's insistence on the compatibility between
materialism and mysticism (a peculiarity characteristic also of Weil) turns

up in the "Theses" in the examination of historical materialism into which Benjamin slips the idea of "messianic time" as the moment that refuses the homogenization and emptying out of the timeline of narrative history and so introduces a new possibility into the world. Under the auspices of historical materialism, time does not unfold in installments along the triumphant axis of Progress, but as non-narrative and fragmentary. Opinions vary on Benjamin's reconciliation between materialism and mysticism. Gershom Scholem believed that "the 'Theses' mark Benjamin's decisive break with historical materialism and a return to the metaphysical-theological concerns of his early thought" (Beiner 423). For Beatrice Hanssen the combination failed to deliver a coherent politics (7), while in "Walter Benjamin, the Arcades Project," J. M. Coetzee regards Benjamin as a reluctant materialist, seduced to Marxism by the love of a dangerous woman (*Inner Workings* 42).

15. For a definition of Benjamin's *Kreatur*, see Hanssen (103–105).

16. See especially Crawford's chapter "Literature of Atrocity" (50–80). Crawford also draws on Benjamin's antiteleological view of history (25).

17. *The Sportswriter* is the first of the Frank Bascombe trilogy, followed by *Independence Day* (1995) and *The Lay of the Land* (2006).

3. The Indignities of Species in Darrieussecq's *Pig Tales*

1. *Truie* is French for sow. Although the compactness of the French pun *Truismes* does not quite survive the English translation, the play of words is maintained in the phonetic interchange of "tale" and "tail." I shall be using the English title, except when quoting sources that stick with the original French. Darrieussecq's use of *truisme* recalls Derrida's play on *bête* and *bêtise* in "The Animal That Therefore I Am" (398).

2. "Piggle-squiggles" is the translation of *écriture de cochon*, literally "pig writing." I will be using the French expression throughout.

3. Michel Lantelme, "Darrieussecq's *Pig Tales*: Marianne's Misfortunes at the Turn of the Millennium," *Romantic Review* 90.4 (1990): 527–536.

4. In its nod toward autobiographical narrative, *Pig Tales* reflects some of Darrieussecq's preoccupations in her 1997 PhD thesis "Moments critiques dans l'autobiographie contemporaine. Ironie, tragique et autofiction chez George Perec, Michel Leiris, Serge Doubrovsky et Hervé" ("Critical Moments in the Contemporary Autobiography. Tragic Irony and Auto-fiction in the works

of George Perec, Michel Leiris, Serge Doubrovsky and Hervé Guibert"). In *Pig Tales* textual opacity is the measure of the heroine's bodily transformation. In Darrieussecq's subsequent novels, language remains turned to the material at the neurological and microbiological levels. Simon Kemp described Darrieussecq's work from *Naissance des fantômes* onwards as "micro-narratives of the mind's surface" (Kemp 429). I will return to Kemp's arguments later in the chapter.

5. In "Dishing the Dirt," Gaudet provides details of the novel's popular success in France and beyond. Jean-Luc Godard bought the rights to the film version of the book, which (perhaps fortuitously) has not yet materialized.

6. Frédéric Badré, "Une nouvelle tendance en littérature" *Le Monde,* October 3, 1998. Although Houellebecq, not undeservedly, holds court here, the 1990s saw an energetic resurgence of writing by women. See Rye and Worton's illuminating introduction to *Women's Writing in Contemporary France* (1–26), Didier Jacob's piece "*Mesdames Sans Gêne*" in *Le Nouvel Observateur,* special issue, 39 (1999); and William Cloonan, "Literary Scandal: Fin du siècle and the Novel in 1999," *French Review* 74.1 (October 2000): 14–30. Despite the difference and variety amongst these writers (in addition to Houellebecq and Darrieussecq, a partial list includes Linda Lê, Annie Ernaux, Christine Angot, Nina Bouraoui, and Virginie Despentes, whose 1999 novel *Baise-Moi* was made into the controversial film in 2000, codirected by Despentes and Coralie Trinh Thi), Jacob underscores the shared preoccupation with the body and with graphic violence and sex of these "nouvelles marquises de Sade." Badré called the new tendency postnaturalist, which, posited against the avant-garde, returns the novel to the fabric of everyday experience. Although it is possible to link Darrieussecq to this (post)naturalist method, she owes at least as much to the antirealism of the *nouveau roman*.

7. *Pourquoi une truie?*

"De toutes les questions possibles, sauf peut-être « comment ça va?", c'est la question qu'on m'a le plus posée depuis la publication de *Truismes* en 1996.

Je n'ai pas vraiment de réponse, sauf statistique. On traite les femmes de truie plus souvent que de jument, de vache, de guenon, de vipère ou de tigresse; plus souvent encore que de girafe, de sangsue, de limace, de pieuvre ou de tarentule; et beaucoup plus souvent que de scolopendre, de rhinocéros femelle ou de koala.

C'est simple. Mais est-ce que ça répond à la question? Posée si souvent, c'est qu'elle porte ailleurs, c'est qu'elle questionne quelqu'un d'autre, ou quelque chose d'autre. On toque au carreau. Mais y a-t-il quelqu'un, quand on écrit? *(Zoo 7–8)*

8. Carol J. Adams has most consistently provided the linkage between the rhetoric of femininity and animality. See *The Sexual Politics of Meat*, *The Pornography of Meat*, and "Identity and Vegan Feminism in the Twenty-First Century," an Interview with Tom Tyler in *Parallax* 12.1 (2006): 120–128.

9. Jordan is quoting from Lidia Curti, *Female Stories, Female Bodies: Narrative, Identity, and Representation* (London: Macmillan, 1998), p. 107.

10. Michel Houellebecq's *Les particules élémentaires* (Paris: Flammarion, 1998) was published in the UK as *Atomised*, trans. Frank Wynne (London: Heinemann, 2000). For a first-rate discussion of the indictments of liberalism in general and of sexual liberation in particular in contemporary French literature, see Abecassis's "The Eclipse of Desire," to which I return later in this chapter. Two other works, each differently pitted against French liberalist philosophy, are relevant in this context: Dominique Lecourt, *The Mediocracy: French Philosophy Since the Mid-1970s,* trans. Gregory Elliott (London: Verso, 2001), which includes a brief but incisive commentary on Houellebecq (66). See also Wolfe's assault on Luc Ferry in "Old Orders for New: Ecology, Animal Rights, and the Poverty of Humanism" (*Animal Rites* 21–43).

11. In *Atomised*, humanity is ultimately transcended by a race of (sexless) posthuman cyborgs, while in *Pig Tales* it succumbs to human-animal hybridity. Darrieussecq and Houellebecq situate many of their literary experiments and social critiques in the convenient period of the near future, as, for example, in Darrieussecq's *White* or Houellebecq's *The Possibility of an Island.*

12. For critiques of classical anthropomorphism, see Tom Tyler, "If Horses Had Hands," *Society and Animals* 11.3 (2003): 267–281. A useful discussion of anthropomorphism and its vicissitudes can be found in Erica Fudge, *Animal* (London: Reaktion, 2002). For challenges to commonly held ideas about the fallacies of anthropomorphism, see Lorraine Daston and Gregg Mitman, eds., *Thinking With Animals: New Perspectives on Anthropomorphism* (New York: Columbia

University Press, 2005). Marc Bekoff has continually written about animals' emotional and moral sensibilities. See, for example, Marc Bekoff and Jessica Pierce, *Wild Justice: The Moral Lives of Animals* (Chicago: University of Chicago Press, 2009); or Marc Bekoff, *Minding Animals: Awareness, Emotions, and Heart* (Oxford: Oxford University Press, 2002). See also Acampora's *Corporal Compassion* (85–86) on the "rehabilitation" of anthropomorphism.

13. "All writing is piggery" (my translation). Artaud's statement appeared in his early surrealist text *Le Pèse-Nerfs*.

14. For a survey of Deleuze's various notions of "becoming," see "Becoming" in Claire Colebrook, *Gilles Deleuze* (London: Routledge, 2002), pp. 125–145.

15. Other examples of mirrors, reflections, and photographs include scenes in the apartment of her first lover Honoré (37, 44), a photo on the political campaign posters "for a healthier world" (55, 74), a passing reflection in a shop window (65), a hotel room mirror (76).

16. This point concerning naïveté carries over to the novel's social/political dimension. As a parody of liberal humanism, the deadpan narration makes perfect sense. For *Pig Tales*'s is a world defined through rampant consumerism, violence, and sex, from which the traces of friendship and love have all but disappeared. If, however, this fictional world is really ours, then it is our own (biased) reading—with its emotional and moral preconceptions—that is outdated and out of touch. In an ironic reversal, it is no longer the protagonist who is dim, but the reader.

17. The face, as the saying goes, is the gateway to interiority; it is what most personalizes, as is evident from the artistic form consecrated to the revelation of personality: the portrait. The uncanny proximity between apes and humans lends itself particularly well to the portrait form. One example of the use of the portrait to convey individuality is the 2004 exhibition Face to Face by photographer James Mollison at London's Museum of Natural History. The exhibition's blurb read: "Extraordinary portraits of orphaned apes, highlighting the vitality and intelligence of these magnificent threatened animals—our closest biological relatives." This approach to the subject of conservation and animal rights hinges on the invocation of kinship (intuitive and biological) between "us" and "them." A revaluation of kinship is important for the understanding of a variety of interactions between kindred beings, including violence. This is one of the implicit concerns of this

study, which moves beyond the question of animals as a matter of kinship versus otherness. One problem with rights discourse is that it does not problematize the space of kinship. Kinship is, in fact, a contradictory and difficult zone. It makes possible amity and moral inclusion, but also and perhaps just as significantly, aggression. An assumption common in human rights discourse is that systematic violence (like torture or genocide) requires the "dehumanization" of victims. But although violence entails a distancing between perpetrator and victim, neither is it thinkable in the purview of complete otherness. A (qualified) recognition kinship is thus present in the perpetrating of violence. One can wreak violence on she or he who— like me—is recognized as capable of suffering: my kin. *Pig Tales*'s interspecies economy crucially shifts the discussion away from the register of kinship (resemblance versus difference) to that of power. Michael Nichols and Jane Goodall's book of photographs *Brutal Kinship* (New Jersey: Aperture, 1999) illustrates the contradictory status of kinship. Homi Bhabha has recently spoken about "neighbourliness" as a complex, paradoxical space of agency. "'Also, I know that a man can become of an incredible wickedness very suddenly . . . ': Time, Agency and the Banality of Evil"; CCSR Annual Lecture, June 10, 2009, University of East London. I thank Erika Rundle for the reference to Nichols's book.

18. On Lévinas's humanism see Derrida's "The Animal that Therefore I Am" (381). *Animal Rites* devotes considerable space to critiquing Lévinasian humanism, while Calarco's chapter on Lévinas in *Zoographies* explores the limitations and the potentialities in Lévinas for a nonanthropocentric philosophy.

19. "My novel is anything but psychological," a statement made by Darrieussecq to Shirley Jordan in an unpublished interview (qtd. in Jordan 147).

20. Additionally, one can read bestiality in the novel following Derrida's ironic lead in "The Animal That Therefore I Am," which makes bestiality the only thing which is truly "proper to man," since animals are by definition exempt from this transgression (409). For another literary take on bestiality, see Edward Albee's play *The Goat; or, Who Is Sylvia?* (London: Methuen, 2003).

21. For a reading of the overlap between gender and species in *Pig Tales*, see Naama Harel, "Challenging the Species Barrier in Metamorphosis Literature: The Case of Marie Darrieussecq's *Pig Tales*" in *Comparative Critical Studies* 2.3 (2005): 397–409. Harel makes a similar point to the one made here,

that whilst "interpretations of *Pig Tales* as a political or a feminist fable are well established, they all ignore the interspecies aspect of the story" (1). The novel's feminist focus must not take precedence over its preoccupation with species.

22. I should note that hybridity or transhumanity need not be monstrous. Acampora's *Corporal Compassion* includes quite a number of interbodily points of contact between humans and animals, with a distinctively "convivial" feel:

> The convivial challenge for humans . . . is to interpret the skin-boundary not as an impermeable *barrier* encapsulating corporeality but as a surface of somatic *contact*. In Paul Shepard's words, "the epidermis of the skin is . . . like a pond surface or forest soil, not a shell so much as a delicate interpenetration. It reveals the [human] self ennobled and extended . . . because the beauty and complexity of nature are continuous with ourselves"; as John Compton puts it, "what is characteristic of embodied, inter-subjective, world-related human life . . . is structurally analogous to what is found in other [living] regions of the natural world." (39–40)

23. *Zoo* uses a similar play between linguistic ability and animal needs. In "Connaissance des singes," for example, a sullen talking chimpanzee called Marcel (his various hang-ups are indeed reminiscent of Proust) explains to the narrator (a woman writer with writers' block) that eating reduces his capacity for speech. In *Pig Tales* the narrator discovers that reading books reduces hunger.

24. Nietzsche's "transhumanism" is also important here. See Jami Weinstein, "Traces of the Beast: Becoming Neitzsche, Becoming Animal, and the Figure of the Transhuman," which tracks Nietzsche's impact on the rethinking of humanity and animality (*A Nietzschean Bestiary* 301–318).

25. See for example Jacques Derrida, *Writing and Difference* [*L'Écriture et la différence*, 1967], trans. Alan Bass (New York: Routledge, 1981), which, incidentally, includes an essay on Artaud. Derrida's central notion of writing cuts across all of his work. It reinstates writing as nonsecondary to speech (or the voice) and reveals language as a heterological system, internally other and "othered." This includes recognizing the *in*human within human language, within literature. See also Barthes, *Writing Degree Zero* [*Le Degré zéro de L'Ecriture*, 1953].

26. More recently, Hamsun has begun to enjoy a critical revival. See, for example, Jeffrey Frank, "In from the Cold: The Return of Knut Hamsun," *New Yorker,* December 26, 2005. http://www/newyorker.com/archive/2005/12/26/051226crat_atlarge.In 2009, the year that marked the 150th anniversary of Hamsun's birth, the Norwegian government met with the (routine) Israeli remonstrations over the author's commemoration. See Cnaan Liphshiz's "Row Grows Over Norway Honor for Pro-Nazi Nobel Laureate," *Haaretz,* June 21, 2009, http://www.haaretz.com/hasen/spages/1094430.html.

4. Cine-Zoos

1. I am grateful to Richard Kerridge for drawing my attention to zoos' air of dreariness, not unlike the tedium of the inner city or suburban neglect. One film that illustrates this point clearly is Frederick Wiseman's 1993 *Zoo.*

2. On the cultural, ideological, as well as commercial structures of (in particular) wildlife television, see Cynthia Chris's *Watching Wildlife* (Minneapolis: University of Minnesota Press, 2006).

3. Acampora is explicit about the "pattern of pornography" that underlies zoos. See also Bob Mullan and Garry Marvin, *Zoo Culture* (London: Weidenfeld and Nicolson, 1987); Paul Shepard, *The Others: How Animals Made Us Human* (Washington, DC: Island, 1996); and Randy Malamud, *Reading Zoos: Representations of Animals and Captivity* (New York: New York University Press, 1998).

4. On taxidermy and animal art see the *Botched Taxidermy* special issue of *Antennae* 7 Autumn (2008), http://www.antennae.org.uk/ANTENNAE%20ISSUE%207.doc.pdf.

5. Baker's discussion is partly a response to moral objections to postmodern animal art. The strongest objections Baker cites are by John Simons in *Animal Rights and the Politics of Literary Representation* (Basingstoke: Palgrave, 2002); and Anthony Julius, *Transgressions: The Offences of Art* (London: Thames and Hudson, 2002).

6. Jonathan Burt explains that in postmodern art "ideas of pet-keeping, sentimentality, anthropomorphism, and a literal depiction of animal beauty are rejected in favour of bleak and figuratively transgressive versions of the animal" (Burt 26). Examples abound. Corinne Rusch's 2009 installation piece *Thinking Around—Metaphors in Nature*, for example, uses the hides of taxidermied animals (a deer, a badger) to question the cultural "embalming" of

feminine beauty. The animals are cut in half and mounted backward on the wall, so that their backsides face the viewer. The piece also includes photographs of women posing amongst an array of stuffed animals, mimicking still life paintings. The mounted rears are witty inversions of hunting trophies. But there is also confusion in this piece that simultaneously flaunts and disavows the animal. During a Q&A with the artist, Rusch was asked if she was vegetarian—a question that frequently acts as shorthand for raising the sort of ethical questions Baker examines. "No, not at all," Rusch replied, "I love meat." The reply illustrates just how taboo sentimentalism, nostalgia, and melancholy (in Benjamin's sense) have become in contemporary art. "Repeating with a difference" is now the ultimate ethical gesture. But this can seem more deflecting than either sentimentality or nostalgia; reality is present as pure confrontation but emptied of its vulnerability for both artist and viewer. For an overview of recent animal art, see Massimiliano Gioni, "Where the Wild Things Are," *Tate Magazine* 11 (Autumn 2007), http://www .tate.org.uk/tateetc/issue11/wildthings.htm.

7. See Hilda Kean, *Animal Rights: Political and Social Change in Britain Since 1800* (London: Reaktion, 1998).

8. In " . . . From Wild Technology to Electric Animal," Lippit discusses Francis Bacon's account of being "moved" by photographs of slaughterhouses. "Since the animal possesses no discernible subjectivity," writes Lippit, "the human subject cannot rediscover itself in the place of this other. While a human being can project anthropomorphic characteristics onto the animal or experience emotions (such as pathos or sympathy) in response to its being, an impenetrable screen—language—divides the loci of animal and human being. If Bacon has indeed effected an identification with this image, then where does one locate the source of Bacon's identification: in the animal or in the photograph?" (" . . . From Wild Technology" 120). The difference between Lippit's project and mine lies in the way we treat the dominant history of thinking about animals. Lippit is acutely aware of the problems of Western metaphysics: what or who is "the animal" this tradition is referring to? In what "discernible" sense do animals lack subjectivity? And how can the assumption of the absence of language categorically distinguish between humans and animals? Lippit's critical reflections result in the emergence of cinema as *symptom*: an apparatus symptomatic of the dominant tradition's

own aporias or lacks. My approach is less diagnostic. It attempts to find a position outside the dominant tradition that reads the animal as otherness and lack, in order to reframe the question of the animal. As is my method throughout the book, I am conducting my inquiry from the reverse perspective, one that rejects the accepted parameters (subjectivity, language, identification) of the human. I proceed from what *is* discernible in both humans and animals: their existence as embodied, finite beings.

9. Bazin describes the actors in Antonioni's *Cronaca di Amore* as "caught in the maze of the plot like laboratory rats being sent through a labyrinth" ("De Sica" 66).

10. Bazin is sometimes called a "Catholic humanist"; see, for example, Colin MacCabe's "Barthes and Bazin," in Jean-Michel Rabaté, ed., *Writing the Image After Roland Barthes* (Philadelphia: University of Pennsylvania Press, 1997), p. 75. Bazin's roots in phenomenology and Personalism, his association with the journal *Esprit*, make the label perfectly acceptable. My point is certainly not to argue against a humanist reading of Bazin, only to follow through the (nonhumanist) implications of the realism he espoused.

11. Between 1940 and 1943 Simone Weil was in contact with the anti-Nazi publication *Témoignage Chrétien*. She helped distribute its first three issues (*Three Women in Dark Times* 157–158). In his foreword to the 2004 edition of *What Is Cinema?* vol. 1, Dudley Andrew writes that in 1943 Bazin was to publish the essay that would become "The Ontology of the Photographic Image" in a special issue of *Confluences*, printed at the same publishing house responsible for *Témoignage Chrétien*. Publication was delayed when the Gestapo raided the journal's office (1:xiv). Incidental affinities continue via Roberto Rossellini's 1952 film *Europa '51* (which Bazin wrote about in "In Defense of Roberto Rossellini"), whose main character (played by Ingrid Bergman) is based on Weil.

12. The revived interest in Bazin confirms his importance to contemporary film theory and (new) visual media. See, for example, Daniel Morgan's "Rethinking Bazin: Ontology and Realist Aesthetics," which considers Bazin's adaptability to "a rapidly changing media landscape" (443). Similar to my own rereading of realism, Jennifer Fay considers "the absence of man in Bazin's formulation" ("Seeing/Loving Animals" 52) as the opening up of his aesthetics to posthuman ethics (43).

13. Tyulkin's films were first shown to Western audiences as part of the Fallen Curtain screenings programmed by Marcel Sthwierin at the 2005 Oberhausen

International Short Film Festival. On the program, see George Clark, "Seeking the Other," *Vertigo* 9.2 (Autumn/Winter 2005): 12–13.

14. See Ruslan Janumyan, "Kira Muratova," *Senses of Cinema* 28 (2003), http://archive.senseofcinema.com/contents/directors/03/muratova.html. See also Jonathan Rosenbaum, "Kira Muratova's Home Truths: *The Asthenic Syndrome*," in *Essential Cinema: On the Necessity of Film Canons* (Baltimore: Johns Hopkins University Press, 2004), pp. 43–47.

15. "Play. A cat plays with a mouse before eating it. What is that play? It's theatre. It's an étude. When she's eaten enough, a thousand mice, and begins to play with a piece of paper . . . that's art in nature" (Muratova qtd. in Taubman 106). Taubman writes that "throughout the film she used domestic animals—dogs, cats, even canaries—to provide a mute protest. Muratova, like the post-conversion Tolstoy, is a vegetarian. She attributed the turn that led her to make *Asthenic Syndrome* to 'the presence of Lev Tolstoy in my life, to his ideas and world-view . . . I so dislike the way nature and matter are arranged, how animals suffer, I don't like the fact that some of them eat others'" (Taubman 48).

5. Scientific Surrealism in Franju and Wiseman

1. Franju is not the first to film animal slaughter, but he is the first to devote an entire film to it as a complex theme. An earlier film that uses documentary footage of animal slaughter in a similar way to Franju is Alberto Cavalcanti's 1926 *Rien que les heures*. Cavalcanti's is one of the so-called city films of the 1920s, along with Walter Ruttmann's *Berlin: Symphony of a Great City* (1927) or Dziga Vertov's *Man with a Movie Camera* (1929), which revel in cinema's unique ability to probe urban space and time. Cavalcanti's film includes an episode in which a typically bourgeois man is having his lunch. The camera focuses on his plate as he cuts his steak, then, in superimposition, framed by the plate, we see the origin of the meat in the slaughtering of an animal (a horse?). Violence fractures the civilized facade of middle-class existence. This works conventionally enough as an allegory and social critique of the brutal underbelly of modern urban life. But, as in Franju's own city film, the slaughter sequence also carries an inalienable literal power.

2. The exhibition Undercover Surrealism at London's Hayward Gallery (May-July 2006) examined the contribution of *Documents* and the Bataille milieu

to a range of disciplines, from anthropology and ethnography to cinema. It featured Lotar's photographs with the accompanying text from the journal. The images and text are reprinted in *Encyclopaedia Acephalica* (London: Atlas, 1996), pp. 72–74.

3. *Sang des bêtes* (1949), *En passant par la Lorraine* (1950), and *Hôtel des invalides* (1951) form a documentary triptych whose main theme can be defined as modernity's slaughterhouse. The films deal with the abattoir, technology and factory work, and the ravages of war. Franju explores his theme across several contexts and species. Like *Primate*, *Sang des bêtes* belongs to a series whose subjects include both humans and animals.

4. Not everyone agrees that Franju's cinema is explicitly political. For a counter-reading of *Eyes Without a Face* that rejects the predominance of historical allegory see Curtis Bowman, "A Film Without Politics," *Kinoeye* 2.13 (2002), http://www.kinoeye.org/02/13/bowman13.php.

5. One example of this surrealist "lagging" is Luis Buñuel and Salvador Dali's famous *Un Chien andalou* (1928), in which the surgical eye slicing moment (in reality the eye of a calf) easily "outruns" the film's other surrealist images. I recently watched again Hans Richter's *Dreams That Money Can Buy* (1947) and was struck by a certain loss of pitch in some of the film's more wondrous and "shocking" images. To an extent, canonical surrealism suffered the consequences of its own success, especially in terms of its influence in ubiquitous areas like advertising and television. And, although the movement was internally conflicted (Breton versus Bataille), it on the whole failed to realize a truly radical political program.

6. On the success of Dr. Von Hagens, see Virilio,"A Pitiless Art" (41). Cary Wolfe's "From *Dead Meat* to Glow in the Dark Bunnies: Seeing 'The Animal Question' in Contemporary Art" addresses Eduardo Kac's controversial transgenic animal art. "Animal Beings" special issue of *Parallax* 12.1 (2006): 95–109.

7. "Je te frapperai sans colère et sans haine, comme un boucher."

8. Liz Ellsworth's *Frederick Wiseman: A Guide to References and Sources* (Boston: Hall, 1979), pp. 102–158, meticulously compiles statistical information on Wiseman's films. Ellsworth's statistics are repeated in several studies of *Primate*, for instance, in Thomas Benson's "The Rhetorical Structure of Frederick Wiseman's *Primate*." Benson writes: "The film is 105 minutes long—feature

length—and contains . . . 569 shots. That works out to an average of 11 seconds per shot for *Primate*, approximately half of the average shot length of 22 seconds in Wiseman's *High School*" (Benson 193).

9. Like *Sang des bêtes, Primate* explores the vicissitudes of technological rationalism. Donna Haraway's extensive *Primate Visions* discusses postwar primatology as "largely . . . a result of the extraordinary wartime mobilization of science" (120). The connections between rationalism, technology, and organized violence—and between Franju's and Wiseman's films—are thus traceable along multiple axes: militarily, scientifically, culturally, and aesthetically.

10. For a discussion of the ethics of vivisection, see Diamond, "Experimenting on Animals." For a welfarist approach to animal experiments, see Jean Kazez's *Animalkind: What We Owe to Animals* (Oxford: Wiley-Blackwell, 2010), especially chapter 8, "Science and Survival" (136–155). I have already briefly discussed the distinction between welfarism and abolitionism in chapter 2. Arguments for tighter regulation to reduce pain and increase animal welfare in research do nothing to challenge the rationale that legitimates the use of animals in the first place. From an abolitionist perspective, moreover, welfarism is ultimately counterproductive, since it reinforces rather than combats the rationale of domination. In food production, too, the move toward more "compassionate" forms of exploitation (bigger cages, free-range meat, etc.) avoids the fundamental ethical question: does it make sense to speak of a "compassionate killing" of animals? An abolitionist approach seeks to end all animal exploitation as morally unjustifiable, no matter how "humanely" exploitation may be carried out.

11. On the limitations of mainstream bioethics vis-à-vis some of the ideas I have been discussing throughout this study, see Cary Wolfe, "Bioethics and the Posthumanist Imperative," in Eduardo Kac, ed., *Signs of Life: Bio Art and Beyond* (Cambridge: MIT Press, 2007), pp. 95–114.

12. It is interesting to contrast Haraway's reading of *Primate*'s scientific surrealism to Paul Virilio's assessment of avant-garde science in books such as *Art and Fear, The Information Bomb*, or *The Accident of Art*. Virilio's polemic against the nature and reach of contemporary biotechnology is politically and ethically alarmist, while Haraway celebrates the destabilizing effects surrealist science has on traditional humanist paradigms. Haraway's analysis seems complicit in the discourses she critiques. She sees *Primate* as exploring the

merging of human, animal, and machine. While wholly aware of the hierarchies of power that Yerkes exemplifies (in terms of species and of race), Haraway's focus is on the fluidity of boundaries between species. Haraway's work in this respect embodies some of the difficulties inherent in posthumanist theory that tends to separate the ethical from other aspects of its inquiry.

13. One essay that (lovingly) evokes the haunting visuality of the biotechnological workspace is Sarah Franklin's "The Cyborg Embryo: Our Path to Transbiology," *Theory, Culture and Society* 23 (December 2006): 167–187. Franklin describes in great detail the interiors and ecology of the embryology laboratory, from the "dirty room" (IVF surgery) to the "clean" derivation lab, and down to the individual tools used by embryologists in their work ("it is not uncommon for embryologists to make their own pipettes by hand . . . with a Bunsen burner" [174]). My thanks to Noreen Giffney and Michael O'Rourke for bringing this essay to my attention.

6. Werner Herzog's Creaturely Poetics

1. Alan Singer's remark made at the Werner Herzog: Between the Visionary and the Documentary conference, September 16–18, 2005, at the Goethe Institute, London. My concern is with what Herzog's "regard for nature"—be it great or small—might mean in the context of (his) cinema, the wildlife film, and in terms of Herzog's treatment of the human figure.

2. Singer's keynote "Through the Ruby Looking Glass: Transcending the Visionary," at Werner Herzog: Between the Visionary and the Documentary.

3. In 2007 Herzog released *Rescue Dawn*, a fictional reworking of *Little Dieter Needs to Fly*. As the distinction between fiction and nonfiction in Herzog is tenuous at best, much of what I argue here via Herzog's documentaries applies also to his fiction films, complete with their notoriously arduous shooting expeditions.

4. Errol Morris often uses a similar device of arrested looks (e.g. *Stairway to Heaven*, *The Fog of War*, *Standard Operating Procedure*). The device is interesting for the way it halts motion and suspends (rather than accentuates) the personal expression of the "framed" subject.

5. Throughout this study I try to disclose the stillness and inertness of human beings, a strategy that in my introduction I described as "contraction." In her

superb *Vibrant Matter*, Jane Bennett performs the materialist gesture in the opposite direction, urging us to recognize the "thing-power" of inert stuff, investing matter itself with an "energetic vitality" (5). The two gestures complement one another, as Bennett explains: "the case for matter as active needs also to readjust the status of human actants: not by denying humanity's awesome, awful powers, but by presenting these powers as evidence of our own constitution as vital materiality. In other words, human power is itself a kind of thing-power" (10).

6. Attentiveness implies a mode of seeing that, while remaining undisclosed to (and thus unreciprocated by) the object, does not emanate from a position of power. It eschews scopophilia by falling short of controlling the object as subservient or beautiful. This looking draws on Weil's notion of attention as a kind of absent-minded thinking, an orientation with no specific object or idea. Attention might also invoke Lévinas's notion of the other's face seen in its nakedness. Lévinas gives the example of looking without being able to determine the color of the other's eyes. Voyeurism, on the other hand, belongs to an economy of looking where the other appears as a definite object (of desire) with particular (fetishized) traits—that is, the object of voyeurism is, paradoxically, never naked. My point is that *not all discrete looking falls into the theoretical domain of voyeurism*.

7. In her chapter on Nietzsche's *Ecce Homo* in *Beasts of the Modern Imagination,* Margot Norris uses this lack of reciprocity between subject and object to point out that Nietzsche's (mock-) biography is oblivious to its imagined readers. Nietzsche does not seek to communicate, educate, or persuade. His self is asserted outside of the contractual exchange between author and reader. Thus Nietzsche seeks to free himself from the social as the foundation of individuality. His person is a natural fact, physiologically and metabolically self-generating. "Nietzsche's *Ecce Homo*: Behold the Beast," *Beasts of the Modern Imagination*, pp. 73–100.

8. Benjamin's 1916 essay "On Language as Such and on the Language of Man" introduces the notion of "nature's mourning." In Paul Celan's short prose piece "Conversation in the Mountains," human and nonhuman nature speak, and human language itself emanates from the impersonal expressiveness of nature. *Paul Celan: Collected Prose*, trans. Rosemarie Waldrop (Manchester: Carcanet, 1986), pp. 17–22. See Hanssen's discussion of Benjamin and Celan in *Walter Benjamin's Other History,* pp. 155–160.

9. Weil is discussing the connections between necessity and beauty, between nature and art. In this and other passages, and despite her dislike of him, Weil is echoing Nietzsche's assertion in *The Birth of Tragedy* that nature itself is inherently artistic, regardless of the human agency of the artist. Weil writes: "Matter is not beautiful when it obeys man, but only when it obeys God" ("Love of God" 77).

10. See, for example, the February 2006 issue of *Sight and Sound*, which includes Catherine Wheatley's piece on *Hidden*, "Secrets, Lies and Videotape," and Nick James's "The Greatest Show on Earth" on *Grizzly Man* and *Wild Blue Yonder*.

11. David Lynch's *Lost Highway* (1996) treads similar paranoid ground as *Hidden* and, like *Hidden,* refuses narrative resolution. Unlike *Hidden*, however, *Lost Highway* is genuinely frightening. Its lack of logical structure feeds spookily into the ambience of visceral terror. Few of *Hidden*'s eulogizers ponder the comparison with *Lost Highway*, yet even when Philip French cites Lynch as a precursor, he remains oblivious to the emptiness and sterility that cripple Haneke's film. Philip French, "They're all out to get him . . . " *Observer,* January 29, 2006. http://www.guardian.co.uk/theobserver/2006/jan/29/features .review77. Rather than calling attention to contemporary hollowness, *Hidden* exemplifies it. More successful in dealing with the sort of issues raised by *Hidden* and also invoking the animal as oblique symbol is Dominik Moll's *Lemming* (2005).

12. There is nothing new in cinema's fascination with the animal body as the pure moving image. Thomas Edison's 1903 *Electrocution of an Elephant* is an early example of what Tom Gunning called the "cinema of attractions." The "cinema of attractions" describes the non-narrative, attraction-based origins of film (from 1895 to about 1906). See Lisa Cartwright's discussion of *Electrocution of an Elephant* in *Screening the Body* (13–16; 17–19). My point is that (as far as is legally possible), the animal continues to provide the ideal disposable body as a cinematic "attraction."

13. In an interview for BBC4's flagship documentary slot Storyville, Graham Dorrington, the subject of Herzog's film *White Diamond* (2004), said that Herzog regards nature as "continual murder." See http://www.bbc.co.uk/bbc-four/documentaries/storyville/graham-dorrington.shtml.

14. In *Animal Liberation* Peter Singer famously proclaimed that neither he (nor his wife) loved animals. Despite being a critic of Singer's utilitarianism, Cary

Wolfe also distances himself from the idea of love as the foundation of justice for animals. He explains that "because the discourse of speciesism . . . can be used to mark *any* social other, we need to understand that the ethical and philosophical urgency of confronting the institution of speciesism and crafting a posthumanist theory of the subject *has nothing to do with whether you like animals*" (*Animal Rites* 7). But is not the very notion of a "philosophical urgency" understandable precisely as something other than reasoned calculation?

15. Children are often thought to have an intuitive connection with animals. Current attitudes to the young and to the "ontology of childhood" (from paeans to childhood innocence to moral panics about its violations and the pathologizing and criminalizing of youth by "experts") are partly shaped by the demands of a neoliberal market ideology. Treadwell's "refusal to grow up" challenges this ideology. His special relationship with animals is thus a main symptom of his alleged immaturity.

16. It is remarkable how, in a Western culture obsessed with child protection, the consumption of lamb or so-called veal is seldom thought of in terms of eating the flesh of child or infant animals. The inability to see childhood across the species barrier is not simply a failure of the imagination but an ethical failure as well: a misunderstanding of the extensive nature of attention. People may eat lamb while declaring lambs "cute." This is the difference between "seeing" and "attending."

17. See "Fact and Truth," in *Herzog on Herzog* (Cronin 238–272). In his *Minnesota Declaration*, Herzog proclaimed "ecstatic" or poetic truth over factual or "accountants'" truth. More recently, Herzog announced on his Web site the launching of weekend seminars called the Rogue Film School. The school is "not for the faint-hearted; it is for those who have travelled on foot, who have worked as bouncers in sex clubs or as wardens in a lunatic asylum." The school is not technical but "about a way of life" (http://www.roguefilmschool.com/default.asp).

18. Nietzsche, *The Birth of Tragedy*, hereafter *BT*.

19. In an evocative passage in §9, Nietzsche contrasts Greek and modern cheerfulness. The Greeks possessed an authentic capacity for joy because they also glimpsed "the terrible depths of nature" (*BT* 46). "Only in this sense can we imagine that we correctly understand the serious and meaningful concept of 'Greek cheerfulness'—while today . . . we constantly encounter this concept

of cheerfulness wrongly understood as a state of untroubled contentment"
(46). The contention is central to Nietzsche's critique of modernity and
offers a powerful challenge to our own age in which happiness is mandatory
and unhappiness pathologized and medicalized. Suffering itself is viewed as a
strange aberration, an anomaly to be eliminated or cured.

20. It is tempting to take further the musical convergences between Nietzsche
and Herzog, but this is perhaps the subject for a separate piece. I should
point out, though, that Nietzsche's discussion of the satyr as a Dionysian fig-
ure in §8 of *The Birth of Tragedy* calls to mind Herzog's many versions of "natu-
ral man." The satyr, writes Nietzsche, "is also the 'simple man' in contrast to
the god: the image of nature and nature's strongest impulses, the symbol of
those impulses and also the herald of its wisdom and art—musician, poet,
dancer and clairvoyant in a single person" (*BT* 44). Are not Herzog's "simple
men" and *enfants sauvages* versions of the Dionysian satyr? I am thinking, for
instance, about the character of Stroszek, who, while an apparently naive and
placid simpleton, is also a gifted musician, or of Kaspar Hauser (also played
by Bruno S., himself the original foundling), who clumsily rejoins civilization
from the wild. The wisdom of these figures (all "losers" in the societal sense)
lies in their embodiment of worldly suffering and in their instinctive affinity
with other sufferers (like the prostitute in *Stroszek*). A strong case can surely
be made for Treadwell as a present-day satyr—a wandering goat-man who,
having lost his tragic chorus, finds himself alone in a world without tragedy.

21. Herzog claims he came to music late and knew very little about it. Even if
one treats such a statement with skepticism, it reveals something about Her-
zog's antischolarly attitude to music. For Herzog the role of (preexisting)
music does not appeal to a musically literate audience. Music functions in
similar ways whether it is preexisting or especially composed.

22. For a reading that pins down *Lessons of Darkness*'s ecological, political, and cin-
ematic overlaps, see Nadia Bozak's excellent "Firepower: Herzog's Pure Cin-
ema as the Internal Combustion of War," *Cine Action* 68 (2006): 18–25.

Conclusion: Animal Saintliness

1. Quandt lists the many religious references and allusions in *Balthazar*. But he
believes that "Bresson's art never proceeds by strict or simple analogy ... he is
not an illustrator or allegorist—and his pessimism invalidates the affirmation

this reading too readily reaches for" (Quandt 19). See also Tim Cawkwell's thoughtful reading of Bresson in *The Filmgoer's Guide to God* (London: Darton, Longman and Todd, 2004).

2. The tension concerns the central theological problem of the nature of the relationship between God's grace and free will. Leszek Kolakowski's *God Owes Us Nothing: A Brief Remark on Pascal's Religion and on the Spirit of Jansenism* (Chicago: University of Chicago Press, 1995) is a brilliant account of the conflict between the Jansenists and the Jesuits. Bresson's films clearly grapple with the issue of determinism and divine grace. They beautifully reflect Jansenism's reactionary pessimism with regard to human freedom and salvation.

WORKS CITED

Abecassis, Jack. "The Eclipse of Desire: L'Affaire Houellebecq." *MLN* 115 (2000): 501–826.

Acampora, Ralph R. *Corporal Compassion: Animal Ethics and Philosophy of Body*. Pittsburgh: University of Pittsburgh Press, 2006.

—— "Extinction by Exhibition: Looking at and in the Zoo." *Human Ecology Review* 5.1 (1998): 1–4. http://www.humanecologyreview.org/pastissues/her51/51acampora.pdf. September 14, 2009.

Adams, Carol J. *The Pornography of Meat*. New York: Continuum, 2003.

—— *The Sexual Politics of Meat*. New York: Continuum, 2002.

Agamben, Giorgio. *Homo Sacer: Sovereign Power and Bare Life*. Trans. Daniel Heller-Roazen. Stanford: Stanford University Press, 1998.

—— *Remnants of Auschwitz: The Witness and the Archive*. Trans. Daniel Heller-Roazen. New York: Zone, 2002.

—— *The Open: Man and Animal*. Trans. Kevin Attell. Stanford: Stanford University Press, 2004.

Andrew, Dudley. "Foreword to the 2004 Edition." *What Is Cinema?* 1:ix–xxiv. Trans. Hugh Gray. London: University of California Press, 2005.

Asibong, Andrew. "*Mulier sacra*: Marie Chauvet, Marie Darrieussecq, and the Sexual Metamorphoses of 'Bare Life.'" *French Cultural Studies* 14.2 (2003): 169–177.

Badiou, Alain. *Ethics: An Essay on the Understanding of Evil.* Trans. Peter Hallward. London: Verso, 2001.

—— *Saint Paul: The Foundation of Universalism.* Trans. Ray Brassier. Stanford: Stanford University Press, 2003.

Baker, Steve. *The Postmodern Animal.* London: Reaktion, 2000.

—— "'You Kill Things to Look at Them': Animal Death in Contemporary Art." In the Animal Studies Group, *Killing Animals,* pp. 69–98. Urbana: University of Illinois Press, 2006.

Barthes, Roland. *Writing Degree Zero.* Trans. Annette Lavers and C. Smith. New York: Hill and Wang, 1977 [1953].

Bataille, Georges. "My Mother." *My Mother, Madame Edwarda, The Dead Man,* pp. 23–134. Trans. Austryn Wainhouse. London: Marion Boyars, 1996.

Baudrillard, Jean. "The Animals: Territory and Metamorphosis," *Simulacra and Simulation,* pp. 129–141. Trans. Sheila Faria Glaser. Ann Arbor: University of Michigan Press, 1994.

Bayley, John. "The Impersonality of William Golding: Some Implications and Comparisons." In John Carey, ed., *William Golding: The Man and His Books,* pp. 126–137. London: Faber, 1986.

Bazin, André. "Cinema and Exploration" *What Is Cinema?* 1:154–163. Trans. Hugh Gray. London: University of California Press, 2005.

—— "Death Every Afternoon." *Rites of Realism: Essays on Corporeal Cinema,* pp. 27–31. Ed. Ivone Margulies. Trans. Mark Cohen. Durham: Duke University Press, 2003.

—— "De Sica: Metteur en Scene" *What Is Cinema?* 2:61–78. Trans. Hugh Gray. London: University of California Press, 2005.

—— "In Defense of Rossellini" *What Is Cinema?* 2:93–101. Trans. Hugh Gray. London: University of California Press, 2005.

—— "The Virtues and Limitations of Montage." *What Is Cinema?* 1:41–52. Trans. Hugh Gray. London: University of California Press, 2005.

—— "*Umberto D*: A Great Work." *What Is Cinema?* 2:79–82. Trans. Hugh Gray. London: University of California Press, 2005.

—— *What Is Cinema?* Trans. Hugh Gray. 2 vols. London: University of California Press, 2005.

Beiner, Ronald. "Walter Benjamin's Philosophy of History." *Political Theory* 12.3 (1984): 423–434.

Bellow, Saul. *Henderson the Rain King*. London: Penguin, 2007 [1959].

Benjamin, Walter. "Theses on the Philosophy of History." In *Illuminations,* pp. 236–255. Trans. Harry Zorn. London: Pimlico, 1999 [1955].

—— "The Storyteller: Reflections on the Works of Nikolai Leskov." In *Illuminations,* pp. 83–107. Trans. Harry Zorn. London: Pimlico, 1999.

Bennett, Jane. *Vibrant Matter: A Political Ecology of Things*. Durham: Duke University Press, 2010.

Benson, Thomas. "The Rhetorical Structure of Frederick Wiseman's *Primate*." In William L. Nothstine, Carole Blair, and Gary A. Copeland, eds., *Critical Questions: Invention, Creativity, and the Criticism of Discourse and Media,* pp. 189–205. New York: St. Martin's, 1994.

Berger, John. "Why Look at Animals?" *About Looking,* pp. 3–28. London: Bloomsbury, 1980.

Bernstein, J. M. "Bare Life, Bearing Witness: Auschwitz and the Pornography of Horror" *Parallax* 10.1 January (2004): 2–16.

Blanchot, Maurice. "Affirmation (Desire, Affliction)." In *The Infinite Conversation,* pp. 106–122. Trans. Susan Hanson. Minneapolis: University of Minnesota Press, 1993.

Burkeman, Oliver. "Fatal Attraction." *Guardian,* January 27, 2006, p. 6.

Burt, Jonathan. *Animals in Film*. London: Reaktion, 2002.

Calarco, Matthew. *Zoographies: The Question of the Animal from Heidegger to Derrida*. New York: Columbia University Press, 2008.

Cameron, Sharon. *Impersonality: Seven Essays*. Chicago: University of Chicago Press, 2007.

Cartwright, Lisa. *Screening the Body: Tracing Medicine's Visual Culture*. Minneapolis: University of Minnesota Press, 1995.

Cavell, Stanley. "Companionable Thinking." In *Philosophy and Animals Life,* pp. 91–126. New York: Columbia University Press, 2008.

—— "Knowing and Acknowledging." In Stephen Mulhall, ed., *The Cavell Reader*, pp. 46–71. Cambridge: Blackwell, 1996.

—— *The World Viewed: Reflections on the Ontology of Film*. Cambridge: Harvard University Press, 1979.

Céline, Louis-Ferdinand. *Journey to the End of the Night*. Trans. Ralph Manheim. London: John Calder, 2004 [1932].

Chris, Cynthia. *Watching Wildlife*. Minneapolis: University of Minnesota Press, 2006.

Coetzee, J. M. *Diary of a Bad Year*. London: Vintage, 2008.

—— *Inner Workings: Literary Essays 2000–2005*. London: Harvill Secker, 2007.

—— *The Lives of Animals*. Ed. Amy Gutmann. Princeton: Princeton University Press, 1999.

Condee, Nancy. *The Imperial Trace: Recent Russian Cinema*. Oxford: Oxford University Press, 2009.

Conway, Daniel W. "How We Became What We Are: Tracking the 'Beasts of Prey.'" In Christa Davis Acampora and Ralph R. Acampora, eds., *A Nietzschean Bestiary: Becoming Animal Beyond Docile and Brutal,* pp. 156–177. New York: Rowman and Littlefield, 2004.

Corrigan, Timothy. "Producing Herzog: From a Body of Images." In *The Films of Werner Herzog: Between Mirage and History*, pp. 3–20. New York: Methuen, 1987.

Cowan, Bainard. "Walter Benjamin's Theory of Allegory" *New German Critique* 22 (1981): 109–122.

Crawford, Paul. *Politics and History in William Golding: The World Turned Upside Down*. University of Missouri Press, 2002.

Cronin, Paul, ed. *Herzog on Herzog*. London: Faber and Faber, 2002.

Courtine-Denamy, Sylvie. *Three Women in Dark Times: Edith Stein, Hannah Arendt, Simone Weil*. Trans. G. M. Goshgarian. Ithaca: Cornell University Press, 2000.

Cunneen, Jospeh. "Sacred in Bresson: *Au Hasard Balthazar*." In Kenneth R. Morefield, ed., *Faith and Spirituality in Masters of World Cinema*, pp. 37–46. Newcastle: Cambridge Scholars Publishing, 2008.

Daney, Serge. "The Screen of Fantasy (Bazin and Animals)." In Ivone Margulies, ed., *Rites of Realism: Essays on Corporeal Cinema*, pp. 32–41. Trans. Mark A. Cohen. Durham: Duke University Press, 2003.

Darrieussecq, Marie. *Pig Tales: A Novel of Lust and Transformation*. Trans. Linda Coverdale. London: Faber and Faber, 1997.

———— *White*. Trans. Ian Monk London: Faber and Faber, 2005.

———— *Zoo: Nouvelles*. Paris, POL: 2006.

Deleuze, Gilles, and Félix Guattari. *A Thousand Plateaus*. Trans. Brian Massumi. London: Continuum, 2004 [1980].

Derrida, Jacques. "The Animal That Therefore I Am (More to Follow)." Trans. David Wills. *Critical Inquiry* 28 (2002): 369–418.

Diamond, Cora. "Eating Meat and Eating People." In *The Realistic Spirit: Wittgenstein, Philosophy, and the Mind,* pp. 319–334. Boston: MIT Press, 1991.

———— "Experimenting on Animals: A Problem in Ethics." In *The Realistic Spirit: Wittgenstein, Philosophy, and the Mind,* pp. 336–365. Boston: MIT Press, 1991.

———— "Injustice and Animals." In Carl Elliott, ed., *Slow Cures and Bad Philosophies: Essays on Wittgenstein, Medicine, and Bioethics,* pp. 118–148. Durham: Duke University Press, 2001.

———— "The Difficulty of Reality and the Difficulty of Philosophy." In *Philosophy and Animals Life,* pp. 43–89. New York: Columbia University Press, 2008.

Donovan, Josephine, and Carol J. Adams, eds. *Beyond Animal Rights: A Feminist Caring Ethic for the Treatment of Animals.* New York: Continuum, 1996.

———— *The Feminist Care Tradition in Animal Ethics.* New York: Columbia University Press, 2007.

Dorsky, Nathaniel. *Devotional Cinema.* Berkeley: Tuumba, 2003.

Drevet, Patrick. "Simone Weil est-elle antisémite?" *Cahiers Simone Weil,* June 2008, pp. 207–210.

Druker, Jonathan. *Primo Levi and Humanism After Auschwitz.* London: Palgrave Macmillan, 2009.

Durgnat, Raymond. *Franju.* London: Studio Vista, 1967.

Everett, Barbara. "Golding's Pity." In John Cary, ed., *William Golding: The Man and His Books,* pp. 110–125. London: Faber, 1986.

Fay, Jennifer. "Seeing/Loving Animals: André Bazin's Posthumanism." *Journal of Visual Culture* 7.1 (2008): 41–64.

Fiedler, Leslie. "Introduction." In *Waiting for God,* pp. vii–xxxiv. Trans. Emma Craufurd. New York: Perennial, 2001.

Finkielkraut, Alain. *Remebering In Vain: The Klaus Barbie Trial and Crimes Against Humanity.* Trans. Roxanne Lapidus with Sima Godfrey. New York: Columbia University Press, 1992.

Ford, Richard. *The Sportswriter.* London: Vintage, 2003.

Freud, Sigmund. "The Uncanny." Trans James Strachey. *Standard Edition* 17:217–256. London: Vintage, 2001 [1919].

Friedman, Lawrence S. *Understanding Isaac Bashevis Singer*. Columbia: University of South Carolina Press, 1988.

Fudge, Erica. "A Left-Handed Blow: Writing the History of Animals." In Nigel Rothfels, ed., *Representing Animals*, pp. 3–18. Bloomington: Indiana University Press, 2002.

Gaudet, Jeanette. "Dishing the Dirt: Metamorphosis in Marie Darrieussecq's *Truismes*." *Women in French Studies* 9 (2001): 181–192.

Golding, William. "In My Ark." *The Hot Gates and Other Occasional Pieces*, pp. 102–105. New York: Harcourt, Brace and World, 1965.

—— *Pincher Martin*. London: Penguin, 1962 [1956].

—— *The Inheritors*. London: Faber, 1997 [1955].

Grandin, Temple. *Thinking in Pictures: And Other Reports from My Life with Autism*. London: Bloomsbury, 2006.

Grant, Barry Keith. "Ethnography in the First Person: Frederick Wiseman's *Titicut Follies*." In Barry Keith Grant and Jeannette Sloniowski, eds., *Documenting the Documentary*, pp. 238–253. Detroit: Wayne State University Press, 1998.

Graves, Paul. "New Models and Metaphors for the Neanderthal Debate." *Current Anthropology* 32.5 (1991): 513–541.

Hanssen, Beatrice. *Walter Benjamin's Other History: Of Stones, Animals, Human Beings, and Angels*. Berkeley: University of California Press, 2000.

Haraway, Donna. "A Cyborg Manifesto: Science, Technology, and Socialist-Feminism in the Late Twentieth Century." In *Simians, Cyborgs, and Women*. New York: Routledge, 1991, pp. 149–181.

—— *Primate Visions: Gender, Race, and Nature in the World of Modern Science*. New York: Routledge, 1989.

Heidegger, Martin. "Question Concerning Technology." In David M. Kaplan, ed., *Readings in the Philosophy of Technology*, pp. 35–51. Lanham, MD: Rowman and Littlefield, 2004.

Hillman, Roger. *Usettling Scores: German Film, Music, and Ideology*, pp. 136–150. Bloomington: Indiana University Press, 2005.

Hitler, Adolf. "Nation and Race." In *Mein Kampf*, pp. 120–131. London: Hurst and Blackett, 1933.

Hobbs, Graeme. "The Opened Hand: Reflections on Artur Aristakisyan's *Palms*." *Vertigo* 3.6 (Summer 2007): 18–19.

Hoess, Rudolf. *Commandant of Auschwitz: The Autobiography of Rudolf Hoess*. Trans. Constantine FitzGibbon. London: Phoenix, 2000.

Ince, Kate. *Georges Franju*. Manchester: Manchester University Press, 2005.

James, Nick. "The Greatest Show on Earth." *Sight and Sound* (February 2006): 22–26.

Jordan, Shirley. "Saying the Unsayable: Identities in Crisis in the Early Novels of Marie Darrieussecq." In Gill Rye and Michael Worton, eds., *Women's Writing in Contemporary France*, pp. 142–153. Manchester: Manchester University Press, 2002.

Joseph-Marie Perrin and Gustave Thibon. *Simone Weil as We Knew Her*. Trans. Emma Craufurd. London: Routledge, 2003.

Kaplan, Alice Y. "On Alain Finkielkraut's *Remembering in Vain*: The Klaus Barbie Trial and Crimes Against Humanity." *Critical Inquiry* 19 (1992): 70–86.

Kemp, Simon. "Darrieussecq's Mind" *French Studies* 62.4 (2008): 429–441.

Kinkead-Weeks, Mark, and Ian Gregor. *William Golding: A Critical Study*. London: Faber, 1967.

Koch, Gertrude. "Blindness as Insight: Visions of the Unseen in *Land of Silence and Darkness*." In Timothy Corrigan, ed., *The Films of Werner Herzog: Between Mirage and History*, pp. 73–86. New York: Methuen, 1987.

Köhler, Wolfang. *The Mentality of Apes*. Trans. Ella Winter. London: Routledge, 2003 [1925].

Kouvaros, George. "'We Do Not Die Twice': Realism and Cinema." In James Donald and Michael Renov, eds., *The Sage Handbook of Film Studies*, pp. 376–390. London: Sage, 2008.

Lawrenson, Edward. Rev. of *The Wild Parrots of Telegraph Hill*, dir. Judy Irving. *Sight and Sound*, January 2006, p. 83.

Levi, Primo. *If This Is a Man and The Truce*. London: Abacus, 1987.

Lippit, Akira Mizuta. *Electric Animal: Toward a Rhetoric of Wildlife*. Minneapolis: University of Minnesota Press, 2000.

—— " . . . From Wild Technology to Electric Animal." In Nigel Rothfels, ed., *Representing Animals,* pp. 119–136. Bloomington: Indiana University Press, 2002.

—— "The Death of an Animal" *Film Quarterly* 56.1 (2002): 9–22.

Lowenstein, Adam. *Shocking Representation: Historical Trauma, National Cinema, and the Modern Horror Film*. New York: Columbia University Press, 2005.

Margulies, Ivone. "Bodies Too Much." *Rites of Realism: Essays on Corporeal Cinema*, pp. 1–23. Durham: Duke University Press, 2003.

Meltzer, Françoise. "The Hands of Simone Weil." *Critical Inquiry* 27 (Summer 2001): 611–628.

Miles, Siân. "Introduction." *Simone Weil: An Anthology*. London: Penguin, 2005.

Morgan, Daniel. "Rethinking Bazin: Ontology and Realist Aesthetics." *Critical Inquiry* 32 (Spring 2006): 443–475.

Nietzsche, Friedrich."On Truth and Falsity in Their Ultra Moral Sense." In Oscar Levy, ed., *The Complete Works of Friedrich Nietzsche*, pp. 173–192. 2 vols. London: T. N. Foulis, 1911.

—— *The Birth of Tragedy: Out of the Spirit of Music*. Trans. Shaun Whiteside. London: Penguin, 1993 [1872].

—— "The Four Great Errors." *Twilight of the Idols*, pp. 26–32. Trans. Duncan Large. New York: Oxford University Press, 1998 [1888].

—— *The Gay Science*. Trans. Walter Kaufmann. New York: Vintage, 1974 [1887].

Norris, Margot. *Beasts of the Modern Imagination: Darwin, Nietzsche, Kafka, Ernst, and Lawrence*, pp. 73–100. Baltimore: Johns Hopkins University Press, 1985.

Novick, Peter. *The Holocaust in American Life*. Boston: Houghton Mifflin, 1999.

Prager, Brad. *Werner Herzog: Aesthetic Ecstasy and Truth*. London: Wallflower, 2007.

Qiao, Guo Qiang. *The Jewishness of Isaac Bashevis Singer*. Bern: Peter Lang, 2003.

Quandt, James. "*Au hasard Balthazar* and *Le Diable probablement*." In Mary Lea Bandy and Antonio Monda, eds., *The Hidden God: Film and Faith*, pp. 17–28. New York: Museum of Modern Art, 2003.

Raine, Craig. "Belly Without Blemish: Golding's Literary Sources." In John Cary, ed., *William Golding: The Man and His Books*, pp. 101–109. London: Faber, 1986.

Reader, Keith. *Robert Bresson*. Manchester: Manchester University Press, 2000.

Rhys, Jean. *Good Morning, Midnight*. London: Penguin, 2000 [1939].

Rueckert, William. "Literature and Ecology: An Experiment in Ecocriticism." In Cheryl Glotfelty and Harold Fromm, eds., *The Ecocriticism Reader: Landmarks in Literary Ecology*, pp. 105–123. Athens: University of Georgia Press, 1996.

Rye, Gill, and Michael Worton. "Introduction." In *Women's Writing in Contemporary France: New Writers, New Literatures in the 1990s*, pp. 1–26. Manchester: Manchester University Press, 2002.

Santner, Eric L. *On Creaturely Life: Rilke, Benjamin, Sebald*. Chicago: University of Chicago Press, 2006.

Schor, Naomi. "The Crisis of French Universalism," *Yale French Studies, France/USA: The Cultural Wars* 100 (2001): 43–64.

Schrader, Paul. *Transcendental Style in Film: Ozu, Bresson, Dreyer*. Berkeley: University of California Press, 1972.

—— "Robert Bresson, Possibly: Interviewed by Paul Schrader." *Film Comment* (September-October 1977): 26–30.

Schwarz, Daniel R. "A Humanistic Ethics of Reading." In Todd F. Davis and Kenneth Womack, eds., *Mapping the Ethical Turn: A Reader in Ethics, Culture, and Literary Theory*, pp. 3–15. Charlottesville: University of Virginia Press, 2001.

—— *Imagining the Holocaust*. Basingstoke: Palgrave, 2000.

Simic, Charles. *Selected Poem, 1963–2001*. London: Faber and Faber, 2004.

Singer, Alan. "Comprehending Appearances: Werner Herzog's Ironic Sublime." In Timothy Corrigan, ed., *The Films of Werner Herzog: Between Mirage and History*, pp. 183–206. New York: Methuen, 1987.

Singer, Isaac Bashevis. *Three Complete Novels. The Slave; Enemies, a Love Story; Shosha*. New York: Random House, 1995.

—— "The Letter Writer." In *The Séance and Other Stories*. New York: Penguin, 1974.

Sloniowski, Jeannette. "It Was an Atrocious Film: Georges Franju's *Blood of the Beasts*." In Barry Keith Grant and Jeanntte Sloniowski, eds., *Documenting the Documentary: Close Readings of Documentary Film and Video*, pp. 171–187. Detroit: Wayne State University Press, 1998.

Snyder, Gary. *Turtle Island*. New York: New Directions, 1969.

Sontag, Susan. "Simone Weil." *Against Interpretation*, pp. 58–60. New York: Dell, 1969.

—— "The Pornographic Imagination." In Georges Bataille, *The Story of the Eye*, pp. 83–118. Trans. Joachim Neugroschel. London: Penguin, 1979 [1967].

Stamelman, Richard. *Lost Beyond Telling: Representations of Death and Absence in Modern French Poetry*. Ithaca: Cornell University Press, 1990.

Tanner, Tony. *Nietzsche: A Very Short Introduction*. Oxford: Oxford University Press, 1994.

Taubman, Jane A. *Kira Muratova*. London: I. B. Tauris, 2005.

Thibon, Gustave. "Introduction." *Gravity and Grace*, pp. vii–xl. Trans. Emma Crawford and Mario von der Ruhr. London: Routledge, 2004.

Tiger, Virginia. *William Golding: The Dark Fields of Discovery*. London: Calder and Boyars, 1974.

Tolstoy, Leo. *Spiritual Writings*. Ed. Charles E. Moore. New York: Orbis, 2006.

Virilio, Paul. "A Pitiless Art." In *Art and Fear*, pp. 27–65. Trans. Julie Rose. London: Continuum, 2003.

Von der Ruhr, Mario. *Simone Weil: An Apprenticeship in Attention*. London: Continuum, 2006.

Weil, Simone. "Are We Struggling for Justice?" In Eric O. Springsted, ed., *Simone Weil*, pp. 120–131. New York: Orbis, 1998.

—— "Epilogue." In Eric O. Springsted, ed., *Simone Weil*, pp. 142–143. New York: Orbis, 1998.

—— *Gravity and Grace*. Trans. Emma Crawford and Mario von der Ruhr. London: Routledge, 2004.

—— "Human Personality." In Siân Miles, ed., *Simone Weil: An Anthology*, pp. 69–98. London: Penguin, 2005.

—— *Letter to a Priest*. Trans. A. F. Wills. London: Routledge, 2002.

—— *Oppression and Liberty*. Trans. Arthur Wills and John Petrie. London: Routledge, 2006.

—— "Spiritual Autobiography." *Waiting for God*, pp. 21–38. Trans. Emma Craufurd. New York: Perennial, 2001.

—— "The Iliad or the Poem of Force." In Siân Miles, ed., *Simone Weil: An Anthology*, pp. 182–215. London: Pengiun, 2005.

—— "The Love of God and Affliction." In Eric O. Springsted, ed., *Simone Weil*, pp. 41–70. New York: Orbis, 1998.

—— "The Love of God and Affliction." *Waiting for God*, pp. 67–82. Trans. Emma Craufurd. New York: Perennial, 2001.

—— *The Need for Roots*. Trans. Arthur Wills. London: Routledge, 2001.

"Theory of the Sacraments." In Eric O. Springsted, ed., *Simone Weil*, pp. 99–106. New York: Orbis, 1998.

Weinstein, Jami. "Traces of the Beast: Becoming Nietzsche, Becoming Animal, and the Transhuman." In Christa Davis Acampora and Ralph R. Acampora, eds., *A Nietzschean Bestiary: Becoming Animal Beyond Docile and Brutal*, pp. 301–318. New York: Rowman and Littlefield, 2004.

Wells, H. G. "The Grisly Folk." *The Complete Short Stories of H. G. Wells*, pp. 684–694. Ed. John Hammond. London: Phoenix, 2000.

—— *The Island of Dr Moreau*. London: Random House, 2005.

—— *Outline of History*. New York: Macmillan, 1920.

Wolfe, Cary. *Animal Rites: American Culture, the Discourse of Species, and Posthumanist Theory*. Chicago: University of Chicago Press, 2003.

—— "Exposures." In *Philosophy and Animal Life*, pp. 1–41. New York: Columbia University Press, 2008.

—— "Flesh and Finitude: Thinking Animals in (Post)Humanist Philosophy." *SubStance, The Political Animal*, ed. Chris Danta and Dimitris Vardoulakis. 117, 37.3 (2008): 8–36.

—— "Learning from Temple Grandin, or Animal Studies, Disability Studies, and Who Comes After the Subject." *New Formations* 64. 1. (2008): 110–123.

Žižek, Slavoj. *The Puppet and the Dwarf: The Perverse Core of Christianity*. Cambridge: MIT Press, 2003.

Filmography

Aristakisyan, Artur, dir. *Palms*. Russia, 1993.

Bresson, Robert, dir. *Au hasard Balthazar*. Argos Film, Svensk Filmindustri. France, Sweden, 1966.

Franju, Georges, dir. *Le Sang des bêtes*. France, 1979.

Geyrhalter, Nikolaus. dir. *Our Daily Bread*. Nikolaus Geyrhalter Filmproduktion, ZDF/3sat, Germany, Austria, 2005.

Herzog, Werner, dir. *Bells from the Deep*. Werner Herzog Film Produktion, Momentous Events, Inc. Germany, USA, 1993.

——. *Grizzly Man*. Lions Gate Films. USA, 2005.

—— *Land of Silence and Darkness*. Werner Herzog Film Produktion, Referat für Filmgeschichte. Germany, 1971.

—— *Lessons of Darkness*. Werner Herzog Film Produktion. Germany, 1992.

—— *Little Dieter Needs to Fly*. Werner Herzog Film Produktion, ZDF. Germany, 1997.

—— *Pilgrimage*. Werner Herzog Filmproduktion, BBC, Pipeline Films. Germany, UK, 2001.

—— *The Wild Blue Yonder*. Werner Herzog Filmproduktion. Germany, 2005.

—— *Wings of Hope*. Werner Herzog Filmproduktion, ZDF, BBC Bristol. Germany, UK, 1999.

Munk, Andrzej, dir. *Passanger*. Poland, 1963.

Muratova, Kira, dir. *Asthenic Syndrome*. Goskino, Odessa Film Studios. Ukraine, 1989.

Tyulkin, Vladimir, dir. *About Love*. Kazakhstan, 2005.

—— *Lord of the Flies*. Kazakhstan, 1991.

Wiseman, Frederick, dir. *Primate*. Zipporah Films, USA, 1974.

INDEX

dismissing, 53; Neanderthals in, 52–53

Žižek, Slavoj, 16

Zoo (Darrieussecq), 80–81, 210*n*23

Zoographies (Calarco), 2

Zoomorphic, cinema as, 19, 106

Zoos, 103; colonialism of, 105; conservation and, 104; extinction and, 104–5